BEHIND THE
CURTAIN

Three Days in the Hidden Life of a Special Needs Family

AMANDA SHEPLER

Kevin W W Blackley Books, LLC

For information about this title or to order other books and/or electronic media, contact the publisher:

Kevin W W Blackley Books, LLC
280 E. Treehaven Rd.
Buffalo, NY 14215

www.kevinblackley.com
kevin.blackley@gmail.com

Library of Congress Control Number:
2020907120

ISBN: 978-1-950039-09-8

Printed in the United States of America

DEDICATION

This book was written in stolen moments over eighty days
and is dedicated to those I stole the moments from:

Matthew, Jackson, Marian, Vincent, and Sebastian.

I love you with all my heart.
Thank you for patiently supporting my obsession.

This book is also dedicated to our AUTS2 family, separated by
distance so that our remarkable children are able to shine
their unique light across all corners of the globe.

ACKNOWLEDGEMENTS

Sincere thank-yous are owed to the following people:

To my cousin Deanna, who read the first draft and
knew exactly where to send me.

To the amazing Jennifer Thomas, the extraordinary
editor who took this book to new levels.

To Kevin Blackley, the fearless publisher who
jumped on board and hasn't looked back.

To every one of my nearest and dearest who willingly persevered
through early manuscripts. Your comments were noted and
incorporated, and the end result shines brighter because of you.

To my husband, Matthew, who unfailingly responds
"Do what you've got to do" whenever I dump my share
of household duties onto him to sit at my desk.

To my children, the Beef Buff Band, for being everything
that is beautiful about this world.

PREFACE

We live in incredible times.

Four years ago, my youngest son, Sebastian, was struggling in every area. My husband and I felt terrified and alone—fighting a silent battle against an unknown foe. After eighteen months of begging the medical community to stop brushing aside our concerns, they took his blood.

With a single vial, our lives changed forever.

In the not-too-distant past, before the Human Genome Project, Baby Sebastian would have been tagged with question marks. As the gap continued to widen between his abilities and those of his peers, the paperwork following him would have carried labels, terrifying in their generality: *Disabled. Mental Retardation. Intellectual Disability of Unknown Cause. Birth Defect of Unknown Cause.*

Without a formal diagnosis, accessing Early Intervention services at the levels Sebastian needed would have been nigh impossible, and he would have struggled to reach his greatest potential. He would have faced the same fight for assistance in public school. These battles would have been undertaken in the frightening vacuum of isolation where so many families on a special needs journey exist. Because Sebastian's challenges are singularly unique. Similar in some ways to other children, and vastly different in others.

Odd. Different. Weird. Alone.

But, as I said, we live in incredible times. A time of micro-array testing and international teams of dedicated researchers. And on December 14, 2016, that single vial of blood made Sebastian the fifty-first individual on Planet Earth to be formally diagnosed with a "recognizable new microdeletion": AUTS2 Syndrome. Our geneticist had never heard of it, but she explained that Sebastian's seventh chromosome was lacking information that everyone else has.

If you imagine the human DNA as a set of hardcover encyclopedias, AUTS2 Syndrome means that Sebastian carries around the exact same twenty-six tomes as every other human, but it's as if he cannot access the entry for "Dolphin". He is missing that one single entry from the entirety of fourteen thousand pages.

Happily, in real life, Sebastian knows all about dolphins. In fact, he knows more animal facts than any other elementary student we've met. (And with him being the youngest of four, we've met quite a few!)

If our lives were plotted on a horizontal timeline, noting life-altering events such as births, deaths, and marriages with each dot sized according to impact, Diagnosis Day would be among the largest. That was the day we learned our precious baby was struggling because he was born with a difference that no medicine could fix. It was the day we were directed to an article about zebrafish, because AUTS2 Syndrome is so rare and so newly identified that human-focused research was—and still is—nearly nonexistent. On December 14, 2016, in the face of an answer that merely brought thousands of new questions into focus, we sobbed until there were no tears left to fall.

But like so many life-changing events, Diagnosis Day shines in our memory with a complicated beauty. Knowledge, even the gut-wrenching, heartbreaking kind, bestows a gift. On Diagnosis Day, after our tears were spent, we found that we were no longer helpless, hopeless victims. Because a diagnosis, no matter how rare, creates opportunities.

Armed with our new intel, we met via webcam with the researchers who first identified AUTS2 Syndrome. And we discovered we were not alone. We found the families of other children with Sebastian's diagnosis from around the world and marveled at the similarities in the strengths, weaknesses, and features of our children across the continents. We successfully petitioned the National Institutes of Health in Washington DC to initiate the first formal study of AUTS2 Syndrome in North America.

We were featured in a local news story designed to spread awareness of Sebastian's rare condition—a two-part special that continues to serve as a beacon to families around the globe as they scour the Internet for answers on their own Diagnosis Day.

Sebastian is literally one-in-ninety-five million, but as the critical tests become more commonplace, our global AUTS2 community continues to grow. Social media platforms connect families worldwide, allowing "rare" to no longer be synonymous with "isolated" and "alone."

And while AUTS2 Syndrome is uncommon, the challenges families with special needs face, as well as the Herculean efforts we undertake to appear "normal," are common across all diagnoses. Especially now, as Autism Spectrum Disorder (from which the "AUTS" of AUTS2 is derived) continues to be a topic of international discussion and as adaptive technologies enable individuals with all types of disabilities to engage in their communities at unprecedented rates, knowledge is desperately needed to promote the levels of awareness that can lead to authentically empathetic kindness from individuals worldwide.

In light of this, I've striven to depict a behind-the-scenes transcript of three ordinary November days in our life with Sebastian, chronicled as truthfully as possible. It is the sincere hope of the entire Team Shepler that this glimpse into our day-to-day reality will not only bolster our fellow families on special needs journeys, but also enable those without disabilities to "see behind the curtain" into our unique world, ultimately strengthening the community safety net for our precious and uniquely vulnerable children.

Yours,

Amanda Shepler

DAY ONE

SUNDAY, 3:OO P.M.

The sound of hands sifting eagerly through plastic building bricks floated in through her office door. The cheerful clinks from the dining room wouldn't have been audible over the incessant drone of the television had the listener not been able to recite every line of the current program word-for-word. The practiced repetition made it easier to block out.

Mom smiled ruefully. Somewhere there were families who didn't have to endure hours of cartoon dogs leading daring rescues on a continuous loop every afternoon.

Somewhere.

But here on Hill Street, the residents of Dog Town had provided the household's soundtrack for nearly five months. The entire family could perform along with every episode of the show, detailing the plights of an animated community that inexplicably relied on talking dogs to save them from all imaginable sources of danger.

And depending on the continued obsession of her son, Sebastian, it could remain a part of their world for years.

But if he is going to adopt a new fixation, she thought, glancing at the embarrassingly large heap of cast-aside pirate-themed products that extended along an entire wall of her narrow office, *let's hope it takes hold before we start Christmas shopping.*

The inordinate amassment of pirate booty had happened because everyone just got so excited when Bas finally showed a preference for *something.* Anything. A preference was evidence that somewhere behind her son's wide-set hazel eyes lay a glimmer of awareness. Their family had waited over two years for a sign—any sign—that Sebastian was really "in there." When it finally arrived in the form of a pirate-preference, they'd seized it with both hands, buying stuffed friends, action figures, playsets, books, costumes, and swords, all in a desperate effort to fan that infinitesimal, precious spark of personality.

Sebastian's love for pirates had lasted nearly sixteen months. Then it ended as quickly as it began, fizzling to nothing in the shadow of *Dog Town.* Since then, Mom reminded herself, the improvements incited by his newest fixation were worth any amount of irritation. Sebastian's eating of "pup treats" had rocketed him from size 24-month clothing to size 4 in no time at all. The show had also prompted him to learn his first color—red—and added dozens of words to his slowly growing vocabulary.

Nonetheless, as a new episode began, the upbeat theme song grated on Mom's frayed nerves and the absurdity of the show's premise disrupted her thoughts. *Why doesn't the town have a fire department or police force? Why are dogs the only animals that can talk?*

Mom shook her head and tried to focus on the tasks glaring at her from her computer screen. Out her office window, she saw the wind thrash leaves from the two towering maple trees in the front yard. The red, orange, and golden swirls of fall created a beautiful scene of vibrant chaos.

She allowed herself to stare just a moment, though, before tearing her eyes away. The chart on her computer screen wasn't going to fill itself, and her to-do list for the day extended many hours beyond this particular task. Owning her own grant writing firm was stressful, but the high-stakes, deadline-driven career allowed her to work from home and mold her hours around the family's activities. With four kids playing sports and instruments on a yearlong schedule, the importance of that flexibility more than made up for the deepening creases around her eyes.

As she began the tedium of plotting out goals and objectives, she heard ten-year-old Jack and six-year-old Vince run from the dining room into the living room.

"We built it, Bassie! Look! This train can hold all your doggies! It's a *Dog Town* train! Come on, let's play!"

The boys' creation must indeed be impressive, Mom thought, because Marian, their eight-year-old sister, clicked off the television and four-year-old Sebastian, rather than screaming, squealed in delight. Mom heard the clatter of building blocks being dumped from their bins onto the hardwood floor and Sebastian's toy basket being dragged off the shelf.

"I'm Red the Dog!" Sebastian sang out gleefully. "Ruff, ruff!"

Mom sped up her typing, ever-aware of the clock in the corner of her screen ticking closer to a jam-packed evening agenda of dinner, homework, violin practice, swim practice, and bedtime. As dragons descended on Dog Town only to be repelled by Red the Dog's invention of a cookie launcher, she continued down the seemingly interminable chart. By the time the Dog Town train faced a rockslide that couldn't be moved until Red the Dog fixed the backhoe, she was down to the final rows.

I'm going to have time to hang out with Matt tonight! she exulted. *Everything else on the to-do list can be accomplished while the kids are still awake.*

Then an icy chill rose in her throat. *Everything except the stack of paperwork I still have to complete for Sebastian's orthopedic visit.*

The appointment was tomorrow morning, and she'd put off filling out the medical history forms until the last possible minute. *Again.* She sighed. The volume of paperwork required when your child saw eight different doctors and six different specialists was staggering.

It's not a problem, she assured herself. *This will force me to stop ignoring the big manila envelope from that researcher in Seattle, too—and most of the requests will be repeated. Two birds with one stone. Easy peasy.*

But it wasn't easy. Not really. Recalling important dates was no problem—she could rattle those off in her sleep: *First hospitalization at five weeks for umbilical infection; second hospitalization at thirteen months for influenza; third hospitalization at eighteen months for meningitis*. The list went on without hesitation: *First laugh at fifteen months. First steps at twenty-two months. First word at thirty-five months. First sentence at forty-one months*. These dates were always lurking beneath the surface of her consciousness, easy to ignore but refusing to go away. These were the dates that screamed to the world that her baby was different.

So far, she hadn't been brave enough to even glance at the newest medical forms.

The orthopedist just needs to check his feet, she tried to assure herself. *They won't need to ask about everything.*

But she knew these were lies. The forms always wanted to know everything. The doctors spoke of being a medical "team," but their teamwork never extended to intake paperwork. Though their questions were all similar, providers didn't share, so every doctor's office had its own set.

And while the font changed and the heading differed, each form always had the dreaded box. The box that asked when the problem was first noticed and what the most significant challenges were. That empty box demanding to be filled in with bleak, unchangeable sentences: *Sebastian has a genetic condition called AUTS2 Syndrome. There are less than 150 diagnosed cases worldwide.*

Researchers had thought they'd found a genetic cause for a certain type of autism—that's where the "AUTS" had come from. But "AUTS2" (pronounced "oughts-two") was more than autism. Which she also had to explain.

Symptoms vary and not much information is documented.

We knew, in the delivery room, that something wasn't typical, but no one would listen.

She sighed again. She'd long since learned to use the accepted lingo of "typical" and "neurotypical" rather than words like "normal" to describe those without special needs.

After explaining Bas's diagnosis, she would have to fill the remainder of the box with a heartbreaking diatribe of symptom descriptions, tearing down her precious baby into a cold list of medical terms and cruel deficiencies that overlooked everything that was beautiful about Sebastian.

Overwhelmed, she rose and stuck her head through the doorway to take in the living room adventure. Jack had wedged one end of their purple roll-up foam balance beam onto an upper shelf and was stretching his long arms to hold it in place. Marian had lifted Sebastian in a bear hug, his skinny legs dangling below him, and their light-blond heads clinked together as Bas's shaky arm stretched to put Red the Dog in his car onto the improvised track. Vince was crouched at the bottom of the perilous ramp, pulling it tight to keep it steady. Time seemed to stand still as they all held their breaths, watching and waiting for Sebastian's hand to remember how to unclench. Suddenly, as his brain rediscovered the steps to release the toy, Red the Dog zoomed towards the ground down the makeshift purple slope. Sebastian stiffened in Marian's arms, hands and feet flapping in rigid excitement.

"Go, puppy, go!" shouted Vince encouragingly. "You did it, Bas! You helped Red the Dog escape the dragon lair!"

"You're such a good pup, Sebastian," Marian said, lowering him to the ground.

Bas gave his sister an appreciative bark, and she gave his silky-smooth cheek a quick kiss.

The universe knew what it was doing, Mom thought, watching them. *Sebastian needs us, but we need him even more.*

As the game carried on, she slipped back to her desk and cracked open an energy drink. She downed it in five gulps.

Less than five minutes left to finish this project, she

commanded herself. *Pull yourself together.*

The paperwork, the endless paperwork, was waiting on the green stepstool in the kitchen. She'd taken to stashing all the medical forms there, nearly out of sight. On good mornings, it was easy to pretend that "today was the day" they would be filled out. It was equally as easy, on bad ones, to ignore them completely, refusing to acknowledge what they represented. The current batch had sat untouched for weeks.

They will still be there waiting after the kids are asleep, she reasoned, *whether you waste time worrying about them now or not.*

Minutes later, her chart was complete. She clicked *Save* and *Close* in rapid succession to end her work day.

It's freezing in here, she realized. She scanned the windows and quickly located an improperly latched top pane that had slid open to let in the icy wind. As she hefted it up and pushed the knob to secure it, she saw their old blue plastic water table careening wildly down the sidewalk towards the school bus stop, propelled by gusts that ripped branches loose from the swaying maples. Mom froze, fleetingly wondering if it would be safe to give chase. Then the house abruptly surrendered to the early November darkness.

The power was out.

SUNDAY, 5:30 P.M.

Sebastian's terrified screams pierced the darkness. But they were instantly muffled as Vince and Marian pulled him into a tight huddle.

"It's okay, Bas," Mom heard Vince murmur calmly. "The lights will be back on soon—it's just like that time in Dog Town."

Mom moved toward the plastic cabinet next to her desk, nearly colliding with Jack's lanky body as she and her oldest son fumbled for the flashlight drawer.

"I can't believe how dark it is outside," he said. "I mean, we haven't even had dinner!"

She could hear the anxiety in his voice, but she didn't fault him for it—she'd been afraid of the dark at age ten, too.

Besides, she reminded herself, *he's not off cowering somewhere—he's here, saving the day.*

The flashlight drawer was completely devoid of flashlights, but they dug out four helpful toys: "sonic screwdrivers" with illuminating ends. Jack pressed the end of one, infusing the office with a bright blue glow accompanied by a high-pitched electronic whine.

"Allons-y!" he exclaimed happily.

They grinned at each other and took off for the living room.

"Here we go," Mom said reassuringly, passing out the toys to the kids. "Now, let's see what we can do about dinner. Big Three, head to the kitchen, please."

Mom smiled, recalling the winter afternoon when she'd realized that exercise wasn't helping her pants fit and that the wax company probably hadn't spoiled the smell of her favorite candle, which had just made her run heaving for the toilet.

"Another one?" Matt had asked incredulously. "How are we going to manage? The first three are still so little and dependent."

She'd bitten her lip in worry and then said resolutely: "We'll figure it out. A baby is coming, so from now on they're the 'Big Three.'"

Mom watched Jack, Marian, and Vince weave their way through the shadowy dining room, their dark frames outlined by their glowing toys. That cold day five years ago, calling them the "Big Three" had seemed absurd—they'd been ages one, three, and five, for goodness sake. But, now, watching their confident strides bear them to the kitchen through the darkness, Mom realized it was a title they'd long since earned.

Meanwhile, her fourth child trembled against her legs, refusing to take the screwdriver she held out to him. His body was rooted to the spot, his uncomprehending face awash with terror.

She knelt and pulled him into a tight hug, knowing that actually picking him up would trigger an epic meltdown. Not a tantrum based on poor behavior, but a meltdown: something completely beyond Sebastian's control that was forever looming, waiting to assert its wild and unreasonable turbulence in response to his world. A world where sounds boomed louder, colors shone brighter, and odors smelled stronger. A world where the logic of cause and effect was muffled, leaving every event unexpected and unpredictable. Existence within the tumult of his perception relied on consistency.

"I love you, Sebastian," she whispered in his ear. "You are safe, and I love you."

Almost imperceptibly, his body relaxed in her embrace. But

as the stiffness receded, tremors moved in, and Sebastian's entire body quaked.

"The lights go out, Momma?" his panicked voice asked. "You turn them on?"

"The wind knocked out the power, my little man," she said softly. "But workers are fixing it right now. The lights will be back in a few minutes."

His body stiffened again and he whimpered.

"You turn them on?" he repeated in rising dismay.

Even through his thick maroon sweater, Mom could feel his heart thumping in his frail chest. She swept her hand to floor, fumbling around for whatever toys might be lying in reach. She recognized by touch a plastic Red the Dog, some salad tongs, and an action figure they'd dubbed "Mayor Sneak." She grabbed them all and held them under the glow of the incessantly buzzing screwdriver.

"Sebastian!" she said, taking on an urgent tone without much effort. "Mayor Sneak used a giant grabber to steal the sun from Dog Town, and now he's getting away!"

It wasn't her best attempt at make-believe, but her invented storyline captured his attention. Sebastian's expression shifted from unequivocal alarm to rapt concentration.

She quickly pressed the toy dog into his clammy hands, along with the lit screwdriver.

"Red the Dog invented a device that glows," she said, "but it's not enough. We need to catch Mayor Sneak and put back the sun! You be Red, okay?"

Sebastian remained frozen, not quite convinced it was safe to ignore his fear.

Vince appeared in the doorway, his white-blond hair glowing blue in the illumination of his screwdriver. Bouncing towards them with the frantic energy of a cooped-up Sunday afternoon, Vince swept his light across the floor and grabbed a handful of toys.

"Dogs to the base!" he called out.

Then his sweet six-year old voice broke into the cartoon's

theme song, with two voices immediately joining in from the kitchen. Mom hugged Sebastian tightly, her heart filled with grateful pride.

Sebastian brings out the very best in everyone. It's his superpower. Listen to the Big Three singing for him.

Marian and Jack poked their heads through the doorway and headed toward their panic-paralyzed brother. They made it three steps before the room exploded in shrieks.

"Ouch! Ouch! Ouch!" shouted Marian. *"Ja-ack!"*

Sebastian, who'd begun to relax with the song, went rigid again at the unexpected clamor.

"Momma!" Marian complained in crescendo while hopping in place. "Jack left building bricks on the floor again, and I just stepped on one!" She reached her highest pitch with gusto. "Now my foot *really* hurts! I'm probably bleeding, Momma!"

Alongside Sebastian's freshly rising panic, a sigh built within "Momma." She took deep breath. But before she could release it, Jack gave a theatrical, villainous laugh. As if awaiting his cue, he lit up his face with the blue tip of his sonic and spoke in a high, nasally voice.

"That wasn't Jack!" he proclaimed. "That was me, Mayor Sneak! You can chase after me, but my pointy building-brick traps will make sure you never catch me! The Dog Town sun is mine!"

He laughed again, emitting the perfect cackle of a cartoon evil genius.

Sebastian's arm shot forward.

"I see that May-Sneaky!" he yelled. "Red sees that bad guy! Go, puppy, go!"

Laughing, Bas ran forward and chased his oldest brother through the dark.

Breathing a sigh of relief, Mom found Vince's hand in the blackness and quick-stepped over to Marian, who was splayed dramatically on the ground, moaning loudly. Mom bent down and scooped up her beautiful daughter.

"It's lucky you're strong enough to hold on to me like a

spider monkey," Mom said, "because you're eight years old now, my darling, and my back isn't getting any younger."

Marian sniffed pathetically in her mom's ear, burying her tear-stained face into her shoulder. Mom reclasped Vince's patiently waiting hand and braved the building-brick minefield toward the kitchen.

Wincing at an unfortunately placed step, Vince looked up at her.

"Bas is lucky, Momma," he said. "With his doggie braces on, he'll never even feel these bricks. I know the braces can leave cuts on the tops of his feet, but at least the bottoms will be safe from stabby toys."

Mom thought about the molded plastic contraptions that covered Sebastian's feet from his toes until well above his ankles. Though decorated with assorted dog stickers, they represented cutting-edge adaptive technology and had given Bas mobility when they'd nearly lost hope of his ever being able to walk unassisted. Still, some days the negatives seemed to overwhelm the benefits. The doggie braces were difficult to strap on, they required Bas to wear socks three hundred sixty-five days a year, and their bulk prevented his tiny feet from fitting into most shoes. They left bruises and welts on his ankles, and in the summer, his sweaty feet were perpetually wrinkled and peeling.

She reminded herself that without his doggie braces, Sebastian would be reliant on a walker. She squeezed Vince's hand, smiling at her happy-go-lucky guy.

"I never thought of it that way, Vincey. You are absolutely correct."

They reached the kitchen and found Jack carefully lighting the big scented jar candle while Sebastian looked on in wonder.

"You no burn yourself, Jack?" Bas asked in a hushed voice. "You okay?"

"I'm okay, Bassie-Boo. When you're bigger, I'll teach you how to light a candle, too. But first, you have to eat lots of food and get HUGE!"

Setting the candle carefully between the stove burners, Jack rounded on Sebastian and tickled him under his arm. Then he reached over and patted his sister on the head.

"I'm sorry about your foot, Marian," he said soberly.

"I think it's going to be okay," she conceded reluctantly, "but you need to be better about cleaning up, Jack! Not just for my poor feet. Bas could have found a toy brick on the floor and put it in his mouth. We have to watch out for our buddy. You know that."

Vince scooted onto the bench next to his sister. "I hurt my foot, too, Marian," he said calmly, "but it's no good shouting at Jack about it. I mean...it *was* Mayor Sneak's fault, after all!"

He snorted, trying to stifle a laugh, but for Vince, that was never really a possibility. In less than three seconds he was belly-laughing with his head on the table, trying to muffle the sound.

Mixing pancake batter at the counter, Mom braced herself for Marian's reaction. Vince loved a good joke—and Marian did, too. But not if she felt like *she* was the one being laughed at. Mom saw Jack choke back a giggle as he lifted Sebastian into his highchair and she realized he was bracing for a squabble as well.

But after an uneasy pause, Marian's laughter pealed across the kitchen.

"What's up with that Mayor Sneak guy anyway?" she asked between giggles. "Who keeps voting for him? He's terrible!"

With the kids dissolving into fits of mirth, Mom poured the first four pancakes onto the hot griddle, giving a silent thanks to the wonders of a gas stove that works uncomplainingly during a power outage.

"Can I scramble some eggs too, Momma?" Jack asked hopefully.

"Red the Dog loves eggs!" Sebastian cheered. "Yes! Eggs! Yummy, yum, yum!"

"I'll help you, Jack," Marian offered, jumping off the bench onto a miraculously healed foot.

"Fine. But I get to crack six of them because it was my idea," Jack bartered.

"Here, honey," Mom said, holding out a plastic cereal bowl. "Crack your eggs one at a time into this and then dump them into the big bowl with Jack's. It'll be easier to fish out shell pieces that way."

She turned back to the pancakes as Marian eagerly accepted the proffered bowl.

It's going to be a candlelight egg massacre, Mom bemoaned, recalling Marian's last three ill-fated egg-breaking ventures. *She can't learn if she doesn't practice, but I do wish it was acceptable to let her practice outside.*

"Momma?" Vince was suddenly beside her at the stove, and calm enough to get some words out. "Since Jack and Marian get to help cook, can I be in charge of Bassie's pup tricks tonight? I have some great ideas."

"That would be wonderful, kiddo," Mom replied, sliding the first round of pancakes onto plates. "Here you go. I'll cut up Sebastian's into puppy-treat-sized pieces for you."

"I'll get the syrup," Vince offered, ducking behind his egg-cracking siblings to reach the refrigerator.

As the second round of pancakes turned golden brown, Marian appeared at Mom's elbow, gripping the silver mixing bowl full of freshly whisked eggs.

"They're ready, Momma! And I only had to rescue five shell pieces. That's a new record for me!"

"That's excellent, Marian. Why don't you and Jack work on getting out cups and utensils for everyone while I finish cooking?" Mom laughed. "It's lucky we have pancakes and eggs so often, to give me the super-training I needed for today. Not every mom could recognize when to flip pancakes by the light of a scented Christmas candle!"

Vince had taken a seat on the bench, closest to Sebastian's highchair. He waved a bite of pancake on his fork.

"Okay, Bas. You're a good, smart doggie. Can you tell me what kind of animal floats in the sea and likes to eat lettuce?"

Sebastian extended his arms out stiffly and fluttered his

hands up and down.

"That's a manatee!" he shouted, his voice reflecting excitement and pride.

"That's right! What a good little doggie you are! You've earned a treat!" With that, Vince shoved the pancake-laden fork into his brother's mouth.

"Ruff, ruff!" Sebastian said, giving his best canine imitation through a mouthful of food.

"Here's your next trick, good doggie," said Vince. "Does a manatee like to swim in the cold Arctic water, or the warm Florida water?"

He expectantly held another forkful of pancake before his brother's mouth.

"Manatees like warm!" Sebastian shouted, his arms still out straight, his hands now flapping madly.

"Good doggie!" Vince said, shoving another bite into Bas's open mouth.

"Those are great questions, Vince," Mom said. "Just make sure you're giving Bas enough time to chew in between, okay?"

She laid fresh stacks of pancakes in front of Jack and Marian and then scooped steaming scrambled eggs onto everyone's plates.

"Best dinner ever!" Sebastian cried as the eggs piled up in front of him.

"Pick up your fork and eat some," Mom suggested, but he just smiled and barked at her.

"My turn," Jack said. "Bassie, we know a manatee swims all day long, but tell me: Does a manatee breathe in water through gills, or air through its mouth?"

Sebastian stared blankly as he thought about the new question. Then both his arms and legs shot out stiffly with his hands and feet all flapping.

"Manatee breaths air!" he said triumphantly.

"That's right!" Jack said as Vince shoved eggs into Sebastian's mouth.

"You get a delicious pup treat because you're so smart!"

Vince said sweetly.

"Ruff, ruff!" Sebastian replied. "Yummy, yum, yum!"

"I have an idea," Marian said through a full mouth. "Let me have a turn!" She swallowed. "Bassie! Look at me, you good little puppy. See how I have my arms? Can you put your arms like this?"

Waiting to flip the final round of pancakes, Mom turned from the stove to look at Marian. Her daughter had raised one arm in the air as if waiting to be called on in class, while her other arm bent up to touch her shoulder. Sebastian chewed thoughtfully as he stared at his sister through the candlelight.

You can do it, Bas, Mom silently encouraged. *You can do it.*

The Big Three also waited in anticipation. When Sebastian's left arm lifted tentatively, Jack sucked in his breath. Vince spun and gave him a pointed glare. *Don't distract him,* his look admonished. Jack bit his lower lip and watched in silence.

"Look at my arms, Bas," Marian encouraged. "Make your arms do it, too!"

Sebastian's left arm lifted slowly in the air and a smile spread across his face.

"I do it!" he said.

"That's almost it, Bassie!" his sister encouraged. "Look at my other arm. What is it doing? See? Can your other arm do that?"

Sebastian lowered his left arm from the air and placed it tentatively on his shoulder.

"Now I do it?" he asked.

Vince leaned over and gently touched Sebastian's right hand, which was flapping up and down at the end of his rigid arm.

"Don't forget about this hand," he said kindly. "Where does this hand go?"

Startled, as though he'd forgotten about having two hands, Sebastian suddenly shot his right arm straight into the air, correctly mimicking his sister's unusual position. The kitchen erupted in jubilation.

"You did it, Bassie!" Jack cheered. "You get another delicious pup treat!"

Without skipping a beat, Vince shoved another forkful of eggs into his brother's mouth.

"You're such a good puppy, Bas," he cooed.

Ten minutes later, Jack, Marian, and Vince—having polished off an impressive stack of pancakes and a heaping pile of eggs—were now taking turns offering trivia questions and tasks to Sebastian so he could earn more pup treats. Despite their patience and endurance, Bas's Tigger plate still held more than half a pancake and at least a dozen bites of egg. It was his favorite dinner and he was being handfed, but somehow Sebastian never seemed hungry or motivated enough to eat. The task of cajoling him into finishing meals had become a family affair.

At Bas's last visit, the pediatrician had been concerned about his body mass index of just twelve percent. Although the subject hadn't been broached—*yet*, Mom grimaced—images of G-tubes had haunted her dreams ever since.

Bas's diminutive body needed calories, but he approached each meal as though the act of eating ran far second to the important work of expressing his love for everyone around him. Her thoughts took live form as she abruptly realized Sebastian was lying across his plate, smushing syrupy pancakes into his sweater as he tried to pull Vince into a hug.

"We best, best friends!" Sebastian shouted in his brother's ear.

"Good thing we didn't bring the laundry upstairs yet." Mom sighed. "Marian, my sweet, will you run and grab Sebastian a new shirt from his pile on the couch?"

"Yes, Momma," Marian chirped. "But first I'm putting on shoes. Those bricks are treacherous!"

Glancing at the glowing screen of her phone, Mom realized Matt was late again. At least the kids' activities were all at the same place this evening.

"Okay!" she said brightly. "I'm going to make a plate for Daddy and put it in the oven to keep it safe from sniffing doggies. I'm also going to finish helping Sebastian eat his dinner, which appears to now be covered in sweater fuzz. You kids need to get your homework done, and that includes instrument practice." She looked at the Big Three sternly. "Jack, why don't you bring your violin out here and do music first? Marian and Vince, you two can work on your math and spelling until Jack is done and then it'll be your turns. You all have swim practice tonight, so we need to hurry."

All three kids petulantly stuck out their bottom lips, and she steeled herself for an onslaught of excuses and complaints. But at that very moment, like a Christmas miracle summoned by the pine-scented jar candle burning on the table, the lights flickered on. Everyone cheered—the mutinous glares instantly forgotten.

Smiling to herself, Mom pushed up her black-framed glasses and launched quickly into loading the dishwasher. She'd gotten as far as gathering the utensils when she yelped in surprise at Matt grabbing her from behind and pulling her into a hug. The celebration of re-illumination had obviously masked the sound of the gate clinking and door opening.

The kitchen exploded in a wild cacophony of "Daddy's home! Daddy's home! Daddy's home!" mingled with indignant barking from Alice and Thomas Jefferson, their beloved behemoth dogs who—crouched under the table, ever-hopeful for food to fall—had also been caught unawares by Matt's stealthy entry. Not to be left out, Sebastian contributed to the racket by ruffing and howling with the dogs from his highchair.

Although Mom detested being startled, she smiled. The evening's schedule was hectic, but at least everyone was together now. Life was so much easier when they were all together.

SUNDAY, 9:30 P.M.

She'd done the dishes, scrubbed the counters, swept the back steps, signed the school papers, fed the dogs, picked up the stray toys, and was carrying still-warm laundry to the couch for folding when Matt finally descended the stairs. They took turns with bedtime, and technically tonight was her turn, but lately she'd been falling asleep on Sebastian's bed as she waited for him to settle down. There was nothing worse than waking up in the middle of the night, still wearing your clothes and glasses, and with a stiff neck, compliments of Winnie the Pooh—who in all fairness, never asked to be used as a makeshift pillow. Ever the hero, Matt had taken an extra shift.

"Finally!" he said, shooting her a smile and sighing. "Everyone is in bed, at least for now. Want to hang out?"

"Absolutely, yes!" she enthused. "I've been waiting for this all day." She dumped the laundry on the couch and grabbed his hand. "I've earned a treat," she said, tugging him towards the kitchen. "Want to share some popcorn?"

They'd gotten an air-popper for Christmas two years ago, a mighty marvel that could fill a giant bowl with fluffy white deliciousness while simultaneously melting fresh butter. Matt reached for the fridge and pulled out two cold beers. He cracked them open while she poured kernels into the heating tray.

"Hey! I forgot until right now," he said, holding a can out to her, "I got held up coming inside today. You won't believe what I saw scooting across the street as I pulled into the driveway!"

"I won't?" She grinned, her mind flashing to the moment before the power went out. "Sooo...if I guess correctly, will you get the beers from the fridge all night?"

"Sure," he replied confidently. "But you get only one try. And if you lose, you have to give Alice her medicine."

Mom held out her hand to him.

"Shake on it," she said sternly.

He reached out and playfully squeezed her hand just a smidge too hard.

"It's a deal!" they said simultaneously.

The popcorn began shooting to the top of the popper and pouring out the spout.

"It's a waterfall! A popcorn waterfall!" Mom cried, mimicking the kids' wonderment every single time they used the machine.

Matt rolled his eyes and poked her in the ribs.

"Enough of that," he teased. "That's like saying 'Beetlejuice' three times. You're going to summon our household demons!" They both laughed.

"Come on," she admonished. "We have good kids and you know it."

"Completely wonderful little people," he agreed. "And I love to be with them. But I don't want to be with them right now because I just spent an hour getting them to sleep!"

Laughing, she nodded her agreement. "They're exhausting sometimes. You know, last night, I actually had a dream about *Dog Town*. All the pups were barking at me to save the mayor's chicken. Turns out it was Thomas Jefferson wanting to go outside."

"Ha!" Matt laughed. "Now, stop stalling: What did I see in the road about five houses down? I can't wait to celebrate my freedom from wrapping a smelly antibiotic pill in an even smellier piece of bologna tonight."

Mom chewed her lip, pretending to think. "Hmmm...I only get one guess?"

"Yup," he gloated. "Make it a good one."

The popcorn was done and she flipped off the air-popper. She poured the butter and reached for the salt.

"You saw the water table," she said nonchalantly. "Our old, leaky blue water table." She rose up on tiptoe to kiss his cheek. "Am I right?"

"Hey!" he complained. "You cheated!"

She giggled. "How could I cheat? But I admit I did see it leaving. I was closing an office window and saw it spin past like a whirling dervish! I was going to chase it, but just then the power went out and I forgot about it entirely."

Matt folded his arms and pouted. "Well, I'm the one who rescued it."

She hugged him. "I'm glad you did. The leak isn't that bad, and the kids still play with it when the weather is nice. We should probably put it in the garage tomorrow, though. We're not going to see nice temperatures again until May."

He kissed the top of her head. "I already put it away. So that means you have to get the next round from the fridge, right?"

She slapped him on the arm. "That was *not* the deal!"

Laughing, they headed towards the living room, balancing drinks and popcorn.

"Wait a minute," she said suddenly. "You were way later than a jog to the corner and a trip to our garage. Did you have a late call on the ambulance?"

Matt sat down on the couch and patted the seat next to him. She snuggled in, looking up at him expectantly.

He sighed, and when he faced her, no trace of his smile remained. She'd been studying his moods for nearly twenty years now, and she knew well the expression that clouded his features. A bone-deep weariness drew his cheeks taut while his eyes flashed with fierce conviction.

"What happened, my love?" she asked quietly, reaching up to comb her fingers through his wavy brown hair.

"It's fine," he said calmly. "It wasn't work. I got out on time. I came home and then I ran for the water table. As I was rolling it back, a neighbor stopped me."

"Which neighbor?" she asked. She was sure it didn't really matter, but she was stalling—in dread of what had happened to crush his joy so completely.

"From somewhere across and down the street—I'm not even sure which house. He had some snacks he thought the kids would like. I left them on the steps to the basement."

He took a deep breath, obviously steeling for what came next. He shifted his body so they were face-to-face and held her hands.

"He asked about Sebastian," Matt said, and then added in a rush: "I think the treats were just a ruse, as if he's been waiting to catch one of us alone."

Mom let out her breath wearily. This was a not a new thing.

On any given day, a shocking number of people seemed to feel entitled to an explanation about Sebastian's idiosyncrasies, for no reason other than to satisfy their own curiosity. Strangers at a swim meet. People walking their dogs past their house. The lady cashing them out at the grocery store. They all asked.

Once or twice, people even rolled down car windows to shout questions about it. Just last Friday, a mom and grandma had watched from their car as Mom played with Sebastian on a grassy hill while they waited for Marian to be released from school. The grandma had rolled down her window and, shouting from across the road, asked Mom if she'd ever had her son tested for "problems." The woman no doubt meant well, but she was the fourth person to ask such a question that week. And, frankly, that represented a *light* week. It was exhausting.

They'd memorized a preemptive three-minute explanation about Sebastian's behaviors and diagnosis for friends or anyone they'd be spending considerable time with. This "elevator pitch" had proven an effective method for building an accepting community, which was something they needed. What they *didn't* need was for complete strangers to constantly remind them their kid had challenges.

And this neighbor—the one with the treats—was a man whose name she and Matt didn't even know.

"What did he say?" she asked, adrenaline coursing through her body.

"He came right to the point," Matt said. "'That boy of yours, your youngest,' he said. 'We see the kids playing, and we've been wondering: Is there something wrong with your youngest?'"

Mom was on her feet without knowing she'd stood up.

"Well?" she asked angrily. "What did you tell him?"

"I told him everything," Matt said simply, standing up and reaching for her hands again. "Everything I could think of. I told him that since he'd asked, I was going to tell him, and I kept talking at him until I sensed he felt uncomfortable with the amount of information he was being assaulted with." Matt's eyes flashed again. "*That's* why I was late."

Matt looked at the ground and sighed. "I know we want people to be kind to Bas, and to understand about him, but what the hell? There I was, standing in my uniform in the dark, holding the water table under our trees in the freezing wind. I mean, doesn't he know there's a time and a place? A freaking time and place." Matt paused to swig his beer. "But then I stood there, trying to figure out *when* is the right time and place to ask someone if their child has a disability. And I couldn't think of a single time I'd consider 'right.' So I decided to just roll with it. I don't know if it was the right thing to do, but I believe he was asking out of genuine concern, and we do need allies, right?" He looked up at her pleadingly. "A big part of me wanted to just punch him in the face. Sebastian is incredible. He beats the odds, and beats the odds, and works so hard." Mom felt the tears Matt was fighting burn behind her own eyes. "So how is it fair that people watching him play in our yard from their windows across the street can know there's something different about him? How is that fair?" His voice broke, and he stopped talking and pulled her into a hug.

As they stood there, clinging to each other, the rage she'd felt a second ago seeped out of her, replaced by exhaustion and uncertainty. Because, really, that's what events like this triggered in her. Some days—not often, but some days—Sebastian's challenges made both her and Matt feel afraid. Helpless. Hopeless. They stayed inside on those days, when they just weren't brave enough to shrug off the barrage of questions that always seemed to be out there, waiting.

The shoulder of Matt's gray sweatshirt was dark from wetness when she pulled her face away.

"You did the right thing, baby," she murmured. "I'm not sure I could have done it, but I hope so."

He looked down at her and smiled gently.

"You would have. You're even better at it than I am." His grin broadened. "You would have even pulled off a smile that looked convincing." He chuckled. "I probably looked like an evil possessed robot."

She giggled back. "No wonder he looked uncomfortable—it wasn't his visions of us three years from now, changing the diapers of a seven-year-old, or the looming threat of a G-tube, or us being crushed in a daily hug by a stinky adolescent Sebastian who doesn't understand hygiene or personal space. He was overcome with a dawning realization of the twisted automaton living across the street."

Matt summoned an unsettling leer and stiffened his arm out to make robotic grabbing motions at her chest.

"Hey!" She laughed, swatting his hands away. "Cut it out, creep-o!"

He pulled her back down on the couch and adjusted it to full recline position. Then he pointed the remote at their television and started the search for an evening show.

"It's time to relax," he said. "This popcorn isn't going to eat itself."

Still leaning forward to remain upright, she pulled the blanket up over her and resolutely finished her first can of beer.

"You're right. Let's relax. But first, please fetch me another beverage, my debonair water-table chaser."

24

MONDAY, 2:0I A.M.

She awoke to the shrill cry of Sebastian's screaming.

"Momma is coming, Bassie!"

She and Matt had fallen asleep on the couch, trying desperately to prolong the night. She thought about waking him but immediately opted against it. He looked relatively comfortable, and it took serious effort to rouse him. There was no time for that. More than once, Sebastian had tumbled down the stairs in his frantic attempts to reunite with her faster.

Yawning, she grabbed her phone, straightened up the recliner, and with a surge of adrenaline headed for the stairs.

"Momma's coming. You wait right there, and I'll pick you up...Here I come. Momma's here."

He was standing on his toes in the dark hallway dressed in his rumpled pirate pajamas, his light-blond hair askew. She scooped him up and carried him to the bathroom, holding his trembling body tight while murmuring a soft stream of reassurances in his ear.

"Momma's here. You're safe. Momma's here. Momma's taking you to the potty." She felt his skinny arms tighten around her neck as he burrowed his head into her hair. "It's night and you are in your safe home. Momma loves you."

They reached the bathroom and she planted him in front

of the toilet. He stood there obediently, taking panicked breaths. Meanwhile, she filled him a cup of water and quickly brushed her teeth. Then she risked a quick peek across the hallway at the Big Three, still sleeping soundly in their bunks.

At least it doesn't wake them anymore, she reflected gratefully.

She ducked back into the bathroom to find that Sebastian had grown bored of standing at the toilet and was exuberantly pouring the cup of water she'd given him into the bowl.

Sure, who needs a middleman? she thought wryly. Shaking her head in self-admonishment, she took the cup away.

"We need to change your diaper," she said gently. "We can do it right here if you can stand still."

Sebastian smiled at her and put his hands on her shoulders to steady himself as she knelt down for the quick switch.

As she was congratulating herself for successfully changing a standing four-year-old in the pitch dark, he shifted his grip and pulled her into a hug that caught her off-balance and slammed her knee into the ground with surprising force.

That'll be a bruise in the morning, she thought.

Aloud she whispered, "Thank you for that hug, Bassie. That was very nice."

Reassembling his pajamas, she carried him down the hallway to her own room, her newly sore knee complaining with each step. The clock on the shelf read 2:07, and she silently marveled at Sebastian's internal alarm.

Every single night, she thought. *Two o'clock on the dot, every single night.*

Setting her cell phone on the nightstand, she made sure the alarm indicator was blinking and then crawled into bed and tried to claim headspace on her memory foam pillow before Sebastian could plunk himself on it. His thin body snuggled in impossibly close, and his hand reached up to touch her face.

"I love you, Momma," his raspy nighttime voice said. "I just love you so much."

She yawned and kissed the top of his head. "I love you too, Sebastian. And now it's sleeping time for everyone, so you need to be resting."

"I resting, Momma. I resting in the dark." His voice was trying to whisper, but it more closely resembled a hoarse shout. "It's night out, Momma. The moon is out. There are werewolves out, Momma?"

"No, sweetie. There are no werewolves out tonight. They are all sleeping."

A yawn overtook her, and Sebastian broke through the pause.

"Where do sea lions live, Momma? They live on the rocky coast?"

"That's right, Bassie. Sea lions live on the rocky coast of California. Now, we've got to stop talking for tonight because it's time for resting. Let's get you one last drink of water." She reached onto the nightstand for the cup and helped his slight body sit up. He was getting stronger, but it was still difficult for him to go from lying to sitting without rolling around first—a fact he used to excuse late-night horseplay wherever he got a chance. He finished sipping and she lowered him back down to the pillow.

"Thanks for that nice water, Momma! That was a good, good drink."

"Here we go, Sebastian," she said, adjusting the blanket. "You've got Red the Dog and your sea lion, and you are ready for some good sleeping."

He settled into a comfortable position and his heavy eyelids drooped.

Please, she thought desperately, *Please, please let tonight be the night he actually goes back to sleep.*

After five minutes of fidgeting, his breathing slowed and became regular as he snuggled his two stuffed animals into her side. For one wild second, she thought he had drifted back to dreamland as easily as that. But then his toenail scratched her sore knee, and she realized his feet were pointing and flexing with steady precision under the covers.

At least he's quiet and content, she thought, closing her eyes in relief.

She had almost dozed off when a tiny voice started singing: *"Dog Town Adventures! Calling all the dogs! Time for a rescue! Go, puppy, go!"*

She took a deep breath and reached her arm up to smooth Bas's hair.

"Sebastian," she said softly, "it's not time for singing right now. We need to save our words for tomorrow, when the sun is out."

"Okay, Momma," he replied. "I love you. I sleeping here in your room with you."

"I love you, too, little man, but it's time for sleeping now. That means no more singing."

He closed his eyes again and hugged his animals tightly. As she felt sleep embracing her, she realized Sebastian was quietly humming the tune from Minuet III, the piece Marian had almost mastered on her violin. She wanted to stop him, but she knew it was pointless. It was the same every night: He'd be awake next to her until four in the morning. For Sebastian, AUTS2 meant that his mind just couldn't stay asleep for a whole night.

She felt his soft hand caress her cheek and was struck by the juxtaposition: *It's supposed to be the mom's job to hum lullabies and stroke faces.*

Then the weight of the exhaustion collected over four years of sleepless nights crushed her awareness, and she was unconscious once more, leaving her precious baby to sing quietly to himself in the dark.

DAY TWO

MONDAY, 5:30 A.M.

The alarm buzzed. In one fluid motion, she silenced the noise, extricated herself from Sebastian's draped limbs, and rose to her feet.

Deep sleep to battle-ready in seconds. Who says I'm not a warrior?

She stole a glance at the bed; Bas was still sleeping soundly.

Good morning to me, she thought blurrily, grabbing her clothes from their pre-prepped pile at the end of the bed and shuffling down the hallway for her shower. She wasn't always this lucky. Many mornings began with a sobbing Sebastian clinging stubbornly to her leg as she tried to set a new record for World's Fastest Shampooing.

The house was pitch black. The sun wouldn't be up for another hour. She flipped the light switch in the bathroom before remembering it had shorted out a few weeks ago while Jack and Vince "happened" to be playing Mad Scientist. No one had admitted responsibility and the problem hadn't been solved with new bulbs—her best and only idea, representing the limit of her electrical know-how.

I really need to remember to call an electrician.

She reached for the toy lantern she'd stowed atop the shelf over the towel rack and clicked the chunky plastic knob to the glow setting—passing over the option to cloak the bathroom ceiling in a planetarium-style presentation of Northern Hemisphere constellations.

Don't want to get too crazy! She giggled to herself.

Darkness still pervaded, but the lantern emitted just enough light to spot a plastic alligator, a Red the Dog action figure, and a rubber dinosaur lying in wait for her unprotected feet.

It really is my lucky day, she thought, grabbing them from the bottom of the tub and airlifting them, dripping, over to the sink.

Minutes later, she was fully dressed, her long wet hair soaking her clean sweatshirt as she fumbled with the laces of her trainers. She'd learned to be ridiculously fast in the shower because the less time you were in there, the less likely you were to be joined by a child.

The darkness was still complete. *I must have been really fast today*, she thought, reaching for her cell phone. Even in mid-November, she typically saw at least a hint of sunrise by the end of her shower. She pressed the home key and was puzzled to see the screen read *5:40 a.m.*

Did I just imagine my alarm? I could swear it went off. Why am I up forty-five minutes early?

She fumbled through her phone's camera roll, searching for the screenshot she'd taken of the family calendar for the next two weeks.

The orthopedist, she realized. *Sebastian has an orthopedic appointment this morning at 7:15. Which means we need to leave by 6:45. Which means he needs to be awake by 6:00 so there's a fighting chance he'll eat enough to be full.*

A wave of panic crashed into her stomach and rippled out through her body.

I never did the paperwork. It's still on the table under the green stepstool.

She swallowed and gazed into the mirror. The face staring

back at her in the dim glow of the toy camping lantern modeled an unflattering combination of exhaustion, guilt, and dismay. With dark circles under her eyes, deep worry lines creased in her forehead, and a bottom lip tucked under in consternation, she barely recognized the reflection as her own. She shook her head and tried out a smile, succeeding only in achieving a pathetic pleading look.

Cripes! she chided. *Get a grip. Forgotten paperwork is not a crisis. It's not even an emergency. Chill out.*

But the thumping panic was now awash with cold dread. She contemplated canceling the appointment—inventing an excuse for the opportunity to try again another day—but the fantasy died before it was fully realized.

Sebastian needs this. His pediatrician was very clear. If Bas needs surgery to correct his feet, it won't do anyone any favors to delay his first appointment. This HAS to happen.

She watched her brow furrow and her eyes tear up. Thinking about *why* they had to visit the orthopedist was strictly off-limits. *It's just a precaution,* she told herself. *Just to be safe and sure.* But it was too late. The thought had slipped out and now the tears spilled over. She reached for a tissue and silently dabbed at her face.

That's enough now! she tried again. *Whatever this day is going to dish out, you can handle. Because you're tough. You're stronger than anything today or any day can throw at you. Never forget who you are.*

But that face in the mirror—the depleted, exhausted, frightened face with tears pouring down its cheeks—needed further reminding.

She had to dig deep.

You are the mom who met with a geneticist and told her that Sebastian had a rare genetic mutation—even before any bloodwork or testing had been conducted. You knew. Because you were already an expert in Sebastian. Then you researched and learned and became an expert in rare genetic conditions, too.

You knew. And you told her. And you were right.

She took a deep breath and reached for a tissue.

By that time, Mom had been no stranger to unusual health situations. As fate would have it—maybe the universe's way of preparing her for the challenges of Sebastian's diagnosis—the Big Three had already endured more than their share of medical encounters.

You are also the mom who sat alone, she remembered, *patiently waiting through <u>both</u> of Marian's hernia surgeries.*

You are <u>also</u> the mom who ran into a cloud of swarming, angry hornets to save Vince. <u>And</u> the mom who ran out of the swarm, shielding Vince and baby Sebastian from those hornets with your own body. And even though you fell in that field, you managed to tumble over your babies without hurting them, protecting them from endless stings until help arrived.

She wiped at her eyes and then blew her nose.

Remember: <u>You</u> are the mom who searched and fought until you found a pediatric surgeon willing to attempt the heart procedure Jack needed. You knew the risks—the terrifying risks—but you also knew how ineffective his medication was. You saw how those pills drained him. You saw the half-life he was living. So <u>you</u> are the mom who said it wasn't okay. You said "NO" to having your nine-year-old be too tired to get out of bed before noon. You refused to accept a "solution" that left Jack unable to walk home from the bus stop each afternoon.

Remember the ambulance rides—so many ambulance rides—and the nights in the Pediatric Intensive Care Unit with your little boy who was too tired to be afraid. <u>You</u> put things in motion to make it all stop. And when that day came, the worst day you ever lived, <u>you</u> were the mom who kissed Jack good-bye and kept your confident and encouraging smile as they wheeled him away to the operating theater for the eleven-hour cardiac surgery that saved his life.

Mom filled the bathroom cup with cold water and gulped it down. Then she found her toothbrush and attacked her mouth with vigor.

<u>You</u> are the mom who gets through whatever you need to.

Every time. So right now, I'd tell you to grow up, but you've already taken "adulting" to new levels.

She spat into the sink.

Today is an initial visit with a new specialist. An initial visit. You've faced down monsters; there's no need to fear a squirrel. Cut it out and move on with your morning.

The end.

Her internal pep talk over, she stared at herself in the mirror. The blue eyes peering out from her curtain of wet blond hair were dry. The nervousness and uncertainty were gone. Exhaustion was still there—it was *always* there—but it now served to emphasize the blazing determination that had taken over her expression. To her surprise, she actually looked intimidating.

Pushing on her black-rimmed glasses, she gave herself a steely glare. *So you forgot about the paperwork. Oh, well. You can pretend you left it at home. They'll give you a new set, and you can fill it out in the waiting room.*

Leaving it at that, she opened the bathroom door to creep quietly down the hallway. Although she'd been stealthy in her activities, Vince the Early Riser was there, fully dressed and waiting patiently on the floor for her. Luckily, the acquired reflex of checking for lurking children in dark morning hallways was one of her Supermom powers. This was nothing new.

Putting her finger dramatically to her lips, she gestured toward the stairs. Vince nodded theatrically and followed her like a shadow. They snuck down the stairs and made their way past Matt, still sound asleep on the couch, to the kitchen. Vince turned on the light while Mom hurried down the steps to the back door. She unbolted and opened it so that the dogs could access the exit flap Matt had installed in the outer storm door. Though Alice and Thomas Jefferson hadn't come down yet, when they awoke, heading outside would be their number one priority.

"Good morning, Vincey!" Mom said brightly as she reappeared at the top of the back stairs. "You, sir, are up *very* early today!"

"Good morning, Momma! You were in the shower and I waited. Isn't this the same time I get up every day?"

"Nope," she answered, "but that's okay because now you can be my helper." She pulled him into a hug. "We have to make some good breakfast. Momma's up early because Sebastian has a doctor's appointment this morning. *You* are up early because you pop out of bed like a waffle pops out of the toaster." She grinned at him, her lighthearted third child. "I'm thinking we should serve some fruit, cheese, and cereal. How do you feel about that? Would you prefer to peel mandarin oranges or cut up some apples?"

She knew what his answer would be, but she asked anyway, looking forward to his proud excitement at being trusted with a knife.

"I'm the star potato cutter of this family, so I think I should do the apples," he said. "I know just where my special knife is, and I'm six now, so cutting up fruits and vegetables is easy for me." He tilted his head and squinted his eyes in concentration. "I even remember about the core. That's different from potatoes, but I remember."

Grinning at Vince's confidence, Mom placed four apples by the cutting board in front of him and kissed the top of his head. Then she hurriedly gathered bowls and spoons and set them on the table before heading back to the cupboard to collect a mismatched assortment of plastic cups, which she filled only halfway with water to minimize the effects of inevitable spills.

Vince began singing "Bohemian Rhapsody" as he chopped apples into bite-sized chunks like an experienced sous-chef.

"Momma? I've been wondering. How old is the oldest person alive?"

And so, the random questions begin.

"Hmmm...I'm not sure, Vincey. I left my phone upstairs, but if you remind me later, we can look it up online."

"I think they're about a hundred and ten!" Vince said. "But I'm going to get even older than that because of all the healthy food I eat. Plus, I'm going to be a scientist who discovers how to make people live longer."

Cheese in hand, she turned from the fridge to respond, but Vince's mind was wide awake this morning, and he had already switched topics.

"How many different breeds of dogs are there?"

"I'm not sure, Vince. Quite a few."

"More than fifty?"

"Yes, more than fifty," she replied.

"More than seven hundred?"

"I'm not sure, buddy. I don't think so, but we'll have to research it."

"Okay. I want to have a bunch of different breeds on my farm when I grow up. And also, donkeys. Is there more than one type of donkey? I want to have a farm of dogs and donkeys. They are both very friendly and helpful animals. Plus, dogs and donkeys can be friends with each other. Those are my favorite animals." He paused and looked at her in alarm. "But when I go on vacation, will you watch them? Will you watch thirty dogs and ten donkeys if I go to Disney?"

She laughed out loud. "I don't know, Vince. Are you going to go to Disney and leave me behind?"

The look of shock on his face was genuine and adorable.

"Eek! Oh no! That's a terrible idea. I'll get a donkey-sitter. Is there such a thing as a donkey-sitter? And I'll send the dogs to an overnight daycare somewhere. Or I could hire a neighbor to watch my farm. I can't go to Disney without *you*!"

She rumpled his shiny blond hair and poked him in the ribs. He squealed in delight. All four apples had been hacked into cubes, and she scraped them onto the four plastic breakfast plates shaped like a monkey, an owl, a spaceship, and Tigger.

"I've got to run up and grab Bassie," she said. "Do you want to put five cheese cubes on each plate?"

Mom handed Vince the bag of pre-cut yellow cheese and poked him in the ribs one more time for good measure.

Vince's laugh was one of the happiest sounds she'd ever

heard. It followed her as she jogged through the house, her bruised knee feeling every step. She took the stairs two at a time, chagrined that she was somehow running five minutes behind.

Sebastian was sprawled sideways across her queen-sized bed, mouth open and breathing gently. His long dark eyelashes stood out in stark contrast with his pale skin.

If a Renaissance cherub ever dressed in pirate pajamas, this is how he would look.

She stood perfectly still, admiring her beautiful baby and hating what had to come next. *Never wake a sleeping Sebastian!* Her whole body recoiled at the thought of disrupting him, knowing exactly how hard it was for him to rest.

I haven't found clothes for him yet, she reminded herself. *He can sleep another minute.*

She crept down the hallway to their small spare bedroom that was currently crowded with overstuffed bookshelves and knee-high stacks of books in front of them, a rack of dress-up clothes, giant boxes of assorted diapers, a wardrobe filled with Jack's clothes, and a dresser filled with Sebastian's. After running Sebastian's schedule for today through her head—*orthopedist, school, swim lesson, home*—she grabbed a yellow-and-gray sweater and a pair of elastic-waisted pants with a functional tightening string. *Warm, fancy, and easy to pull off and on*, she basked. *Perfect.* She snatched a pair of socks from his top drawer and smiled at finding a legitimately matched pair on the first try. Then, tucking the outfit under her arm, she dug through the pile of diapers in the corner.

Pull-up, need a pull-up, she chanted. *School day means a pull-up.* At two months past his fourth birthday, Sebastian still didn't seem to recognize when his body needed to visit the toilet. School diligently took him to try every hour, so she wanted to make the process as painless as possible for everyone involved. *Ta-da!* she rejoiced triumphantly. *The last pull-up. We need to get more today, but this will work for right now.*

Outfit sorted, she snuck past the bunk room where Marian

and Jack were still asleep and popped back into her bedroom. Sebastian was snoring softly, his slim three-and-a-half-feet stretched across the disheveled blankets, looking for all the world like a child who had an easy relationship with sleep. She sighed, wishing for the thousandth day in a row that his nighttime schedule was more conventional. Then she flipped on the light.

"Good morning to you!" she sang in quiet cheerfulness. *"Good morning to you! Good morning, sweet Sebastian...Good morning to you!"* She leaned in and kissed his smooth cheek.

He stretched lazily and then his eyes fluttered open. "Good morning, Momma," he said thickly. "I have school?"

"Yes, you do," she replied, helping him sit up and take a sip from the water cup. "But first, we have to eat breakfast. Are you ready to come downstairs with me?"

"Yup. I so, so hungry." He scooted onto her lap and put his arms around her neck. "Carry me, Momma—carry me down. I hungry. Like a walrus."

She stood up with his warm body clinging to her chest. Grabbing his clothes and his two stuffed animals, she headed for the dark stairwell, stepping as quietly as possible to avoid waking Jack and Marian.

"Good morning, Bassie!" exclaimed Vince as soon as they appeared in the doorway. "Look at this great breakfast we have! I cut you up some yummy apples all by myself!"

"Yummy, yum, yum! Walruses eat apples, Momma?" Sebastian asked.

"Oh, yes," she answered quickly. "Walruses *love* apples for breakfast. It helps them to grow big and strong."

Vince was suddenly at her elbow, shout-whispering as only a six-year-old can. "I think, actually, walruses are carnivores, just eating fish and clams and stuff. Or maybe omnivores. But are there apples in the Arctic?"

A steely "mom glare" stopped Vince in his tracks.

"Walruses are car-nee-cores?" Sebastian asked in concern, his hand clutching an apple chunk, now frozen halfway to his mouth.

Vince smiled brightly at his baby brother. "No, Bassie. Walruses *are* apple-eaters!" he asserted. "I'm a *big* walrus, and those apples on your Tigger plate look delicious, so you better eat them quick!" He gave a loud roar and reached out his hand in slow motion as if to steal his brother's food.

Sebastian's arms and legs shot out straight, his hands flapping up and down in excitement, sending the apple he'd been clutching flying across the kitchen where it landed on the floor. Vince ran to collect it and then rinsed it hastily in the sink and put it back on Sebastian's plate with a sheepish glance at his mother.

"I'm not sure why I said that," he murmured. "Sorry, Momma."

Vince gave her a squeeze and then, peeking around her at his younger brother, declared loudly: "Walruses like cereal, too—right, Momma? And *this* walrus wants to have some Cinnamon Bun Crunch this morning. How about you, Bassie Walrus? Do you want some, too?"

"I love cinny-un-unch," Sebastian replied with his mouth full. "Yummy, yum, yum." Then he opened wide and roared the sound he imagined walruses make, shooting apple bits across his tray onto Vince's arm.

Handing Vince a napkin, Mom grabbed the bag of cereal from inside the microwave, stashed safely out of reach of mischievous dogs, and poured bowls for the boys. She sloshed milk, found spoons, and served both walruses their Cinnamon Bun Crunch with a flourish. Then she sat down and pulled her chair directly up to Sebastian's tray and began the morning task of trying to make him eat.

We have only thirty minutes. I hope he's feeling helpful today.

"Let's put on some good eating music," she said cheerfully as she attempted to push a spoonful of cereal into Sebastian's mouth. "What do you think, boys? Violin songs or trumpet?"

"Let's do violin, Momma," Vince urged. "Jack isn't even up yet to hear his trumpet songs, and I need to hear my songs again a few times before lessons tonight. That's how I get so good at playing, you know. Listening to the songs."

Sebastian was chewing away and didn't comment, but as soon as "Twinkle, Twinkle, Little Star" began tinkling from her phone, he hummed along contentedly.

So far so good. He's had two apple chunks and one bite of cereal already.

"Where my walrus, Momma? Where my elephant seal?" Having swallowed, Sebastian turned his head in expert evasion maneuvers to avoid her next spoonful.

"I've got your fluffy sea lion right here, Bas," she said. "Will he work?"

When Bas opened his mouth to answer, she pushed the spoon in.

And immediately regretted it.

Amateur move, she lamented, watching him leave his mouth hanging open, allowing the cereal and milk to dribble out of it down the front of his pajamas.

"Where my walrus? Where my elephant seal?" Sebastian's voice cracked as he geared up for a meltdown. "I *need* them."

"Hey, Bassie! I'll go get them for you, but you need to eat four bites for each of them. Is it a deal?" Vince stood at Sebastian's tray, his own cereal neglected on the table, hopefully holding out his pinky finger.

Sebastian lifted his miniature hand and spread his fingers wide, allowing his big brother to link his pinky. "You get my walrus and my elephant seal, I eat. We best, best walrus friends."

Vince grinned and took off at lightning speed. Mom shoved a spoonful of cereal into Bas's mouth.

"That, one!" Sebastian shouted, proudly counting his bites.

Mom glanced at the clock and jumped up, suddenly realizing her drying hair hadn't been combed and her Survival Bag hadn't been packed.

"You keep chewing, Bassie Walrus. I have to finish getting ready."

At that moment, frantic thundering footsteps on the stairs broke through the violin rendition of "Lightly Row." Jack and Marian were fleeing full-speed from the imaginary monsters that left them terrified of being upstairs alone.

Please let them be dressed, Mom pleaded, recalling yesterday morning when they'd appeared in nothing but underwear. November mornings were cold in the kitchen, but it had proven surprisingly difficult to convince the kids to face those imaginary monsters to collect their warm clothes from upstairs.

Mom grabbed two more bowls, filled them with cereal and milk, and plunked spoons on the table. When Jack and Marian appeared, she was pulling Sebastian's dripping hands out of his own bowl and stuffing another bite of cereal into his mouth.

"That's two," she said, giving Sebastian head's a kiss. "Good morning, kiddos! I've set up your breakfast. Did you sleep well?"

"I cut up the apples for you," Vince said proudly as he reappeared in the kitchen brandishing a small plastic walrus and elephant seal. "How many bites did you do already, Bas?"

"Two," Marian responded with a yawn. "How many does he need?"

"Four per animal," Vince replied. "So you're halfway to your walrus, Bassie! Have another bite of that yummy cereal." He shoved in a mouthful using his own spoon.

As Mom stepped over to hug her two big kids, Jack looked at the stove clock in surprise.

"Why are we up already? It's only six-thirty. That's really early for a school day."

"Awww, man!" Marian protested. "I wanted to sleep in!"

Mom squeezed them tight. "Momma and Bas have to leave in fifteen minutes for a visit to the foot doctor," she explained. "They're going to tickle Sebastian's toes and see if they can make him laugh."

Her story had the desired effect on Sebastian, who extended his arms and legs in excitement. "They tickle my toes?" he asked.

The Big Three, however, were not as easily assuaged. Vince

looked confused, Jack concerned, and Marian on the verge of tears.

"Sit down and eat, love bugs," Mom said calmly. "It's not a big deal. Just a quick appointment so the bone doctor can look at Bassie's feet and make sure he should be wearing his doggie braces all day every day. He's going to school right after, and he'll probably still be on time." She pulled Sebastian's hand out of his cereal bowl again and shoved another spoonful into his mouth. "That's four! Great job, walrus! Here's your walrus friend!"

Sebastian grabbed the toy and plunged it into his bowl with an ecstatic walrus-like bellow.

Jack snorted. "No one is allowed to be surprised at that," he said tightly, fighting back laughter.

"Momma," said Marian, "your hair needs help if you're going to an appointment today. I'll feed Bas. You'd better do something about it quick."

"Eek! I was on my way to do that but got distracted. Thanks, Sissy."

Mom ducked into the bathroom-slash-laundry room—an eclectic but useful room that extended off the back of the kitchen and ran the length of the dining room—and stood before the mirror dragging a brush through her already-dried tangles.

"Lucky thing it's cold out!" she called. "Because this hair is a complete disaster. Looks like it's officially a Hat Day."

With only twelve minutes remaining, Mom ran through her checklist: *Pack the bag for the doctor, dress Sebastian, grab his school stuff, wake Matt.* Her own breakfast would have to wait.

She grabbed an empty cloth bag from the top of the dryer and snuck out the bathroom's side door into the dining room. She jogged through the archway into the living room and turned on her heel. Scanning the built-in shelving units, she threw three books, a squishy ball, Red the Dog, jingle bells that attach to your wrists, and a small container of molding clay into the bag with wipes and a handful of diapers. Reconsidering, she took out the jingle bells. *No time for coffee this morning—don't torture yourself.*

"Wake up, honey," she said brightly to Matt, turning on the

lights. "Sebastian and I have to leave in ten minutes for his orthopedic appointment. I forgot about it until this morning. You have to be in charge of bus stop times today."

Matt groaned and rolled over. She zipped past, remembering that Sebastian's doggie braces were upstairs in the bunk room. *Momma to the rescue*, she thought as she pulled them out from under two damp towels discarded in a heap after last night's showers.

Nine minutes left: *Dress Sebastian, grab his school stuff, get to the van.*

She flew back down the stairs, yanking the blanket off Matt on her way past.

"Hey!" he shouted.

"You *have* to get up, honey. I'm leaving now. The Big Three are here and they need you to make sure they get to their buses on time."

Back in the kitchen, Sebastian was holding his plastic walrus in his right hand and his elephant seal in his left. His toys won, he'd cemented his lips shut.

"Please open up, Bassie," Marian was begging. "You need to eat a few bites more so you can grow big and strong."

"I've got it from here, Sis," Mom said, leaning over to give Marian a hug. "Sebastian, I need you to eat three more bites so your tummy gets full."

Bas looked at her and then turned to his brothers and sister. Satisfied everyone was watching, he opened his mouth, smiled a wide smile, and said, "I love milk!" Then he dropped both toys into his red plastic cereal bowl and, before anyone could stop him, picked it up and dumped it on his head.

Milk and soggy Cinnamon Bun Crunch poured down his face, the back of his head, and the neck of his pajama shirt.

Mom closed her eyes and took a deep breath, feeling Marian's hand slip into hers. The happy chatter had ceased and the only sounds were the steady drip of milk onto Sebastian's tray and the perky notes of Minuet I floating out from the violin playlist.

Kindness. Courage. Understanding. Mom chanted the phrase in her head, trying to draw strength. *I'm just so tired.*

She opened her eyes. "Sebastian," she said calmly, "it's a good thing we didn't get you dressed yet, because now you are all wet and sticky. Cereal stays in our bowl or it goes in our mouth. But cereal is *not* supposed to go on our head."

Licking his face happily, Bas hunched forward to eat bits of cereal that had stuck to the front of his pajamas. He stopped to look up at her. "I have hat, Momma."

The doctors and specialists thought he'd never talk, she reminded herself. *Listen to all his wonderful words.* Except right at this moment, now just seven minutes until she needed to be in the van, it was difficult to revel in the daily miracle that was Sebastian.

Jack's voice broke the silence. "He's wearing a fez, Momma. Fezzes are cool. And you *did* say it was a Hat Day."

Mom looked from Jack to Sebastian. The red cereal bowl *did* look like a fez, precariously perched on Bas's head. She broke into laughter.

Bas squealed in delight. "Hat Day! I wear a hat, Momma. Just like you!"

Taking in the full view of Sebastian, with cereal and milk dripping down his face and pooling on the floor, she laughed even harder.

"Momma, I'm going to go turn on the van for you, okay?" said Jack. "It can have a few minutes to warm up. Is the Survival Bag all packed?"

"Thank you, Jack," Mom said, still giggling. "Take Sebastian's backpack too, please."

"I got towels for the floor, Momma." Vince dumped an armload of clean, folded beach towels on the spill of milk under Sebastian's highchair.

"Good deal, buddy. Thank you." Two towels from the dirty pile would have done the trick, but Mom wasn't going to complain. She needed all the help she could get.

"Okay, Sebastian," she said. "Let's see what we can do with you."

She hefted him onto the counter and began to strip him down.

"Vince, could we use one of those towels?"

He handed her a towel from the floor, and she rubbed Sebastian's milky wet head, shoulders, chest, and arms.

"I don't think we can save his hair, Momma," said Marian, "but what if we use this?"

Marian held out the small jar of hair wax that Jack, who had just recently taken an interest in his appearance, used to spike his hair straight up.

"Perfect! Great idea, Sissy. Arms through, Sebastian. Let's get this sweater on you first."

Mom shoved him into his pull-up, yanked up his pants, and crammed his frozen feet into the matched octopus socks. She then began the process of strapping his feet into his braces and wedging them into his trainers.

At least this part doesn't take me ten minutes anymore, she thought.

"Stand up, Bassie. Go use the potty before I tie your pants. Otherwise they'll fall down off your skinny little buns."

"I have cutie little buns!" Sebastian declared happily.

"I'll help him," Vince offered, leading Sebastian into the bathroom and leaving the door ajar.

Mom zipped up her coat and jammed a striped knit beanie onto her head while Sebastian stood at the toilet.

"I take my walrus and my elephant seal?"

"Here you go, buddy," Marian said quickly. "I rinsed them off for you."

While Sebastian reunited with his toys amid joyful shouts, Mom helped him pull up his pants and tied them. Then she put a blob of wax into his hair and styled it upward as though they'd intended him to look like a miniature punk rocker.

"Okay, now. Coat on, Bas! We've got to go. MATT!!!" Mom shouted toward the living room. "I'm leaving. GET UP NOW!" She heard the creaking of the reclined couch being shoved back into the upright position. "Daddy is here," she told Vince and Marian. "He'll help make sure you don't miss the bus. Don't forget your saxophone and sheet music, Marian."

She scooped up Sebastian and headed for the back door, bumping into Jack.

"It snowed," he whispered excitedly.

Her heart sank. That would add another five minutes to their walk to the van, and at least ten minutes to their drive to the orthopedist.

But she put on a smile. "You were all so helpful this morning," she told the Big Three. "Thank you, guys! It snowed, so wear gloves. That way you can make snowballs without getting frostbite! I love you, and I'll see you at the end of school."

They chorused good-byes as she bustled Sebastian out the door.

Outside, Bas trembled in exhilaration.

"Snow! Cold, cold snow!" he cried. "I touch it!"

He let go his arms from around her neck to reach out for it, causing her to almost drop him.

First snow, she reminded herself. *Kindness. Courage. Understanding.* Wincing at the pain in her knee, she set Bas gently on the driveway. He ran in place, his skinny legs bouncing up and down while he tried to bend over and touch the glistening white covering on the ground.

"How does the snow feel, Sebastian?"

"It so cold! It cold and wet! I eat it?"

Pulling him by the hand, she led him to the gate.

"Here's some fresh and clean snow you can try. It's going to be cold in your mouth, though."

He reached into the fence lattice and pulled out a mini-sized ball of snow.

"Yummy, yum, yum!" he shouted, jumping up and down on stiff legs while his hands flapped frenetically.

She grabbed the elephant seal midair as it flew past her face and then dragged her youngest son out through the gate. She replaced the complicated series of latches and locks that kept Thomas Jefferson—their expert escape artist—from leaving their yard and tugged on Sebastian's arm to make him walk. Shivering as she tromped through the thin layer of snow to the van, she silently thanked Jack for thinking to warm it up.

The sliding door didn't open on her first pull, but a strong yank freed it from the ice that had tried to freeze it shut.

I really need to remember to thank Jack, she thought again, leaning over to pick up Sebastian. *That could have been awful.*

She put her hand on Sebastian's leg to hoist him into his car seat. *What the...?*

He was saturated.

He didn't fall in the snow, did he? He couldn't have. She'd held his hand the entire time. *It can't be milk. And I just changed him.* That's when she realized: *Pull-up. He's wearing a pull-up.*

Perfect for kids who were potty training, pull-ups were great at containing a small dribble to allow the wearer to get to the bathroom in time. Pull-ups were *not,* however, designed for kids who didn't realize they were going. And Sebastian, who had stood at the toilet not more than three minutes ago, still did not realize when he was going.

Mom sighed and picked him up, feeling the wetness soak her coat sleeve as she sprinted back towards the house.

We're going to be late.

MONDAY, 7:35 A.M.

"Next."

She slung the Survival Bag higher on her shoulder, re-tucked Sebastian's winter coat under her arm, held her steaming café mocha out with her right hand to prevent spillage, and grabbed Sebastian's arm with her left hand to drag him along to the window.

"Hi there," she said, trying for an upbeat smile. "This is Sebastian. Our appointment was for seven-fifteen but we're a bit late. We had a soggy pants incident in our driveway, and it wasn't a fast fix. I'm so sorry."

There'd also been an I-need-to-stop-for-coffee-or-I'm-going-to-have-a-breakdown moment, but that was nobody's business.

"Do you have your paperwork?"

"No." She'd originally intended to act surprised, but she didn't have energy to spare for the charade. "I left it on the kitchen table."

The secretary tutted for a moment and then handed her a clipboard with a thick stack of forms attached.

"These will all need to be completed and turned in before I can put you on the list to be seen. It's going to take you some time. It would have been better to bring them."

Releasing Sebastian's hand to reach for the paperwork, Mom

locked eyes with the woman behind the counter. "It's been a rough morning."

It took only three seconds to secure the clipboard and a pen, but three seconds is a lifetime for a small child who suddenly finds his hand free. As Mom stowed the paperwork alongside the coat under her arm, she caught a strange wobbling movement out of the corner of her eye.

Somehow Bas had worked his way onto the strap that was affixed between two posts to serve as a line indicator, to keep waiting patients from crowding those at the window. He'd pulled it down under his bottom and was trying to use it as a swing. Unfortunately, the posts weren't designed to support twenty-eight pounds of excited preschooler.

Oh no no no! This is going to be bad!

She lurched forward and—covering an impossible distance in a nanosecond—managed to snag the nearest pole as it careened towards the ground and prevent it from smashing into Sebastian's head as it lost its battle with gravity. The second pole tipped backwards in slow motion, and to her horror, fell hard against a man on a crutch with a prosthetic leg who was awaiting his turn at the window.

"No worries," the man grunted, pushing the post back upright. "Not like it's going to leave a bruise, right?"

Completely unfazed by his fall and the ensuing commotion, Sebastian smiled up at the man from his landing spot.

"Phew! That a close one!" he said brightly. "You want a donut? I having a doctor donut party!" He held out the cardboard box of donut holes that had also been acquired during their coffee pit stop.

"Sebastian," Mom told him, "the line guides aren't for sitting on. Are you okay, buddy? Did you bonk your head?"

"I okay. I just fall. That swing not work."

"Stand up, then, and let's apologize to this man. This isn't a swing, Bassie. You made the pole tip over onto him."

Sebastian clumsily rolled onto his knees and hoisted himself unsteadily to his feet. Then, after picking up his donut box, he launched himself into a full-body hug of the stranger's prosthetic leg.

"I sorry! I try to swing. But I had a great fall."

"That's okay, buddy," the man said graciously, hopping against his crutch to adjust to the unexpected exuberant hug. "No one got hurt."

"I'm so sorry," Mom said, returning the poles to their original positions while noticing for the first time the warm heat on her legs that meant she'd spilled at least half her café mocha across her pants.

"No worries at all, ma'am," the man replied, awkwardly patting Sebastian's spiky head.

Mom smiled at him and decided not to dwell on the look he was giving her, recognizing it immediately as the expression people get as they decide whether or not it would be appropriate to ask questions or, worse, offer condolences.

"Look, Bas!" Mom deflected. "They have bead tables over there to play with! Want to check them out with me? Momma has some homework to do, and you can play."

"I eat donuts, too?" Sebastian asked, unwrapping himself from the man, rising onto his toes, and flipping his take-along cardboard donut box up and down with his excited hands.

"Absolutely, yes! You can eat your donuts and play with your toys."

"Yay! Best. Morning. Ever!" Sebastian shouted, before taking off running towards the colorful bead tables on his tippy toes, his arms extended straight out at his sides.

Twenty minutes. It won't take longer than twenty minutes. She took a deep breath. *Time to face the music.*

She piled her armloads onto an empty chair, placed her half-cup of café mocha on the magazine table, and got to work reducing their family's trauma to dates, symptoms, and deficits.

When she reached the privacy statement signature pages fifteen minutes later, she looked up in triumph...before realizing in panic that she hadn't heard Sebastian since giving him the molding clay three pages ago. She leapt to her feet and saw his blond hair spikes in front of the water cooler, where he was eagerly dispensing fresh, ice-cold, filtered water into his clay container.

At least the paperwork is done, she thought as she hustled across the carpeted waiting room. The sleeves of Sebastian's chunky gray-and-yellow sweater were saturated from the elbows down and the molding clay was certainly destroyed, but it was the smell emanating from the corner that worried her the most.

"Bassie, my love, did you go potty?"

"Hi, Momma! I so thirsty! This water is yummy, yum, yum!"

"Let's not drink out of the clay cup, buddy. They have paper cups, see? Here." She filled a cone-shaped cup. "Have a nice drink from this."

When he finished with a loud, theatrical slurp, she took him by the hand.

"Momma is done with her homework. Come with me to turn it in, okay?"

"Okay, Momma. Sure! I bring my donuts?"

"Of course, Sebastian."

She dropped the clay container into a trashcan on their way to the window and stood at the line entrance to await their turn, holding Sebastian's hand tightly to avoid another swinging incident. The voice came almost immediately.

"Next."

"Hi, again. Here's our paperwork all filled out." She cleared her throat nervously as she handed over the clipboard. "Also...do you have a changing table in the ladies bathroom?"

The woman behind the glass leaned from her chair to get a full view of Sebastian.

"Well, it has an infant changing station that folds down from the wall." She met Mom's eyes. "But he's far too big to fit on it."

Feeling her adrenaline surge, Mom blinked hard and forced her mouth into a massive smile.

"Thanks! We'll go check it out. It'll take us a few minutes, so if you call us and we don't respond, that's where we are."

She hurriedly bent down to pick up her precious baby and to escape the woman's disapproving glare. But from his new height, Sebastian could see a potential best friend through the glass.

"Hi!" He waved animatedly at the receptionist. "I'm Sebastian. I here to have my toes tickled. You want a donut? I share with you!"

Mom glanced at the woman, not bothering to hide whatever her face revealed, and then walked purposefully back to the chair to grab her Survival Bag.

Kindness. Courage. Understanding, she chanted. *She can think whatever she wants. She doesn't know us. It doesn't matter.*

Mom piled their coats, Survival Bag, donut box, and café mocha in the carpeted hallway outside the ladies room, recoiling at the thought of setting their belongings on a public bathroom floor. She whipped out a package of wipes and a regular diaper.

School can put him in back in a pull-up when he gets there, she consoled herself. *No big deal.*

Miraculously, after the driveway incident this morning, Marian had found one more pull-up hiding in the living room diaper basket, but now they were truly, officially out until Mom got to the store.

"Come on, Bassie, let's get you changed."

With a sinking feeling, she saw that while the receptionist may have been rude, she was also correct. Bas's astonishing growth spurt over the past year was wonderful in every way—except in moments like this. Now nearly forty inches in height, Sebastian was far too long to lie on a changing table designed for babies. Complicating matters, AUTS2 robbed him of balance—helped only slightly by his braces—which made it difficult for him to stand during the process.

To top things off, Sebastian had a fear of the loud, echoing abruptness of toilets being flushed in public restrooms. Mom could feel his heart pounding through the front of his sweater.

"You no flush?" he whimpered.

"No, I won't flush. I promise. You're wearing a diaper, and wipes can't go down the drain, so we don't need to use the toilet at all. That's lucky, because both of these stalls are too small to fit us both. We'll change you here by the sinks. And if we're fast, no one else will come in and flush either."

"No loud flush?" he whimpered again.

"I promise," she said, kissing his cheek. "Now, you're going to have to stand, Bassie-Boo. And it's yucky in here, so you're going to have to try to hold still. But we can do it, right?"

"Right, Momma. We are best, best friends!"

Suppressing a shudder of disgust at touching the floor and ignoring the throb of her bruised knee and the chilly dampness of her coffee-saturated pants, she smiled tenderly at her baby and knelt down to get to work.

She finished in record time and was washing his hands inside her own when she heard their name being called outside.

"Here we come!" she shouted, turning off the faucet and shuffling Sebastian out of the ladies room.

The nurse was waiting in the hallway.

"Sebastian?"

"Yes," Mom confirmed breathlessly. "That's us."

"I Sebastian!" shouted his sweet, cheerful voice.

"Follow me. We're going this way."

Coats, bags, café mocha, and Sebastian in tow, Mom proceeded down the long hallway.

"Here we are!" said the nurse. "The doctor will arrive in just a few moments. Usually I take initial notes and he comes later, but since we've never met anyone like Sebastian before, today I'm just going to stay. If you'd like to take off his shoes and socks, that would be great."

The nurse smiled and turned to her laptop, clicking through tabs until colored scans of their freshly completed paperwork showed up on the screen.

"You tickle my toes?" Sebastian asked the nurse hopefully as Mom unlaced his trainers and unfastened his ankle braces.

"Yes, Sebastian!" the nurse responded genuinely. "As soon as the doctor gets here, he and I are going to tickle your toes." She looked up as the door opened. "And here he is!"

Putting a now-barefoot Sebastian on the floor, Mom stood to shake hands with the specialist.

"It's nice to meet you," she said. "Thank you for fitting us in. This is—"

"I Sebastian!" Bas's voice cut her off. "You tickle my toes?"

Arms stiffly out, Bas tiptoed awkwardly across the examining room and hugged the orthopedist.

"Ha! Good morning, Sebastian." The doctor crouched so he was eye-level with his perky patient. "We'll tickle your toes for sure. But first, could I have you walk over to Nurse Sarah? I want to see your feet in action."

Sebastian cheerfully obliged, traversing the room with light, hopping steps.

"I'd like to see him walk when he's not so excited," the orthopedist told Mom gently.

"Hey, Sebastian! Come here and see the toys I brought for you," she said. "Your walrus and elephant seal borrowed Red the Dog's boat, except they don't know how to steer it! Red wants to help, but he's stuck on the island. The doggies are having an emergency!"

Grabbing the toys, Sebastian shouted, "Emergency! Emergency! Doggies to the rescue!"

"Maybe we can go over your questions while he calms down?" Mom asked hopefully. "New friends and new places are a bit overwhelming sometimes."

"That sounds perfect," the orthopedist replied. "First, tell me about Sebastian's diagnosis: what it means and what brings you here today."

Mom took a deep breath and began the recitation: "Our Sebastian here has differences in his DNA that make him completely unique. We guessed something was going on right away. He got sick all the time, and he missed every single developmental milestone there was to miss. But we met resistance from the medical community, hearing again and again that 'all children develop at their own pace.' It wasn't until we applied for Early Intervention Services that we found the right people to help us." She sighed. "Even then, it was a long process. Sebastian finally got genetic testing right after his second birthday. And *that*," she said with a smile, "is when we found out he's a proud member of the X-Men."

"I have superpowers!" Sebastian proclaimed. As they all smiled encouragingly at him, his cherubic face turned dark. "But no flying. Sebastian no fly."

"That's right, Sebastian," Mom said, pulling him into a hug. "Flying is not your superpower."

He gave her a quick peck and then hopped back to his pile of toys.

"Bassie has anomalies in his seventh chromosome. There are actually fewer than a hundred fifty people in the world diagnosed with the mutation he has. Since the individuals are spread out over all six inhabited continents, the deviation is probably not linked to common ancestry like some genetic mutations. But almost no research is available, so that's just a guess.

"AUTS2 was discovered only a few years ago," Mom went on. "It seems to impact boys and girls equally, but again, that's based solely on research we ourselves have conducted, seeking out other AUTS2 families across the globe."

Mom paused for a sip of café mocha and bent down to pick up the elephant seal, which had skittered across the floor into her foot. She handed it back to Sebastian, who roared loudly, launching the elephant seal and the walrus into an extended conversation, presumably about how to pilot Red the Dog's boat.

"What AUTS2 means for Sebastian," Mom continued, "is that he's missing a chunk of information everyone else has. There's a particular length of DNA space linked to AUTS2. Any change in that space—a deletion, a bit out of sequence, or a duplication—results in an AUTS2 Syndrome diagnosis. On his seventh chromosome, Sebastian is missing exon 6, along with the information before and after it. The symptoms and severity of AUTS2 seem to be linked to which exons are involved and how much information is missing or repeated, but again, there's almost no research." She smiled ruefully. "When we got our diagnosis, the geneticist had nothing but an article about zebrafish and mice to share with us."

The nurse gasped, and Mom shook her head in commiseration.

"That didn't lead us to much information about what to expect or what to do—though apparently zebrafish with AUTS2 have a larger jaw bone." Mom giggled at the absurdity. "But having no human-based information at all was unacceptable. So we got in touch with the researcher in Amsterdam who identified and named AUTS2, and had a video conference with her about a week after our Diagnosis Day. She told us Bas's symptoms are what she considers common to AUTS2: cognitive delays, mobility challenges, short stature, troubles with chewing and swallowing. She told us that the few people diagnosed with AUTS2 whom she's been able to study have displayed profoundly autistic characteristics uniquely mixed with a 'cocktail party personality' common to a condition called William's Syndrome. The William's Syndrome mutation takes place just down the genetic street from the AUTS2 zone, so I suppose it makes sense."

She paused to watch her diminutive son, now fully absorbed in the important task of painstakingly arranging the entire contents of the Survival Bag into a straight line.

"In the personality sense, Sebastian is a prime example," Mom said. "He loves to walk on his toes, he flaps when he's excited, he hangs out upside down, and he spins on his therapy swing for hours each day. He likes to line things up, loud or unexpected noises are traumatic and disorienting, and although his communication skills are exploding, he still relies heavily on a set of stock phrases." She gulped the remains of her coffee. "Those things all scream 'autism.' Many of our AUTS2 kiddos have multiple diagnoses, including autism. Sebastian does not. I took him in for an autism evaluation before we had any genetic testing done, and he climbed onto the doctor's lap to pet his beard. The guy couldn't see past it. Bas displays so many behaviors that could be considered 'profoundly autistic,' but then his magical personality cancels it all out. His social empathy is incredible, and he loves *everyone*." She chuckled. "For a while, we didn't think he knew the difference between us and strangers at the supermarket. But that's not true. He knows his family and friends, and he loves us. He simply loves the mailman, the bus driver, and you two exactly as much. It's one of his superpowers." She snorted, realizing that, right on cue, Sebastian had relocated his play into the nurse's lap and was cuddling in as though they were old friends.

"I just missed you so much!" Sebastian cooed.

The nurse leaned down and kissed Sebastian's head. "He's an innocent," she said in hushed awe. She hugged the wriggling boy and then wiped inconspicuously at her eye.

"Bas is very lucky," Mom told her. "Many of his AUTS2 counterparts don't speak at all. His words exploded out about eight months ago, and they keep coming."

"I new Bas! I talk and talk!" Sebastian slipped off the nurse's lap and ran clumsily for a hug from the orthopedist.

"That's right, Bas!" Mom cried. "You found your words! Anyway, we're here because he uses what we've nicknamed 'doggy braces' to keep him steady." She held up the sticker-adorned contraptions. "This is actually his third pair. He took his first steady, consecutive steps the day he got his first pair; now he can climb stairs safely. He's working on running smoothly and jumping with bent knees. He sees his physical therapist three times a week, which is where we got our initial recommendation for the braces two years ago. So now, our pediatrician wants *you* to confirm that he should still be wearing them every day, and to make sure he doesn't need anything in his feet corrected. Our online AUTS2 family shares every detail we can, so we know a few kids have had procedures to address foot issues. We figured it was worth investigating."

The orthopedist lifted Sebastian onto the examination table and Bas stretched out his feet in anticipation.

"Get my toes!" he shouted.

"Those are nice toes." The orthopedist tickled Sebastian's soles and his patient squealed in laughter.

"What other issues should we be aware of?" the doctor asked.

"Hmmm," Mom considered. "Bas typically doesn't register pain. So, for example, if we accidentally strap his braces too tightly, we'll take them off that night to discover wounds. But it's always a complete surprise to him—he goes about his day without indicating any discomfort whatsoever. That's typical within our AUTS2 community. At first, it sounds like another superpower, but we've heard some terrible stories. The world is a scary place when your baby doesn't reliably recognize pain."

The orthopedist nodded his understanding.

"Well, the great news today is that Sebastian's feet look pretty good to me." He tickled Sebastian's toes again before setting the delighted child back on the floor. "I was going to recommend X-rays, but I honestly think we can hold off until next year. There are certainly some underlying issues, particularly the restricted length of his tendons, the lifting toe, and the arch of his foot. But for now, the braces serve as a great solution."

"We'll be coming back then?" Mom asked tentatively, trying to hide her aversion to adding yet one more appointment to their already-packed medical schedule.

"Oh, yes. I'd like to keep Sebastian on an annual schedule so we can monitor his progress. But for now, I'd say the braces are exactly the right response." He ruffled Sebastian's well-waxed hair. "Yikes! Those are some serious spikes!"

"I made the mistake of dubbing today 'Hat Day' while Sebastian still had a full cereal bowl," Mom explained with a sigh. "It made a surprisingly convincing fez."

The orthopedist and nurse both laughed.

The orthopedist patted Bas's head gingerly. "You just keep working hard and wearing your doggie braces, okay? You can come back and see us again next year."

"Ruff, ruff, ruff!" Sebastian shouted.

MONDAY, 9:15 A.M.

"How'd it go?"

Matt had been putting away dishes, but when she walked into the kitchen he froze, a colander and a pan suspended midair on their flight to the cupboard. His quick question and tension in his eyes told her she hadn't been the only one dreading today's appointment.

"Really well, I guess," she told him. "The orthopedist watched Bas walk and felt his feet and ankles, but he decided not to even order X-rays yet. The doggie braces are the best plan for now. We have an appointment for Bas to be checked again next November." She smiled. "And even though we were late, we didn't have to wait and Bas still made it to school right on time."

Matt set the cookware on the counter, stepped around the open dishwasher door, and pulled her into a tight hug.

"That's fantastic news! Phew!"

She hugged him back, letting him bask in his relief.

"I know it sucks to add another specialist to the list," he added, "but if we only have to visit once a year, that's not *too* bad—right?"

She pulled away and nodded. "Agreed. I was so worried about this one, but it turned out to be much easier than I thought. Bas was so well-behaved in the examination room and they loved him."

She felt like she was rambling. She knew it was to avoid talking about the next part of the morning, so she stopped. Matt deserved a few minutes to revel in the happy conclusion of one problem before another reared its head. But he could read her face as adeptly as she read his.

"What's wrong?" he asked.

She sighed. Forcing a small smile, she pulled a sheet of paper from the Survival Bag and handed it to him.

"Sebastian's teacher gave *this* to me when I dropped him off."

His eyes scanned the paper, and she watched confusion spread across his forehead.

"We knew conferences were tomorrow," he echoed her thoughts, "but why did they block off so much time for us?"

Sebastian attended a full-day preschool for students with special needs, and short parent conferences were held three times a year to ensure each child's Individualized Education Plan reflected his or her changing needs.

She pulled the paper out of Matt's hand and slammed it on the counter. "I don't know why. Because right there at the top it says every family has a twenty-minute conference window, but then there's our time: three consecutive spaces circled in thick black felt-tip ink."

"Did they give you a reason?" Matt sounded angry. "Didn't you ask?"

"I didn't. You know drop-off is a hectic rush. The buses were unloading, and I was reminding them that we'll pick up Bas early on Monday for swim class. She handed me the paper and just said something about finalizing everyone's time for tomorrow. I didn't really look at it until I got back to the van. And by that time, I couldn't go back inside because I was crying." She hung her head. "The only reason I can think of for their scheduling a giant conference is to propose a major change. Just thinking about it makes my stomach churn."

"Sebastian *is* progressing, right?" said Matt. "And he's not acting out in class, is he?"

"His daily reports have never indicated behavioral issues," Mom agreed. "Sebastian tries his hardest every day and his teachers seem to enjoy him. But I'm worried. His report cards are terrible because his progress isn't as fast as they hoped." She felt tears threaten. "You don't think they would kick him out, do you? Bassie needs to be in school. Where else would we be able to send him?"

She took a deep breath to calm herself. "You know it usually takes more than a note about a conference to freak me out, but it was a stressful morning and I wanted today to be a celebration. After finding out Sebastian doesn't have foot surgery on the immediate horizon, I believed for ten whole minutes that the rest of the day would be worry-free. Then out of the blue, I'm faced with a mysteriously prolonged evaluation tomorrow. There's just never a moment to catch a breath, you know?"

"Hey," Matt said softly, "it's going to be fine." He tugged off her striped snow hat and smoothed her hair. "Sebastian is awesome. He's doing so many things we thought he *never* would. He's progressing at his own pace and as you said, his teachers love him. Everyone loves Sebastian. Maybe this is all a mistake."

She exhaled loudly. "It's not a mistake. Look at it. If they'd made that circle any thicker, you wouldn't be able to read the times inside it. It's bolded like that to make *sure* we notice."

Matt nodded. "Okay, then look at it this way: Maybe it'll be fun to talk about Sebastian for a whole hour. They might have cookies and coffee. Or maybe you'll actually be done in twenty minutes after all."

She scrunched up her face. "Easy for you to say—*you* get to go to work tomorrow. It'll be just me at the World's Longest Conference, facing whatever they're going to lay out, all by myself."

At her words, the exhaustion she felt deep down to the pit of her soul washed over Matt's face, making her instantly regret her outburst.

"Do you want me to call in?" he offered. "I can take the day off if you want me there."

"Of course I want you there," she said sadly, "but you need to save your days off for an emergency. Remember we're coming up on flu season."

"Sebastian already got his shot," Matt assured her, "and we'll all get ours, too. Besides, last year, Sebastian spent only two nights in the hospital. I really think he's fighting off illness better. If you want me to call in, I'll do it right now."

Her mouth lifted in a half-smile. "No way. I was just being a baby." She kissed his cheek. "Sometimes it's enough just to know you'd do it if I needed you to. I'll be fine. Now let's not think about it anymore today; it's making my head hurt."

He watched her in silence, apparently judging if she really meant it. Deciding she did, he poked her in the arm and smiled.

"I think the headache is actually because you can't absorb caffeine through your pants. If my nose is working correctly, your morning coffee is what stained your jeans such an intoxicating shade of brown."

She looked down at her legs and laughed.

"I told you it was a stressful morning!" she said, punching him in the arm.

"Hey! Why don't you go change, and we'll go out," he suggested. "We can grab fresh coffee and then buy groceries before heading to lunch. It can be a date! If we leave right now, we'll even have time to drop off the cold and frozen food before we pick up Bas for swimming. What do you think?"

Her husband looked so hopeful, she didn't have the heart to remind him that she had three deadlines looming later this week.

I can probably work during violin lessons this afternoon, she reasoned. *And I can always stay up later tonight and work longer hours tomorrow, too.*

"That sounds perfect," she said. "But are you sure I have to change? I think I smell rather...perky!"

He slapped her behind and she yelped.

"I'm going, I'm going," she said. "I'll put on new pants. Especially since these are also covered in germs from the orthopedist's restroom floor. Meanwhile," she admonished, "*you have to finish the dishes before we go anywhere!*"

"NEVER!" he barked teasingly.

Laughing, she ran up the stairs.

MONDAY, 1:15 P.M.

Four hours later, she peeked through the high window of the classroom door to survey the dark scene. Five children lay sleeping on comfy nap-mats across the floor, covered in soft blankets and cuddling stuffed friends as they peacefully dreamed. Meanwhile, Sebastian's red-and-blue *Dog Town* mat lay crumpled and abandoned in the corner. She wasn't surprised; he'd stopped napping before he was two. But that didn't keep her from feeling sad.

He's so tired by the end of school. I wish his body would let him relax.

She scanned the room and found him, the only child sitting at the table. His back was to the door, but she could see him energetically squishing his hands though a sensory bin filled with rice.

She turned the knob and pushed the door gently, so as not to disrupt the other students' naptime.

"Momma!" Sebastian swiveled around. "You come to get me? No more school? I miss you so much!"

"Hiya, sweetie," she cooed, waving at his teachers. "Yes, we're leaving an hour early today, remember?"

"I go swimming with my flappy feet! I swim with Mr. Andy!"

Knowing volume control was outside his capabilities, she hurried him out into the hallway as quickly as possible. One of his teachers followed and spoke through the open doorway.

"He didn't want to nap today," she whispered, "and he didn't eat much for lunch."

Mom nodded and smiled. "I've got some snacks in the van. Thank you!"

She and Bas walked hand-in-hand down the hallway, but as always, Sebastian stopped at the stairs and faced her.

"Carry me, Momma. Carry me."

She bent down and hoisted him onto her hip, secretly grateful to avoid the anxiety of watching Sebastian laboriously traverse the endless staircase. He hugged her tightly and kissed her cheek.

"We go swimming, Momma?"

"Yes, we do! I packed your goggles and you still have your elephant seal in your backpack from this morning." She smiled at him. "*And...*I brought you a snack."

Sebastian squealed in delight. "What snack you bring Momma? You bring donuts?"

She giggled and kissed his cheek.

"No, I did not bring donuts! You already had some today, remember?"

Flopping instantly from unmitigated elation to utter devastation, he let out a whimper.

"But I *did* bring a banana," she said, "and some graham crackers shaped like dog bones. Plus, a vanilla yogurt pouch. All of your favorite yummy things!"

Now downstairs and outside, she stopped, seeing donut-induced devastation overwhelm Sebastian's emotions and his eyes well with tears. She hugged him tightly, desperate to avoid a meltdown.

Suddenly Sebastian stiffened.

"Big Tuna! I see Big Tuna in the van! He waiting for me?"

Mom laughed out loud and spun Sebastian in a circle, taking

in the rare bright November sunshine that had already melted the snow from this morning. Bas had spontaneously begun calling Matt "Big Tuna" on their beach vacation last summer and rarely called him anything else since.

"Yes, Little Tuna! Of course he came, too. We both love to watch you swim!"

Matt hopped out of the driver's seat to help load Sebastian into the back.

"Hi there, Little Tuna! Did you have a good day at school?"

"I play manatees," Sebastian said through a mouthful of vanilla yogurt. "You came to get me, Big Tuna? Where we going?"

"You know where we're going, Bassie. You tell me."

His arms and legs straight out, hands and feet flapping spastically, Sebastian yelled, "We going to swimming!"

Mom automatically reached into the glove box for napkins to sop up the vanilla yogurt that now dripped from her shoulder, her hat, and the ceiling of the van.

"Let's listen to some nice music on our way," she said, hoping to divert Bas from further frenzied food explosions. "Sebastian, do you have any songs you want to hear today?"

"We hear Sebastian music!" he replied unhesitatingly, launching into a wordless version of his favorite movie theme song.

Matt moaned quietly and punched Mom's arm. She knew he forever dreamed of greater song variety and was wishing she'd selected any of the dozens of new albums he'd added to their collection over the past few months. Giggling, she searched her phone's music library, reveling in the benefits of sharing musical preferences with her kids. Sebastian had been singing along with animated film soundtracks since long before he'd discovered words. Today, his lyrics were still largely invented, but despite that, no one would struggle to recognize the song.

Perfect pitch, she thought. *Not a bad superpower.*

"Just embrace it, Big Tuna," she said sweetly as the music began. "It's his very favorite."

"I want ear plugs for Christmas," Matt replied through gritted teeth. "It's been three years straight of that same Sebastian Playlist. Ear plugs, I say!"

"I'll do you one better: How about headphones? Then you can blast death metal for all I care, without bothering the rest of us. You'll miss out on Bas's beautiful voice, though. Listen to him go!"

Matt glanced in the rearview mirror at Sebastian.

"*He's* great," Matt said. "But I am *soooo* tired of those songs!"

"I'm sure Sebastian would be happy to compromise with another playlist," she cooed, struggling to keep a straight face. "I bet we could find *Dog Town* music, or a nursery rhyme station that he'd find acceptable."

Watching horror spread across Matt's face, she lost her battle with stoicism and burst into laughter.

"Never mind," he said firmly. "The Sebastian Playlist is *fine*. Please, let's stick with this!"

MONDAY, 1:45 P.M.

The parking lot was empty and the swim school appeared closed when they arrived. She smiled.

"It's rather like we own the place."

"Sebastian Shepler, Crown Prince of Western New York!" proclaimed Matt, mirroring her grin.

"It used to make me sad," she confessed, "but not anymore. He's made so much progress since we switched from regular lessons to the adaptive swim program. It was the right decision."

Matt nodded. "It's so much easier for him to focus when the pool isn't filled with yelling, splashing kids. It's already distracting enough with the colorful flags, the floating lane lines, the water jets, and the echoes. I'm so grateful they're willing to open early for us."

"You just like being the only parent in the viewing area," she accused with a smile.

Matt peered back at Sebastian in his car seat. "Bas, someday you're going to have to show me how you manage to make graham cracker stick to your face like that," he said. "It's quite a talent."

Mom twisted around to look. Bas had crammed a fistful of banana into his mouth and also managed to coat his entire forehead, cheeks, nose, and chin in crumbs.

"But for now," Matt went on, "let's wipe it off. I don't think

Mr. Andy wants that mess floating around in his pool."

"Where we are, Momma?" Bas exclaimed. "Swimming? Let's go! You get me out of here? I stuck!"

"Big Tuna will get you out!" Matt said in a deep growl as he opened the van's sliding door. "Then I'll tickle your pits and eat your toes!"

Mom couldn't see them from her side of the van, but she could envision the scene as Sebastian squealed in glee at Daddy's game. Joy and excitement were synonymous with flapping hands and flexing feet—a fact Matt was also aware of—so she was surprised to hear him yelp in pain. He emerged from the van with Sebastian in his arms, rubbing at his face.

"I didn't dodge in time," he said with chagrin. "Got a handful of flying fingers to the eyeball."

She shook her head in mock censure.

"Duck and weave, my love," she said. "Duck and weave."

The entryway was dark and the reception desk was vacant, but the front door was unlocked. They were expected. Once inside, Sebastian wiggled out of Matt's arms and ran to admire the pool through the viewing windows.

"Let's go get you into your *Dog Town* bathing suit, Bassie!" Mom said.

Bas took two eager steps towards her and halted. As his face transformed from delight to terror, she felt her heart breaking for him.

"You no press the fan?" he whimpered.

"No, baby," she reassured him, pulling his body into a tight hug. "We're the only ones here. No one will press the hand dryer." She shot Matt a pointed glare as she reiterated, "*No one* will press that button today."

Matt broke into another roar: "*I'm* going to press the button. *Muahahahahaha!*"

"No, Big Tuna!" Sebastian's hysteria was real and Mom could feel his heart pounding through his coat. "No press the fan!"

"No one is going to press the button, Bassie," Mom

repeated. "Big Tuna is just joking around." Staring up at Matt, she kissed Bas's head. "No one wants to make you upset before your swim lesson starts."

Emitting an exaggerated sigh, Matt nodded.

"Come on, Bas," he said resignedly. "We've got to get you dressed, buddy. I won't turn on the blower."

They worked together in the family locker room, efficiently pulling off Bas's trainers, unstrapping his braces, and yanking off his sweaty socks.

"You eat my toes, Big Tuna?" Sebastian asked hopefully.

"These stinky things?" Matt teased. "No way! These toes are only good for one thing: tickling!"

"Okay, guys," Mom interrupted. "Bas can't swim in his sweater. He'll sink! We need to calm down for a minute so I can get his clothes off."

"Pants with a string would have been better," Matt whispered as he tugged at Sebastian's jeans.

"I tried!" she said in exasperation. "We started the day in the perfect pants. But Sebastian's pull-up wasn't up to the task, remember?"

"Of course I remember." Matt chuckled as he shoved Sebastian's leg through the swim diaper and then the inner net lining of his swimsuit. "Will you ever figure out how to tell when I'm making a joke?"

She reached out to swat him, but he grabbed her arm and pulled her into a kiss.

"I ready to swim!" Bas cried. "You have my elephant seal, Momma?"

Mom pulled away and looked at her son. "I sure do, Bas. You're all dressed and ready? Let's go find Mr. Andy!"

"I'm going to sit out here and watch through the window," Matt reminded Bas. "It's too hot in there for me."

"Momma come with me?" Sebastian asked, grabbing her hand in panic.

"Of course I'm coming with you! Momma will bask in the

heat on the deck like a gecko and watch you swim with Mr. Andy. And you can wave at Big Tuna through the window."

Sebastian roared, holding his elephant seal aloft in one hand and tugging his mother along with the other.

"Come on, silly Momma gecko! Let's go!"

The sliding glass doors opened and her eyes immediately watered at the potent odor of chlorine wafting on warm air currents. But her discomfort subsided after two blinks and Sebastian seemed not to notice the smell at all.

She kept a firm grip on her son's tiny hand as he dragged her across the pool deck towards the chairs where they would wait for class to start. Bas was unsteady without his braces, and his excitement exaggerated his already clumsy movements. Though she knew the water was at least ninety degrees, that didn't mean she wanted to experience it firsthand in a rescue mission.

That's the whole point of these lessons, she reminded herself. *Eventually, he'll figure it out. He'll be taller and he'll be stronger and he'll know enough about swimming to get himself safely to the edge.*

Mom had harbored a fear of her child drowning since before Jack crawled his first inch, but the fear had blossomed into abject panic when Sebastian arrived. He spent his first three years unable to walk steadily or communicate with words. He didn't seem to understand or remember directions, and despite his clingy reliance on his parents, when least expected, something as mundane as a pinwheel, a dog, a dripping faucet, or even a ceiling fan could catch his attention and freeze him in place, with no apparent recognition that time was passing. Mom's concerns had transformed into vivid nightmares when she subsequently realized that balloons, squirrels, and fluttering wind socks didn't hold a candle to the entrancement of sunlight on ripples and waves. Sebastian was utterly incapable of resisting any and all bodies of water. It was the most intoxicating substance in the universe, and her baby boy wanted nothing more than to be a part of it. Suddenly the backyard swimming pools in the neighborhood, the creek at their property in the Southern Tier, and their summer week at a lakefront cottage became terrifying in their potential for tragedy.

After Sebastian's second birthday, a season of weekly aquatic therapy sessions had uncovered another wrinkle in the challenge. They'd already known reflexes were difficult for him: He'd struggled to swallow. He'd required training to learn how to use his tongue and teeth to chew and eat. He didn't attempt to catch himself when he lost his balance. But they'd never guessed it was possible to lack the inherent instinct that kept you from trying to breathe underwater.

It doesn't matter, she lectured herself. *He learned to chew. He learned to swallow. He hasn't choked in months. Sometimes he puts his arms out when he trips. It takes work, but Sebastian is a hard and uncomplaining worker. He can learn this, too. He can learn not to breathe underwater.*

In the safety of the viewing corner, Sebastian was gaily flinging his elephant seal into the air. It landed on the concrete standing upright.

"Ta-da! Elephant seal do a trick, Momma!"

She laughed. "Hey, Sebastian! Let's try on your new swim goggles. Remember how great they worked last week? Let's get them set on your eyes so you're ready."

"You put them on me?"

"Sure, kiddo. Let's see."

She slid the rubber strap behind his head and centered the viewing cups over his wide-set eyes.

"Hmmm. Do those feel all right?" she asked. "Your beautiful hazel eyes are so big it looks like the goggles don't quite fit."

"They great!"

The automatic glass door slid open, delivering a draft of refreshing air as Mr. Andy entered the pool area.

"Yay! It's Mr. Andy! Look! I have my elephant seal!"

"Hello there, Sebastian." Mr. Andy smiled. "Those are some serious spikes on your head. It's like a blowfish costume!"

"I not a blowfish!" Sebastian laughed. "I Sebastian elephant seal!"

"Well, Sebastian elephant seal, I have something I want to show you before we get in the pool. Come and see."

Sebastian hopped towards his swim instructor and wrapped Mr. Andy's legs in a massive hug.

"Look," said Mr. Andy. "I took a picture for you at the Science Museum. See that? It's not an elephant seal, but it *is* a walrus."

Sebastian studied the photo. "That a walrus?"

"Yup." Mr. Andy nodded emphatically. "I saw him mounted on the wall and I thought of you. That's a *big* walrus."

"Look at his big, big tusks!" Sebastian shouted. Then his face paled. "He a scary walrus?"

"Nope!" Mr. Andy assured him. "He's just a walrus head on the wall. He's got thick whiskers, too. See them?"

"Where a walrus live, Mr. Andy?"

"Well, they like to swim in the ocean and lie around on big rocks."

Sebastian's face lit up. "Walrus live on the rocky coast? Like a sea lion? Like elephant seals?"

Mr. Andy grinned. "You sure know a lot about aquatic mammal habitats, Sebastian!" He laughed. "Yes, I believe walruses also live on the rocky coast."

Sebastian's hands flapped vigorously. "I swim like a big, big walrus!" he shouted. "You—you swim like a big, big fish, Mr. Andy!"

Mr. Andy laughed again. "Okay, Sebastian! Let's sit down and slide into the pool, and then you can show me your walrus swimming moves."

Mom cracked open an energy drink and watched with pride as Sebastian obediently sat down on the pool deck and carefully lowered himself into the water.

A far cry from when we first started, she thought, recalling the afternoon a year ago that he'd taken his swimming assessment to determine the safest class placement. Deep down, she'd known that Sebastian would only be safe with private lessons, but it had seemed wrong—limiting, somehow—to simply enroll him in one-on-one sessions without giving the swim school a chance to see him in action. She'd worried about unintentionally holding him back if she didn't let him try the assessment.

No. She examined her motivations dispassionately. *I felt like the one-on-one program was akin to accepting defeat. Signaling that Bas was too different to participate with the other kids. I'd just wanted so badly to be able to enroll him in a "normal" class.*

She sighed quietly. *Hope springs eternal, but realism is important too.*

She'd brought Bas to be assessed during Vince's lesson, begging the universe for a miracle. Sebastian—overwhelmed by the noise and the splashing, entranced by the shining, rippling water, and fixated on the floating buoy lines—had simply leapt into the lane as though he were an old pro. He couldn't swim, of course, and was far too short to stand up in the shallow end. So while she watched from behind the window, her precious baby had simply disappeared beneath the surface. She could still see his open eyes staring calmly ahead as his chest gently rose for his first underwater breath.

The whole incident spanned only three seconds, but they were three of those magic seconds—a deceptive microcosm with the capacity to encompass an eternity of trauma and guilt.

Three seconds of horror, she thought, *and then the universe delivered that miracle. Not the one I thought I wanted; the one we needed.*

Sebastian was fine. The instructor yanked him onto the deck before the scream left her throat. By the time she burst through the sliding door and ran to him through the chaotic pool area, Sebastian was coughing and sputtering—and also trying his best to get back into the water.

I haven't sat behind the window since, she realized, waving at Matt through the glass. At first, her presence had been necessary because Sebastian was nonverbal and easily overstimulated by the cacophony of noises from other swimmers around him. Now it was simply Standard Operating Procedure.

Sebastian does better with a predictable routine, she justified.

She turned her attention back to the pool to see Sebastian kicking furiously down the lane with just the support of a floating barbell, chasing after his elephant seal, which was balanced on Mr. Andy's head. She giggled and fished her camera out of her bag.

This picture needs to be turned into a Christmas ornament, she decided.

She caught Matt's eye through the glass and saw that he was laughing, too.

She snapped pictures and shot a short video of Sebastian propelling himself through the water with nothing but a floating barbell to help. She briefly focused on her phone, uploading the clip to the AUTS2 social media page.

Accomplishments need to be celebrated, she thought. *A video like this two years ago would have been a lifeline for us. Maybe it can help someone else.*

She looked up quickly when she realized it was too quiet.

To her utter amazement, Sebastian was swimming the lap again, *underwater.* The floating barbell had been abandoned and lay dripping in the gutter. Completely unassisted, Bas was kicking like a maniac as he chased Mr. Andy, who remained just six inches out of his reach.

They surfaced together, and Mom jumped to her feet, cheering.

"Sebastian! You are swimming! You're a swimmer!" She blinked back tears.

Clinging to Mr. Andy in the pool, Sebastian smiled at her in his blue and orange goggles. She snapped another picture.

"I'm so proud of you, Bassie," she sang, flailing her arms in the air. "You are a swimmer!"

"I Sebastian!" he replied. "I get my elephant seal from that big, big fish!"

Grinning, Mr. Andy pulled the toy out from under the surface.

"I dragged it along the bottom with my foot," he admitted, "and it worked!"

"I am just so grateful to you for starting the adaptive swim program," she said fervently. "Sebastian just *swam*. Like, real swimming!"

"Just like Jack and Marian and Vince," Mr. Andy said, grinning.

"I swimming! Sebastian Walrus swimming! You Big Fish, Mr. Andy!"

The swim instructor laughed. "I've certainly been called worse things in my life, Sebastian. I'll be Big Fish if you want me to."

Mom looked over at Matt.

"Do it again, buddy!" she cried. "Big Tuna missed it. Do it again!"

She sent an exclamation point text to Matt, who was absorbed in his cell phone behind the viewing glass and otherwise unreachable. Puzzled, he looked up and she waved her arms around like a nutter.

As they both now watched, Mr. Andy disappeared beneath the surface and Sebastian followed, moving steadily under the water through the powerful motility of his skinny chicken legs. When they came up for air seven seconds later, Sebastian gasped. He hadn't tried to breathe the water!

Sebastian stiffened when he realized Big Tuna was tapping on the glass in celebration and Momma was giving a standing ovation.

"I swim again!" he cried, splashing water everywhere in his jubilation. "I catch that Big Fish under the water!"

Mom shook her head, almost in disbelief. They'd hoped swimming lessons would show Bas how to get safely to the edge and use a ladder. She'd hoped that when he was tall enough, they'd work on bobbing, to allow him to travel short distances in relative safety. But this? She'd never dreamed swimming lessons would result in actual swimming. And yet here it was! She'd seen it! Sebastian was swimming!

She locked eyes with Matt and saw her own emotions mirrored in his expression. If Sebastian was swimming, maybe anything was possible.

MONDAY, 2:30 P.M.

She'd brought along the largest, thickest beach towel they owned, but she still felt her sleeves absorb water from Sebastian's shivering body through the double layers.

Swim diapers. A necessary evil.

"Thank you!" Sebastian called from within his fluffy cocoon. "Thank you for swimming!"

"I'll see you next week, Sebastian!" replied Mr. Andy. "I'm so proud of you!"

Mom waved good-bye to Mr. Andy, feeling that a "thank you" would be woefully inadequate and hoping that her smile said enough. She bustled Sebastian through the sliding glass door and into the cool hallway.

"I so cold, Momma."

"Don't worry, my swimming fishy. We'll get you dried off and bundled into your sweater in just a minute."

She was four steps from the family changing room when Matt squeezed past her at a jog and disappeared through the open doorway.

He could have grabbed the Survival Bag at least! she thought. *What the heck.*

Her cranky complaints halted in her throat as the whirring

mechanical rush of three activated hand dryers flooded the hallway. She froze midstep as Sebastian went rigid in his towel, emitting a howl like a strangled animal.

Seriously?! she fumed. *What is that man thinking? Bas is petrified of that noise and those things take forever to turn off. What would possess Matt to do that, and what am I supposed to do now? Our baby is cold and wet.*

Paralyzed with indecision, she stood cradling her shaking baby just two feet from the changing room.

Matt appeared in the doorway, grinning. He grabbed Sebastian, soaking towel and all, and popped back inside—whisking their sound-sensitive baby into a wild melee of loud, blowing machinery.

Mom stood in the hallway, incensed, listening to the disaster unfold.

"Ahhhhhh!!" said Matt. "This hot air is so nice! It warms you right up!"

"No! No! NO!" screamed Sebastian. "I no like it. No! No!"

"Ahhhh...you just need to feel it on your head, Sebastian. Feel how warm that is?"

"I no feel it on my head. No. No. No. No! No! No! No!"

"This nice warm air will dry you right off!" said Matt. "See? It's so nice and warm!"

"No! No. No. No. No. NO!"

"I'm going to put you under the blower, Sebastian. It's going to warm you up."

"NO! It scary, Big Tuna! It blow my head off!"

"No, silly! It's just nice warm air. Feel how nice it is? Your hair is already almost dry! Let's take off your swimming clothes and let the warm air blow on your body."

She could hear Sebastian hesitate. "It not a scary loud monster? It not loud monster breath?"

"Nope!" breezed Matt. "It's just warm and comfy air drying you off. It's going to stop in a moment, so do you want to help me press the big silver button to keep it on?"

"No!" cried Sebastian. "No. You press it, Big Tuna. You press that monster button."

"Okay," agreed Matt. "I'll press it. But you have to help me. Come on, Bassie. Reach up with me and we'll press it together. You're going to get cold without the nice warm air blowing on you."

"It make a loud noise?" asked Sebastian.

"Yes," said Matt. "It's going to turn back on, and that means there will be noise. It's an engine noise. The engine turns on so that the warm air can blow out."

"NO!" cried Sebastian again. "You press it. I no press it. You press it, Big Tuna. I afraid."

"Whoa, Bas," she heard Matt say. "Don't fall off the bench! There we go; you're steady now." The hand blower loudly resumed. "See! I pressed it," said Matt, "and now the warm air is coming back. Doesn't that feel nice? It's helping you to dry off so fast!"

"That loud monster noise scare me," Sebastian pouted.

"But it's not a monster, remember?" urged Matt. "It's an engine noise. Let's call Momma and tell her about the engine noise."

"Momma!" Sebastian called. "Momma, where you are? Momma?"

Responding immediately to the rising panic in his already hysterical voice, she walked into the dressing room with what she hoped was an encouraging smile plastered on her face. Deliberately avoiding eye contact with Matt, she strode to her son, who was standing naked and nervous under three roaring hand dryers.

"I think these blowers did the trick, Sebastian!" she said. "You're so brave, and now you're dry enough for your clothes. So how about if we get your diaper on?" She leaned in to kiss his head and pulled back. "Pew! Your hair might be dry, but it's still very stinky!"

"It's monster breath, Momma," Bas replied soberly. "Stinky monster breath on my head."

She snorted. "It's not monster breath, silly," she said, strapping Bas's diaper tabs while he stood. "It's chlorine from the pool! And now you've gone and made Momma laugh when I was trying to be mad at Big Tuna."

Matt pulled her into a hug and unwrapped his arm to enclose Sebastian as well. He gave her a quick kiss.

"Hand dryers are a part of the world Sebastian lives in," he said softly. "He's got to learn to cope."

"He didn't need to learn to cope *today*," she argued. "The adaptive program runs when no one else is here, in part so that those hand dryers are not, actually, part of Bas's swimming experience. That wasn't nice."

The dryers turned off again, and she stopped talking, not wanting Sebastian to overhear.

"Let's get your sweater and jeans on, little man," she said.

As she dug through the Survival Bag for his clothes, she was startled by the reactivated roar of the blowers.

"I press it, Momma!" Sebastian squealed. "That hot stinky monster breath warms me up! I press it!"

Matt raised his eyebrows at her, gloating, and she shook her head in resignation.

"Help me get him dressed, please," she said. "We don't want to be late picking up the other kids."

"It was the right thing to do," he pressed. "Admit it."

"It worked," she conceded, "but that's not the same as being the right thing." She sighed. "But, yes, it worked. And I'm glad you did it. Life will be easier without the bathrooms of the world being so terrifying."

"Teamwork." He smiled. "It takes teamwork."

She rolled her eyes and then returned his smile.

"So, what's up for the rest of the day?" he asked.

"It's Monday," she replied. "Every Monday has been the same since September. You really don't know?"

Matt shrugged. "Nope. That's your part of the teamwork." He gave her an innocent smile. "One of *my* jobs is to scare Sebastian into overcoming his noise aversions. *Your* job is to remember the schedule and remind me of it every couple of hours for the rest of our lives."

She laughed and slapped him on the arm.

"That actually sounds about accurate!" she said, snickering. "Come on—we need to pick up the Big Three from school." She rose and grabbed Sebastian's hand. "Let's go, Bassie! Wave good-bye to Mr. Andy when we pass the pool area."

They exited the restroom and made their way back down the hallway past the row of windows overlooking the pool.

"Bye-bye, Big Fish!" Sebastian yelled. "I going home!"

Matt turned to Mom and smiled. "Really, though—what's up for the rest of the day?"

"On Mondays," she said, "the Big Three have violin lessons as soon as school is over—that's my job. You get to hang out with Bas and then come pick up Vince as soon as his lesson is done so he can get to his dance class on time. You're in charge of dinner, which is tricky because Vince has to eat by 4:30 to be ready for his dance carpool to pick him up, but I won't be home with Jack and Marian until an hour later."

"It's all coming back to me now," said Matt. "Monday is pizza night."

"Sebastian, honey," Mom interrupted, "hold still, please, so I can get your strap buckled."

"We watch a show?" Sebastian asked. "Please, Momma?"

"Absolutely," she agreed. "Here, have a nice drink of water and then we'll put on *Dog Town*."

"I so, so hungry," he said.

Mom put her hands on her hips. "Well, I'm looking at your banana, here, smushed on the van floor, so I guess I'm not surprised that you're hungry. And is that most of your vanilla yogurt stuck to the side of your seat? Bassie, we brought you so many snacks, and you've wasted them. You can't grow big and strong if you don't eat."

Matt reached back into the second row and retrieved a strawberry cereal bar.

"Here you go, Little Tuna." He handed it to Sebastian. "I was saving this special for you."

"Yay! Yummy, yum, yum!" Bas cried. "Thank you, Big Tuna!"

Mom had *Dog Town* running on the portable DVD screen before they reached the highway, and Sebastian's clear voice sang happily along with the theme song, his cereal bar clenched in his petite fist, forgotten after a single bite.

She sighed, and Matt reached over to take her hand.

"No sighing allowed," he said. "Did you forget already? Sebastian was *swimming* today. Swimming *underwater*. And he didn't drown. And if that's not enough, he finished up the lesson standing under a hand dryer—while it was blowing!"

Mom smiled. "You're right. It was an amazing afternoon. It's just the 2:45 exhaustion. I need some caffeine." She glanced at Matt slyly, her eyes dancing. "Also, can we talk about his goggles?"

"This new pair is better," he said seriously. "At least they seem to be watertight."

"But did you get a good look at our poor baby in them?"

He bit his cheeks, trying to keep a straight face. "The bridge of his nose is so wide, I'm *glad* we went with the teen size," he said firmly. "We finally found a style that keeps his eyes dry. I think that's why he was so brave underwater."

She wasn't letting him off that easy. "Yes, but did you *see* him in them? I don't usually notice the 'slightly dysmorphic features' the doctors describe in his files, but you can't miss it in those goggles! It's like his eyelids are too wide to fit inside the cup pieces." The giggles were coming and she couldn't stop them. "He looked like a frog."

Matt glanced at her and chuckled.

"I was thinking he looked like a crazy lab assistant. You know, the kind with enormously thick glasses and a pocket protector."

She peeked guiltily back at their precious baby. His beautiful multihued eyes were glued to the screen, his whole face smiling in delight at whatever was happening with the puppies in Dog Town.

"To be fair," Matt reasoned, "no one really looks stunning in swim goggles."

"But our poor guy is a special case!" She tried desperately not to resume laughing.

"Hey," he said, "remember when Marian was his age? Her nose was too tiny to hold up sunglasses, so we had to special-order her the kind with the strap."

"How could I forget?" asked Mom. "Poor Marian. She had the smallest nose I've ever seen on a kid!"

"Right," Matt said. "But she grew, and things normalized without a problem. She can wear sunglasses now just like everyone else. So maybe, just maybe, Sebastian's features will calm down a bit, too."

She raised her eyebrows in doubt. "I'm just glad we found a pair of goggles that work for him. *And* I'm glad I have you." She squeezed Matt's hand. "Because Bas does look like a frog in them. And it makes me laugh. But there aren't a whole lot of people I'd admit that to."

"Look, you've got to be able to laugh," Matt insisted. "We'd laugh at Jack if his googles did that. We'd laugh at Marian or Vince." His voice took on a hard edge. "It needs to be okay to laugh about Bassie, too."

Mom nodded in agreement. "But I'm sensitive about it," she said slowly. "I don't want to be, but I am." Her brow furrowed. "It's a double-standard, you know? *We* can laugh about our frog baby, because he's ours. And if I felt like telling someone about it and they laughed, that'd be okay, too. I'd *expect* them to laugh if I described those goggles honestly." She paused. "But if someone mentioned it on their own?"

"Oh no!" he exclaimed. "I think everyone you know is smart enough not to do that. You'd rip their head off!"

She stuck out her bottom lip.

"Really," he said. "You're very scary sometimes. Not to me," he added quickly. "But to everybody else? I don't think anyone would intentionally piss you off."

She smirked. "But you know what I'm talking about, right? It's like..." She paused. "This morning was a perfect example. There was this guy in line behind us at the orthopedist who noticed Sebastian. I've seen his expression enough times to dread it; he was gathering the courage to say something." She turned to Matt, searching his profile for understanding. "Don't people know by now that if you feel the need to *gather courage* to say something to a stranger, then maybe you could simply NOT SAY IT?! Anyway, I ran. I grabbed Sebastian by the arm and I literally ran away from the man before he had a chance to ask a question or offer sympathy." She felt anger and frustration bubble in her chest. "That's the worst, you know? When a stranger tells you that they're *sorry* about your kid. Your beautiful, happy, friendly kid. The one standing *right there.* Sympathy is great for funerals; it doesn't belong when you're talking about energetic kids—even ones who are obviously a bit different."

They were speeding along at 65 miles per hour, but Matt turned and locked eyes with her anyway.

"I like to tell those people 'I'm *not* sorry' and then walk away," he said.

"Maybe." Mom sighed. "But it still hurts. It hurts every time. And the most unbearable part is they think they're being kind. And it takes too much energy to explain to them why their remarks are *not* kind. So when running is an option, I take it. Of course, I couldn't run from the lady behind the reception counter—the one who acted like I'm a negligent parent who doesn't know how to raise a kid. I had to just smile and let her believe whatever terrible conclusions she'd drawn. But I *could* run from that man, and I did."

"There's nothing wrong with running," Matt reassured her.

"It's crazy though, you know? Unpredictable. I ran from that man because he was making assumptions about Sebastian and I didn't want to spend a single minute setting him straight. In the meantime, I post to social media all the time about our Bassie. His challenges and his successes—I put them out there for people to see." She took a deep breath. "We even did that news special! Putting our entire family on display for a double segment. We presented all four of our kids on television so people could learn about AUTS2 Syndrome and be a better community for our Bas. We let the reporters follow us all the way to Washington DC and the National Institutes of Health, for goodness sake. *We* did that. We're

Team Shepler. We share information. We build knowledge. But I ran from that man."

She looked down, feeling ashamed.

Matt rubbed her shoulder. "Then you went into the examination room and shared a million details with the doctors, didn't you?"

She nodded.

"There you go, then. You're allowed to be selective. You're allowed to take a break. You can share as much—or as little—as you want, every single day. And you can change your mind whenever you want. There's no law that says you have to share with every single person Sebastian meets. Especially random dudes in the waiting room at the doctor."

She shook her head. "That poor guy. I know he was just trying to be nice. Did I tell you he had a prosthetic leg and that Sebastian almost knocked him over...twice?"

"*WHAT?!*" Matt averted his eyes from the road. "I thought you said Sebastian behaved himself."

"No," Mom clarified. "I said he was well-behaved in the *examination room.* In the waiting room, we had some struggles."

"Apparently!" Matt exhaled through his nose. "He almost knocked over a one-legged man?!"

"Well, first he crashed a pole into the guy as he tried to swing on the guide ropes, and *then* he gave him an apology power-hug that nearly landed the guy on the floor."

At the shock on Matt's face, she burst out laughing.

"It wasn't funny and I shouldn't be laughing right now, but those weren't even the worst moments in the waiting room, if you can believe it."

Matt looked at her incredulously. "We've been together all day, and you didn't think to mention any of this before?! And there was something *worse* than knocking over a guy with one leg?"

"Hey! He didn't knock him over. He just *almost* knocked him over."

"Twice!"

"Okay, okay." She chuckled. "But he also soaked the floor in front of the water cooler by playing with the spigot and then pooped his pants while drinking water from his half-filled molding clay container."

Matt laughed. "Dangerous question, but what were *you* doing while all this was going on?"

She grimaced. "Pages and pages of paperwork. I never filled out the forms they sent in the mail. I'm quick, but it still took me fifteen minutes. Bas can accomplish a lot of shenanigans in fifteen minutes."

Matt nodded. "I'm impressed you escaped without a worse disaster!"

"Just call me Supermom," she said, smirking.

"You my best girl, EVER!" shouted a little voice from the second row. "I love my momma so, so much!"

MONDAY, 5:25 P.M.

Thomas Jefferson came trundling through his gigantic dog flap the moment she touched the back door handle. In his exuberance, he managed to loop his massive head through the strap of Vince's violin case dangling from her arm.

"Oh no!" she hollered as the heavy bag of music notebooks slid off her other arm and she was pulled across the driveway, refusing to relinquish her son's instrument to a dog-led adventure. Somehow Thomas Jefferson knew the gate wasn't fully latched, and all one hundred thirty pounds of the full-grown Norwegian foxhound headed there with determination, oblivious to the case entangled around his neck and the mom being dragged behind it.

"Kids! Help!" Mom screamed towards the car. *If he escapes, it's my fault. Why didn't I fully lock the fence?* "Jack! Ahhh! Marian!"

Trying to regain her footing, Mom managed to trip over an abandoned green plastic snow shovel and for the second time in less than twenty-four hours landed squarely on her knee. She yelped.

"Momma! Oh no!" Marian grasped the situation quickly. "Move it, Jack! Thomas is going to get out!"

Dropping her own violin, saxophone, and backpack on the ground, Marian squeezed between the car and the van in their narrow driveway and reached the fence just in time.

"Help me, Jack!" she called out. "I can't get the lock in!"

Jack, the only child finally large enough to sit in the front seat, was hopping through the mud on the passenger side of the driveway. He ducked between the front of the car and their overgrown Rose of Sharon bush to find himself eye-to-eye with Thomas Jefferson, now on his hind legs, pushing the gate with all the strength his front paws could muster.

"Hello, Thomas Jefferson!" said Jack. "What did you do to Momma? There'll be no walkabouts today, buddy."

Three inches from the dog's brown-and-white snout separated by nothing but a lattice fence, Jack backed away quickly. "Blech! Your breath smells disgusting!"

"Jack! Don't leave me here!" Marian screamed. "You've got to power through the stink! Just hold your breath!"

Laughing from her spot on the ground, Mom watched as, together, Jack and Marian managed to slide down the lower latch and slip the padlock through the hole in the upper latch, trapping themselves outside the fence. She was still holding Thomas Jefferson back as best she could by the violin case, ignoring the freezing chill seeping from the concrete into her jeans.

"Are you okay, Momma?" Marian's stricken face peered at her through the gate. "That was a close one!"

"I'm fine," she said, standing slowly. "You two are heroes! You stopped Thomas Jefferson's escape!"

"He probably wouldn't have gotten far," Jack replied, giggling. "He was dragging a pretty heavy anchor."

"Jack!" Marian gasped, punching her brother on the arm. "Did you just call Momma fat?"

"No, *you* just called her fat. I called her a heavy anchor! You know, because she didn't let go." He turned to his mother. "Thomas Jefferson was dragging you like a water-skier, Momma!" He gave a pointed look back at his younger sister. "A beautiful and athletic water-skier. That was crazy!"

Mom could feel a warm trickle of blood running down her

leg, but she laughed out loud anyway. "You kids are too much," she said, shaking her head. "I'm going to take the big lug inside. I'll shut the inside door behind us, and then you two can come in and lock the gate again behind you. Sound like a plan?" She smiled at them gratefully. "Don't forget to close the car doors and grab your backpacks."

"We need to bring in our instruments, too," Marian reminded her.

"Absolutely. Just find all your stuff and come on inside. I'll bet there's some delicious pizza waiting for us in the kitchen, right?"

"Dad's specialty," Jack agreed, grinning. "Takeout!"

Mom lifted the violin case and carefully extricated the dog's neck from the strap. "Come on, Thomas J, you big goof." She patted his gigantic head lovingly. "It's time to go inside." Pulling firmly on his harness, she dragged him off the fence and towards the back door, trying not to limp.

Matt was in the kitchen when they entered. "Hey! I didn't think you were ever coming home!"

She dropped the ten-pound music bag on the floor and gave him a crazed look.

"What happened?!" he asked in alarm, eyeing the ragged, bloody hole in the knee of her jeans.

"Jack and Marian and I deserve a hero parade. Thomas Jefferson was running away with Vince's violin to join a dog band," she said with mock-emotion. "But we got in the way."

"What?" Matt asked in confusion. But that was as far as he got, because someone else had noticed Mom was home.

"Momma! M-m-m-m-m-my Momma! Y-Y-Y-Y-You come back!" Sebastian, already in pajamas, threw himself into her arms and gave her the type of hug typically reserved for the long-lost reunion love scene in a Hallmark movie.

Just then, Jack and Marian came tromping up the steps and blundered into the kitchen behind her, a jumble of backpacks, lunchboxes, and instrument cases.

"The gate's closed and Jack shut the car doors, too," Marian reported. "But Momma, Alice is out in the driveway now, licking the spot where you fell."

Mom sighed. "Of course she is. I was bleeding."

"Eeww!" Jack exclaimed. "Alice is one weird, disgusting dog."

"So she's part vampire—leave her alone," said Matt. "Now, sit down and eat. The pizza is getting cold." He untangled Sebastian from Mom's legs, lifted him high in the air, and plunked him into his highchair. "Jack, I'll get you pepperoni. Marian, do you want cheese...or cheese and green peppers?"

Though he held open the lids hopefully, they all knew it was a lost cause.

"None," Marian said crossly. "You know I hate that kind of pizza, Daddy." She gave an exaggerated sigh. "I guess I'll just have breadsticks and be hungry."

"My darling," Mom said with full dramatic flair, "our fridge is loaded with your favorite yogurts, cheese sticks, grapes, and melon. We have all the ingredients for six different kinds of lunchmeat sandwiches. Oranges and bananas are on the counter, and the cupboards are overflowing with all sorts of delicious healthy snacks. We also have cereal, and those prepackaged peanut butter sandwiches in the freezer. You have a million options, so no one is going to join you in your pity party. Find some food and make yourself full. It's been a very long day and I just don't have the energy to deal with this ridiculousness right now."

Uncrossing her arms, Marian looked around sheepishly. "Sorry, Momma. I'll try a skinny piece with just cheese, Daddy, and I'll get myself a yogurt."

"Y-Y-Y-Y-Y-Y-You cut up m-m-m-my pizza, Momma?" Sebastian asked hopefully.

"I certainly will, Bassie. Then you can eat it up just like a hungry pup!"

"Ruff, ruff!"

"Did Bas have a busy day?" Jack asked through a mouthful of cheese. "He's so exhausted he can barely get his words out."

"Monday is swimming day for Sebastian, remember?" said

Mom. "And it's no wonder he's bushed. Just wait until you see the video I took. Sebastian was actually swimming!"

"What do you mean?" Marian sounded alarmed. "Swimming how?"

"Wait until you see!" Mom enthused. "I'll show you. But first, Sebastian has to eat two bites of pizza."

"Vince started a new song today," Matt said, turning to Jack and Marian as he fed Sebastian a forkful. "How did lessons go for you two?"

"My *Star Wars* songs are going to be amazing at the talent show," Jack responded. "Momma, we've got to order my Jedi robes."

"February is a long way off, my child," she said. "We've got time. Remind me after Thanksgiving, okay?"

"I did sight-reading today, Daddy." Marian beamed. "And my teacher played a duet with me. It sounded like a real performance. I'm getting really good at reading music!"

"All three kids had great lessons this week," Mom agreed. "It's amazing how that happens when they actually practice every day like they're supposed to." She shot Jack and Marian a sidelong glance.

The pair giggled, attempting to look innocent and failing entirely.

"Hey—that's Bassie's second bite!" Jack cried in a brazen attempt to shift the conversation away from their practice habits. "Let's see that video!"

Mom turned to Sebastian. "Shall we show them your incredible swimming skills?" she asked.

"I-I-I-I-I swim un-un-un-under the water!" Bas shouted, his arms and legs stiffening, his hands and feet flapping.

Mom pulled up the video on her phone, and three blond heads crowded around the miniature screen, watching in wonder as Sebastian leapt from the side and swam four feet underwater to his instructor.

"Sebastian!" Marian exclaimed, kissing Bas's head and

wrapping him in a hug. "You actually did it!"

"I'm so proud of you, Bassie!" chimed in Jack. "You were swimming like a big boy! Just like me! Just like Marian and Vince! You were swimming like a sea lion!"

"I-I-I-I-I-I swim like my b-b-b-b-b-best, best friend, Jack!"

Smiling, Mom glanced at the microwave clock and jumped up. "I've got to go! Vince needs to be picked up in less than an hour, and I have to hit the store first!"

Matt laid his hand on her shoulder and pushed her back onto the bench. "You just got here. What do you need from the store?"

"Pull-ups! I forgot to grab them when we were out earlier, and Sebastian has zero left."

"Sit down and enjoy a relaxing dinner," he said with a smile. "I'll get Vince when it's time. You can take off your shoes and stay home."

"But the diapers!" she cried. "He needs them for school. We've got to get pull-ups."

Matt held up his fingers in a V-shape. "Two reasons why that's not a problem: First, tomorrow is Election Day, remember? Conferences, and no school."

Mom cringed, suddenly remembering the hour-long conference looming on the horizon. Then she mentally added a trip to the store with all four kids to her solo workload tomorrow and scowled.

"Hey, don't make that face!" said Matt. "I said there were *two* reasons. You think I'm going to stick you with a shopping trip tomorrow? Give me some credit! The second reason you can relax right now is that Sebastian and I already got the pull-ups!"

"What?!" she asked. "When?"

"While you were at violin." Matt smiled. "After the carpool picked Vince up for dance, we ran to the store. It gave us something fun to do, and I figured it'd save you a trip later. Teamwork, right?"

Mom leaned over and kissed her husband. "That is the *best*! *You're* the best! Thank you!"

94

"What do I look like—a slacker? It was no trouble at all. But you're right," he added, turning to Jack. "Sebastian is totally wiped now. We spent a long time in the toy aisles, bouncing balls and trying out ride-on toys."

"D-D-D-D-D-Daddy Monster ch-ch-ch-chase me!"

Matt looked reproachfully at Sebastian. "You're not supposed to tattle on me!"

"You can't get away with anything now, Daddy," Marian admonished. "Bassie's too good at his words and too forgetful to remember to keep a secret!"

"I don't think he's forgetful," said Jack. "I think Bassie is just innocent. Right, Momma? He doesn't understand how to be anything but honest and kind."

"You might be right, Jack," said Mom. "The nurse at the foot doctor indicated that very thing this morning. But the important question is: Did Daddy and Bas get in trouble at the store for running around and shouting?"

Matt rolled his eyes. "Of course not. Do you think I'd let it get that far? Seriously! I *do* know how to watch a kid in a store."

"I-I-I-I-I-I h-h-h-h-help Daddy Monster p-p-p-pick up all the balls!"

Mom raised her eyebrows at Matt, whose indignant expression morphed into a sheepish grin.

"There *may* have been a small collision with an endcap display. But nothing got broken, no one got hurt, and we fixed it all up, good as new!"

"Sebastian, you must have worked up a big appetite escaping from that Daddy Monster!" Marian suggested, stepping up to redirect the conversation. "I'm hungry, too. Let's eat three bites of yummy pizza together!"

"Y-Y-Y-Y-Y-Y-You sh-sh-sh-sh-sh-share your yogurt with me?"

"Sure, I will. Here you go!" Without hesitation, she shoved a heaping spoonful into his mouth.

"The foot appointment went well this morning—right, Momma?" said Jack. "But I don't remember you saying: Does

Sebastian have to go back again soon?"

"Nope!" Mom grinned. "He doesn't have to go back until next November, a whole year away."

"Phew!" Marian exclaimed. "I worried about that all day." She leaned over the highchair tray to give her baby brother a kiss. "Have a bite of pizza, Bassie! Sea lion swimmers need to eat good food!"

"Jack and Marian, you still have to practice your band instruments today. Jack, I want to hear your scales and trumpet solo when you're done eating. Marian, you can set up your saxophone and get your music sheets in order. You need to practice your solo competition song and your Christmas concert solo."

At the pair's crabby expressions, their father interjected. "You don't have swim practice or dance or anything else tonight," he said, shoving another bite of pizza into Sebastian's mouth. "You don't even have to worry about homework because there's no school tomorrow. So don't give Momma a hard time. It'll take only a few minutes."

"Oh, come on!" Marian whined. "We already did all our homework while we were waiting for our turn at violin!" She eyed everyone at the table angrily. "Why didn't someone remind us we didn't have to?"

"We were just putting first things first, Marian." Jack stifled a laugh. "This is a good thing! Now we won't have to think about schoolwork all day tomorrow!"

Marian sighed heavily. "I guess so. But my math assignment was just awful and it took forever. Long division makes my head spin. I would have broken it into two sessions if I'd remembered we have tomorrow off."

"Would you have divided it evenly, or would there have been a remainder?" Jack asked impishly.

His sister punched him in the shoulder.

"Now your Tuesday is wide open for fun adventures," Mom said, rumpling her daughter's hair. "And we have a busy day planned, so you'll be glad your work is done."

"W-W-W-W-What we doing tomorrow, Momma?" asked Bas. "No school?"

"Nope. No school tomorrow, Bassie. We're going on some adventures! In the morning, you can watch a movie with Jack and Marian and Vince. Maybe your favorite fish movie? Then we'll go vote and then we get to go bowling!"

"B-B-B-B-B-B-B-Bowling!" Sebastian squealed. "I love bowling!"

"Why are we watching a movie, Momma?" Marian asked quietly. "Where do you have to go?"

Mom explained about the conference at Sebastian's school. "I'll zip out there for an early appointment and then be right back. I'll leave out donuts for breakfast, which you can munch on while you watch an ocean adventure. I'll be home before it's over."

"That's no trouble, Momma," Jack assured her. "Marian and I both have our watch phones and we know what to do if there's an emergency. Plus, Grandma is just a quick minute away if we need her. We'll have lots of fun—right, Bassie?"

Sebastian grinned and then launched into his favorite song from the live-action fish show at the amusement park.

"Fish swim all day in the ocean blue."

Marian and Jack joined in: *"From the deep coral reefs to the shore."*

Then both big kids held their breaths in wordless agreement, leaving the third line for Sebastian to sing alone in his tiny voice: *"All the creatures love to splash and explore!"*

In unison, they all sang the final line: *"Protecting our waters starts with you!"*

Mom and Matt applauded vigorously.

"I just love it when Sebastian sings the word 'creatures,'" Marian whispered.

"Me too," Jack concurred. "It's so funny!"

"That was a beautiful trio," Mom said. "Now get your trumpet going, Jack." She pushed him towards the dining room. "Sebastian wants some lovely bombastic dinner music to eat his pizza by! Marian, you're done with your yogurt, so come help me empty the dryer before you find your band folder."

Marian looked pathetically up at her mother and grabbed her hand. "Momma, I think it's finally time to tell you something..." She took a deep breath. "I love to hang out with you, but I don't like doing laundry. I don't mind helping with chores, but I really hate emptying the dryer and moving the wash." She gave her mother's hand an encouraging squeeze. "So, it's probably not fair if I take your favorite job away from you, since I don't even like it."

Mom blinked in confusion and then laughed. "Are you under the impression that laundry is my favorite thing to do?"

Marian nodded solemnly. "You find time to wash clothes and move them into the washer and then the dryer and then onto the couch for folding, every single day. And then you make sure they get upstairs and into the right closet, drawer, or cubby. Usually, it's the first thing you do when you get downstairs in the morning, and sometimes you even stay up extra late at night to do more."

"And you're always smiling by the time you're done," Jack interjected from the living room.

Are they serious? Mom looked at Marian carefully. *Holy cow, they ARE serious!*

"Gracious me!" Mom said. "When you put it that way..." She shook her head incredulously. "I guess I never realized the extent of my laundry addiction before."

She glanced at Matt and saw him peering back at her through cracks between his fingers, shielding himself from whatever was to come.

"We all like spending time with you," Marian repeated gently. "But you have us helping flip laundry loads every day, and we don't want to steal your favorite thing."

"Especially when we don't even like it!" came Jack's voice from the living room.

"Wow." Mom put her hands on her hips. "These are some well-reasoned arguments. It sounds like there may have been some in-depth conversations about this topic. I should thank you both for being so generous and selfless. But first—" She raised her voice: "Jack! Come out here for a minute."

Jack appeared in the doorway, trumpet in hand.

"Sit down, please." They both complied. "I need you sitting down because this might come as something of a shock." She looked each child in the eye and smiled. "You see, the secret is, I actually loathe doing laundry. *Loathe* it." Seeing the kids' confusion she explained, "The word 'loathe' is a fancy, powerful adjective that takes the term 'hate' and amplifies it by twenty."

The kids stared at her in awe.

"But—" Jack started. "But you do laundry all the time!"

Marian looked horrified. "Why do you do it every single day if you don't even like it?"

Standing up, Mom kissed the top of Jack's head, followed by Marian's and then Sebastian's.

"I do three loads of laundry *every day* because I love my family, and it's our responsibility to take care of each other. You kids need clean towels for swimming and clean uniforms for violin. You need leotards for dance class and pajamas for cold nights. Daddy needs clean uniform pants and shirts for work. You need clean sheets on your beds and outfits for school." She smiled at them again. "I hate—no, *loathe*—doing laundry. But I do it because you need me to. And I love *you*."

The room fell silent.

"Wow," Jack breathed.

"I really didn't know," Marian whispered.

"Well, now that you *do* know..." Matt jumped into the conversation brightly, "you two can work together to empty the dryer and shift the wet clothes for a new cycle. Because Momma deserves a break. And because that's what families do."

Jack and Marian exchanged a look. Marian's mouth opened to say something, but Sebastian was quicker.

"W-W-W-W-W-We have the b-b-best family EVER!"

MONDAY, 7:45 P.M.

"Momma!"

She was hanging the never-ending pile of clean shirts in the wardrobe and cramming pants and pajamas into the dresser drawers, while at the same time, actively ignoring Jack, who was hollering from the shower.

"*Momma!* Come here quick!"

Sighing, she shoved the final three pairs of Sebastian's sweats into his pants cubby and headed for the bathroom. The door was open, so the hallway was steamy. Peering inside, she looked down and shook her head. *It's going to be raining downstairs!* she mourned. She reached for two towels from the rack and tossed them onto the lake that was spreading across the linoleum floor.

"Momma!" Jack screamed again.

She cracked open the shower curtain and stuck her head in. "What's up?"

"Something's wrong with this picture," Jack said, pointing to the back of the tub.

She followed his finger and realized Sebastian was sitting in the bathtub, fully clothed in his fire-truck pajamas, splashing with glee. Reflexively, she closed her eyes.

Kindness. Courage. Understanding. She repeated her mantra. *Yes, this is the fourth or fifth time in a week. But he truly doesn't understand.*

She felt the flutter of panic that tried to edge in every time Sebastian's struggle to comprehend behavioral expectations was plainly evident. *He'll figure it out in his own time*, she told herself. *He won't be fifteen and jumping into someone else's shower fully clothed. He'll figure it out by then.*

Misreading her expression as anger at *him,* Jack interrupted her thoughts with panicked excuses. "He was already in here when I got in! He must have climbed in with Marian, but she didn't even mention it."

Mom rubbed her head, realizing too late her hand was soaked. Recovering, she mustered a smile.

"First," she said, water dripping down her face, "the curtain isn't tucked in all the way and the bathroom is flooding. Let's fix it before we turn the kitchen into a rainforest again."

"Oh no!" Jack cried. "It *was* tucked in. I checked!"

He bent down and adjusted the plastic, only to have Sebastian immediately pull it loose, place his elephant seal on the newly exposed ledge and launch it into the standing tub water.

"Mystery solved," Jack said wryly.

"Now, Sebastian," Mom said, pulling the curtain aside at the back of the tub, "you already took a shower today, remember? You had swimming and then you took a nice warm shower and put on your pajamas."

"I-I-I-I-I wearing my f-f-f-fire-truck pajamas!" Sebastian stuttered brightly.

"Yes, you are! But, now, you're wearing them in the shower. And that means they're all wet."

"I t-t-t-t-take a shower with my-my-my-my elephant seal and my b-b-b-best, best friend, Jack!"

"Come on, Bassie," Mom said, pulling him to his feet. "We need to take your clothes off. Diapers and a shower are not a good mix." She softened her voice. "You make me feel sad when you get in the shower with your clothes on. You have to take your clothes off first, okay?"

Jack broke into the conversation. "Momma, do I have to

wash Sebastian?" he asked. "I washed him yesterday, so today is supposed to be Marian's turn." He sighed dramatically. "But since he's still wearing his clothes, I doubt she did it."

It actually didn't need to be *anyone's* turn to wash Bas on swim days—a huge relief for the Big Three because Sebastian was a squirmy nightmare in the shower, constantly falling and banging his head as he tried to evade the application of soap. But in the current situation, the schedule was a moot point.

"I just heard Daddy pull into the driveway." Mom gave a hard yank and managed to peel the arm of Sebastian's soaked pajamas off his body. "Vince will need a shower after three hours of dance class, so Bassie can stay in with him. It's the perfect night to be Vince's turn, since Sebastian's already been scrubbed."

Jack laughed. "Vince is like that kid in the Snoopy cartoons who's surrounded by a cloud of dust. Sometimes Vince washes his head with bar soap and claims that the suds running down his body are good enough to wash everything else."

"Exactly," Mom said from the other side of the curtain. "We'll let Vince practice washing his brother on a night that Sebastian starts out already clean."

Jack smiled. "I'm all done, but should I stay in with Bas until Vince gets up here? Otherwise he's just going to pull the curtain and soak the floor again."

"W-w-w-we play sea lions!" Sebastian exclaimed.

"Great idea," Mom said, holding out their toothbrushes. "Work on some dental hygiene while you're in there."

Jack grabbed them and Mom headed for the door. She stopped at the sound of his worried voice. "Uh, Momma? Are you still out there?"

"What's up?" she asked.

"Did you see Sebastian's back?"

Mom quickly walked over and pulled back the curtain.

"E-E-E-E-Elephant seal says SPLASH!" Sebastian roared and threw his toy to the front of the tub. As he leaned to retrieve it, Mom saw why Jack looked horrified. Stretching from Bas's left shoulder all the way to his hip was a deep, raw wound. Sucking in her breath, Mom leaned over the tub to examine it more closely.

"It must have just happened," she said aloud. "It's still bleeding."

"How?" Jack asked. "And doesn't he know? Doesn't it hurt?"

Without replying, Mom reached up for the bar of soap and worked up a quick lather in her hands.

"Bassie," she said brightly, "Momma is going to wash your back for you, okay? Just like the zookeepers wash the sea lions."

"S-S-S-S-Sea lions take a bath, Momma?"

"They sure do," she said, rubbing soap over the bleeding twelve-inch gouge. "Sea lions love to play in bubbles!"

"I-I-I-I play in the b-b-b-bubbles with my Jack!"

Satisfied that the wound was clean, she maneuvered Sebastian's thin back under the stream of water. Then she closed the curtain again and examined his soaking pajama shirt.

"His jammies are bloodied, too," she murmured to Jack. "But that doesn't really tell us anything. He might have done it on the tub faucet, or it could have been something else. It looks too deep to be a dog scratch." She paused. "There were about three minutes between when I left him playing in the loft room and when you shouted from the bathroom. Maybe it was an open dresser drawer, or the window frame?" She held back a sigh and tried to put some cheer in her voice. "But I'm so glad you spotted it, Jack! I'll put some antibacterial ointment on it when he's dry."

It's just a scratch, she consoled herself. *It's deep and ugly, but it'll heal. It should hurt, of course, but it doesn't. And why does that upset you so much? Nobody wants their child to be in pain. You don't want him to cry.* As she struggled to calm her mind, she could feel the what-ifs pushing to the forefront. *What if it's something terrible someday and we don't notice? What if he breaks his leg and we've got him walking around on it? What if he gets strep throat and we don't even realize he's sick until it becomes scarlet fever?* She clenched her fists, trying to stop the flow of worries, but it was too late. The last one was coming, and even the sharp stabbing of her nails into her palms couldn't silence it: *What if he's got the same cardiac condition Jack had and we don't find out until it's too late because he can't report the symptoms?*

She snapped her eyes open and bit her lip. Hard.

We check his temperature every night, she lectured herself, *and again every morning. We do a visual inspection every time we get him dressed—even the Big Three know to check. He sees the cardiologist three times a year. We're doing everything there is to do. Cut it out. No hyperventilating allowed.*

Gripping the tube of antibiotic ointment and a handful of Band-Aids, she crossed the hallway in search of her daughter. Marian was in the center of the bunk room, her slim body huddled on the carpet under a massive beach towel designed for two bathers. She appeared to be imitating a rock.

"Marian, why didn't you mention your shower had an intruder?"

Marian peeked out from under the towel, her face in an impish grin.

"Ummm...what happened was, well, it happened really fast. As I was getting out, Sebastian came into the bathroom to ask me for the millionth time where elephant seals live. I wrapped myself up in Towel-zilla here, and he was gone! Except then I heard splashing and I knew: He wasn't gone. He was bathing in his pajamas again. I was going to call out to you, but just then Jack came in and I thought it would be funny to surprise him." Her smile broadened. "Surprise!"

"Surprise..." Mom echoed faintly.

"Surprise!" shouted Vince, bursting into the bunk room, his face flush with excitement. "Look what I got!" he said, pointing to his puffed-out chest. "I was a great listener in tap class, and I finally figured out my snappy shuffles. So I won an 'On the Spot' pin!" He held out the white award stuck to his tuxedo t-shirt. "I was the only one in class who got one, and my teacher took my picture!" His eyes were shining. "Just like you, Marian! I won an 'On the Spot' just like you!"

His big sister was already on her feet wrapping him in a huge hug.

"I'm so happy for you, Vincey!" Marian exclaimed.

"That's quite an honor, Vince!" Mom said, joining their huddle. "Congratulations! Now, let me take the pin off carefully so we can put it somewhere special."

"I want to hang it by my bed," said Vince. "Is that okay, Momma?"

"We can attach it to the yarn that holds up your yellow bird," she agreed quickly. "It'll be safe there, and you'll be able to admire it when you're getting ready to sleep. Now hop into the shower, please. It's your turn to wash Sebastian. And Vincey? Don't worry about the boo-boo on his back. I already scrubbed it."

"Sure thing, Momma!" Vince said happily. He took off towards the bathroom.

"Marian, did you brush your teeth yet?" Mom asked.

"Yes, I did," Marian replied, sitting back down on the carpet and pulling her bathrobe over her pajamas. "I put on lotion, too. Are you reading anything out loud to us tonight?" she asked.

"Just a little book for Sebastian and Vince," said Mom. "Not a new chapter book yet. Since we just finished the Little House series, I think we need to wait a few days before jumping into anything else."

Marian looked crestfallen. "I understand. Your voice probably needs a break, too. But I'm still so sad about Laura Ingalls. I wish I didn't know she was dead."

Jack appeared, and Mom noted that he'd once again failed to dry himself. Water ran in rivulets down his face and neck, and his pajamas clung to his body in wet splotches. Immediately, he jumped into the conversation.

"Marian, Laura Ingalls was born before cars, telephones, and even electric lights. She crossed the prairie in a covered wagon, for goodness sake. I can't believe you ever thought she was someone you'd be able to meet in real life."

Marian had tears pouring down her cheeks. "She's like a best friend to me, Jack. She was real, once. And when we read her books, it was like I was there with her. It's so sad to think that she's gone now."

Kneeling down to Marian's level, Mom pulled her over-emotional daughter into a tight hug, ignoring Jack who was rolling his eyes as his dripping body soaked the carpet with shower water.

"I know how you feel, Sissy," Mom soothed. "Sometimes I imagine book characters are my friends, too."

"Well, I don't cry about it," Jack conceded grudgingly, "but I also feel sad when I finish a good book or a series, Marian."

"It's just…" Marian paused to sniff. "We have so much in common with Laura. There were four kids in her family, too, and they all worked together with the laundry and cooking dinner and stuff, just like we do. Pa played the fiddle, and we play the violin. They worked hard at school, and they took care of each other. We're the same, you know?"

"Plus," Jack said, "Laura tricked that girl she didn't like into getting covered with leeches in the stream! And she helped Pa work in the wheat fields, and she only took a bath once a week." He smacked his leg. "You could be twins, Marian. You're living parallel lives."

Marian giggled. "So, we aren't *exactly* the same," she agreed. "But still! They named their dog 'Jack,' don't forget. And when she grew up, Laura named her new dog 'Shep.'" Marian punched her big brother's wet foot. "I wish we could go back in time and stay with the Ingalls family for a summer. Laura and I would be the best of friends."

"I just want to play with their dog and ride their horses," said Vince, entering the bunk room a sodden and dripping. "Maybe they had a donkey Laura forgot to write about."

"That was only about three minutes, Vince!" Mom cried. "How could you have had time to wash yourself *and* your brother?"

She jokingly lifted his dripping arm and pretended to sniff… but then she froze, realizing Vince had come into the room alone.

"Did you leave Bassie alone in the shower?" she asked, leaping to her feet.

"He didn't want to get out," Vince said quickly. "I turned it off. He's just playing in the water that hasn't drained yet."

Go! Go! Go! She was only vaguely aware of her internal voice as she flew from bunk room to the bathroom in three frantic leaps. Adrenaline coursed through her as she saw Sebastian—who could barely maintain his balance on dry, solid ground—crouched on the tub ledge, attempting to stand. Without a sound, she dropped into a kneel and slid across the soaked bathroom floor, arriving between Sebastian and the floor without a millisecond to spare. She snatched his saturated body out of the air and pulled him close to her chest.

"Y-Y-Y-Y-Y-You love me so much, Momma?" Sebastian's muffled voice asked.

"I do," she answered thickly. "I love you so much, Sebastian."

Without moving from their position on the floor, she reached up into a storage cubby and pulled down a bulky colorfully striped towel. Expertly maneuvering her arms, she wrapped her soggy, shivering baby in its plush warmth and then stood up.

"You can't stand on the tub ledge, Bassie," she said forcefully. "It's too slippery. You almost fell. If Momma hadn't been here, you would have gotten hurt."

"I g-g-g-g-get hurt?" he asked quizzically.

He doesn't understand. How do I keep him safe when he doesn't understand?

"That's right. When you fall, you get hurt. That means you have to be careful. You're not allowed to stand on the tub ledge, Sebastian."

"W-W-W-W-W-Where sea lions live, Momma? They l-l-l-live on the rocky coast?"

Mom carried Bas gently to the bunk room and placed him, still bundled in his towel, on the floor next to Marian.

"Yes, Bassie," she replied. "Sea lions live on the rocky coast of California."

"Momma?" Vince was instantly at her side. "I'm sorry I left him there." He reached for her hand and gave it a squeeze. "Before you get Bassie dressed for bed, maybe you should put on your own jammies. Your boo-boo is looking gross."

She followed his gaze and saw that her spectacular emergency slide-save in the bathroom had come at a cost. Her jeans were soaked, and her knee was having a terrible day, bleeding afresh.

"I'm going to be a doctor when I grow up," Vince said solemnly. "Then I can give you stitches. But for now, I'll stay right here, and sing songs with Bas until you get back."

"We'll help, too," Jack offered. "You'll need that ointment and Band-Aid for yourself before you can help Sebastian."

She bent down to kiss each of her children on their head. "Thanks, love bugs. You're right. I don't want to get blood all over the carpet, but my knee seems to have other plans. I'll change really fast."

Marian stood and grabbed the first-aid supplies off the bookshelf. "You'd better take two Band-Aids, Momma; that's a gnarly cut. But no need to rush!" She choked back a giggle. "The Beef Buff Band is all together here." Laughter exploded, and Marian choked out, "We'll sing beautiful songs!"

The boys immediately joined their sister in raucous laughter. As chorused shouts of "Beef Buff Band!" echoed throughout the second floor of the house, Mom shook her head, joining in the levity. She headed down the hallway to her room with Sebastian's "B-B-B-B-Beef Buff Band" stuttering after her.

They're so silly! she marveled. *I don't even remember why they started calling themselves the Beef Buff Band. It must have been over a year ago, and it still makes me laugh. Matt and I are raising a bunch of kids who are just as weird as we are!*

It was going to be a cold night, so she threw on her winter snowflake pajamas as quickly as she could. Then she rolled up her flannel pant leg to inspect her wound. The bruise from the night before had expanded and was now decorated by two separate gashes—one from the driveway, the other from the sharp edge of the bathtub wall unit.

Baby wipes have so many uses, she thought as she scrubbed

at the injury. *It's going to need some ice while I'm at my desk tonight.* Leg sorted, she grabbed her cell phone and called Matt, who answered on the second ring.

"Hey, I know you're doing the dishes and stuff, but we're turning out the lights in a moment if you want to give good-night kisses to the Beef Buff Band."

"I'll be right up," he said. She could hear his footsteps on the stairs.

By the time she got to the hallway, he was bounding up the final four steps from the landing. She held out her hand, which he grabbed and pulled her into a kiss.

"Hey!" she protested.

"You're the one who invited me up for good-night kisses!" he said. "Complaining is not allowed."

Laughing, they headed toward the four young voices singing "You Are My Sunshine" in the bunk room.

"That was beautiful," Mom told them genuinely. "Thank you for keeping Bassie company while I got changed."

"This has been a special performance of the Beef Buff Band," Vince monologued in his best TV announcer voice. "Look for our album *The Beef Buff Band* in stores near you this summer!"

They are never going to calm down enough to sleep, she bemoaned as all four kids dissolved into wild giggles.

"It's time for Sebastian to put on his dinosaur pajamas," she said sweetly, unwrapping him from his beach-towel cocoon and quickly strapping on a diaper.

"Y-Y-Y-You get my Fluffy Red the Dog?" Sebastian asked pitifully.

"Ruff, ruff! Here he is," Matt replied instantly, pulling the stuffed dog out from underneath the bunk where he was wedged.

"Could the Beef Buff Band perform one more song?" Mom asked hopefully, indicating the Band-Aids and ointment as she pointed surreptitiously to the slice down Sebastian's bared back. Marian's eyes widened and Matt sucked in his breath.

Thankfully, Vince, who had already seen the injury, was fast on his feet. "Let's perform the title track from *Dog Town*!" he said, launching into the opening lines.

Rigid with excitement, Sebastian dropped Red the Dog, rose up onto the balls of his feet, and flexed his hands up and down as he focused on trying to interject the lyrics he'd memorized at the appropriate moments.

Distraction for the win, Mom congratulated herself as she slathered antibacterial ointment on his mystery wound and stuck Band-Aids over the sections that looked the worst. When she was satisfied that the injury was infection-proof, she stuffed his head through his dinosaur pajama top.

"It's probably best to wait until the excitement is over," Matt whispered, recognizing the impossibility of forcing Sebastian's stiff arms through the long tight sleeves of his jammies.

Mom nodded in agreement and consciously stopped to enjoy the moment, pulling Sebastian into a tight hug while the Big Three progressed toward the final lines of their song.

Everyone cheered when they were done.

"That was awesome!" said Matt. "Now," he boomed, "all members of the Beef Buff Band, it's time for bed. Climb that ladder, Jack! Get up there, Marian! Get started on your silent reading."

Valiantly trying to stifle a fresh wave of giggles brought on by hearing their father say 'the Beef Buff Band,' the kids hugged him good night and scurried into their bunks, clicking on their lamps.

"You get one book, Vince and Bassie," Mom said calmly as she retrieved Fluffy Red from the floor and handed him back to Sebastian. "Let's do *The Arctic Search*."

The Beef Buff Band forgotten with the thrill of their favorite book, both little boys crowded into Sebastian's lower bunk and stared at the illustrated scene with interest.

"I found three narwhals!" Vince exclaimed, pointing.

"I-I-I-I spy s-s-s-s-sea lions!" countered Sebastian, his arms straight, hands flapping again.

"Those are orcas—a momma and her baby!" Vince said eagerly. "And there's two killer whales!"

"I see, I see, I see...I see elephant seals!" Sebastian countered, his face stretched into its widest smile and his hands twisting. "W-W-W-Where elephant seals live?"

After another five minutes of naming and counting animals, Mom said quietly, "That's it for tonight." Closing the book, she said, "Vince, you can read for a few more minutes in your own bed if you'd like." She leaned over and kissed Vince's cheek gently. "Sebastian, it's time to put your head on your pillow."

Sebastian grabbed her arm in panic. "You, you, you, you stay here with me?" he pleaded. "Y-Y-Y-Y-You sit on my bed?"

"I always do," she said.

Matt ducked into each bottom bunk to whisper "Good night" and then started back toward the chores waiting for him on the ground floor. But Marian's faltering voice stopped him.

"Daddy? Momma? Before you go downstairs..." Marian peered over the edge of her bunk rail, hesitating. Gripping her best friend, Bear Teddison, she seemed to be steeling her courage. "We, uh, have a question we've been wondering about."

Mom peered up from the edge of Sebastian's bed, where she'd started on the deep-tissue massage she gave his legs every time it was her turn to oversee bedtime.

"Who's 'we'?" she asked quietly,

"Me and Jack and Vince," said Marian. "We've been talking, and we're thinking about some stuff."

Disney, Mom thought immediately. *We just got back in September, and they're already going to start begging us to go again.*

Glancing at Matt, she saw from his slightly irritated expression that he'd arrived at a similar conclusion.

"Go for it, kiddo," he said quickly. "What's on your mind?"

Mom saw Vince sit straight up, clutching his stuffed chicken, and lean out to give his sister a look of encouragement. She heard Jack's top bunk creak above her and realized he must be doing the same.

"What we're wondering is, well, well, I mean..." Marian stammered, which was terribly unusual.

"It's okay, Marian," Jack said quietly.

"You say it best," Vince encouraged.

"Well," she continued, emboldened, "you know the Little House books?"

Quickly, Matt caught his wife's eye, narrowing his own in confusion. Mom knew her own expression was a mirror image.

"Yes, of course, Sissy," Mom said. "We just finished reading the last one."

"Well, we loved them," Marian said slowly. "But we've been wondering for a while now…" She took a deep breath and rushed ahead. "You know how Laura has three sisters, Mary, Carrie, and Grace?"

Mom nodded. "Sure, Marian. What about them?"

"Well, Jack and Vince and I were wondering: Is Sebastian like Laura's sister Mary?"

Mom squinted, trying to understand the question.

"Mary got sick and lost her sight," Mom said slowly. "Is that what you mean? Because Sebastian has a lot of challenges, but we had his eyes checked, remember? He can see just as well as you can. He gets all of his shots, and doctors know more now. Kids don't often go blind from sickness anymore."

"No," Marian pressed. "We know Bassie's not blind." She paused, thinking of how to rephrase her question. "What we mean is: Mary never got to have a husband, or kids of her own, because she had a disability. Even though she went to that special college where she learned to read with her fingertips and play the piano, when she came back, she always lived with Ma and Pa. And after they died, she had to go live with her sister Carrie. Because even though she learned so much, Mary couldn't live alone."

Marian paused for a breath, and Jack's voice took over.

"So, we're wondering if Bas is like that," he said. "Like Mary. Will he always live with you until he has to come and live with one of us?"

Mom was silent as the world shifted into slow motion and an unexpected flood of adrenaline unleashed inside her body. Sitting frozen in the relative darkness of Sebastian's bottom bunk, holding his wiggling bare feet, she felt her heart shatter into a thousand pieces as she silently acknowledged the momentous weight the night now carried. She saw Matt paralyzed in the doorway and could read his thoughts, because they were her own.

What choice do we have? she asked herself. *It's not fair. For any of them. But what else can we do? What do we say?*

Three seconds had passed in silence. Knowing eye contact was crucial to the next moments, Mom shifted herself out from underneath the bunk, surprised to find that her eyes were dry. As soon as she lost contact with Sebastian's skin, he started whimpering, so she scooped him up, holding her four-year-old like a baby and rocking him gently.

"That is a great question, kiddos," she said, sounding much more confident than she felt. "You three are very smart to have made those connections." She smiled at each of them in turn and then answered with a quiet, honest sadness. "We can't know for sure what the future will hold. No one does. But if we had to guess... probably." She stopped to breathe deeply. "Probably, yes. Sebastian's best life will be living with his family."

Matt was beside her now, his arm lightly around her shoulder, being careful not to add to the weight she was already carrying.

Vince's voice broke the silence. "Sebastian needs us to help him every day, so we already get a lot of practice. I bet by the time we're grown-ups, we'll be really good at it. Maybe I'll be a veterinarian, and he can be my assistant! I could drive us to work every day."

"We thought so," Marian said simply. "Bas picked us. Out of the millions and millions of families in the world, he came to us. And he makes our family special." She paused in thought. "Not because of AUTS2. That's rare—but being rare doesn't automatically mean special. I meant, our family is special because we all get to be loved by someone as cool as Sebastian." She reached down from her bunk to gently pet her baby brother's hair. "Helping him is a good way to thank him for choosing us."

"It'd be pretty cool to live with your best friend," Jack added.

Sebastian lifted his sleepy head from Mom's shoulder and said groggily, "Y-Y-You all my best, best friends. W-W-W-We a best friend family."

Holding Sebastian tightly, Mom walked with Matt down to the head of Vince's bottom bunk and leaned in to start the round of good-nights again.

"Night-night, Momma. Night-night, Daddy." Vince said softly as she kissed his head. "Sleep tight, Bassie-Boo. I love you."

Mom stood and saw Jack leaning over the edge of his bunk, with his stuffed dog, Bella, clutched to his chest.

"Sweet dreams, Bassie," he said, leaning down further to give them all kisses. "Maybe you can dream about swimming with sea lions tonight!"

Marian was waiting at the foot of her bunk, where it connected to the foot of Jack's. "I'm climbing down partway so I can hug you better," she said quietly as she descended the first two rungs of her ladder. "Good night, Bas. I'll see you in the morning, okay? We can play *Dog Town*."

"There's no school tomorrow!" Mom said, suddenly remembering. "We'll have donuts for breakfast and then you'll all watch a movie. Or you can even sleep in, if you want," she added hopefully.

In unison, Jack, Marian, and Vince broke into giggles. Hearing his siblings, Sebastian perked up and joined in, laughing harder and longer than anyone else.

"All right, all right," Matt said firmly. "We all know you'll be up before seven a.m. Just know that someday when you're all lazy teenagers, your Momma is going to wake you up at 6:30 in the morning just for fun, and I'm not going to stop her."

Mom laid Sebastian back on his pillow and resumed her bedside vigil.

"Deeper than the ocean and higher than the sky," she said gently. "Nobody loves you more than Daddy and I. Sleep fast, kiddos. Morning is coming."

MONDAY, 9:15 P.M.

She'd never had an easier time staying awake. It took Sebastian another hour to stop wiggling and settle down to sleep, but she didn't doze. Not even once.

Alone in the silence, watching her baby boy struggle to find rest, she was the outward picture of stillness—barely moving to blink. But within, her mind clung to sanity as a storm raged, threatening to drown her soul in desperation. She'd gotten through the initial crisis: maintaining her composure as she watched her precious children face the questions that haunted her own mind day and night. But now she sat in torment as the Big Three slept through the first night of their newly recognized reality.

Will they remember this day? she wondered. *Laura Ingalls certainly remembered the day Pa told her she was forevermore to serve as Mary's eyes. Will they remember discussing it among themselves and working up the courage to ask us?*

Mom felt pride trying to push away devastation as she relived their sweet, upbeat assessments of her response. But then anguish rose like bile in her throat as she pictured the future her adult children would face together.

When Sebastian finally reached the depth of sleep that would allow her to slip away unnoticed, she gritted her teeth and headed downstairs.

Matt was standing at the large couch, folding laundry. The floors were clean and she noticed that a lilac candle, her favorite scent, was burning on the television stand. Without a word, she joined him at the pile the kids affectionately called "Mount Laundrious" and mindlessly began folding a sweater, bracing herself to fend off Alice, who in a few moments, at best, would try to climb the heap of clean clothes for a smell-transferring nap.

She and Matt stood side-by-side, pulling clothes in silence, needing a distraction as much as they needed togetherness. She risked a glance and saw that Matt's eyes were rimmed in red.

Crushed with guilt, she released her words in a torrent. "It's my fault!" she cried. "It wasn't intentional when I first started reading them the Little House series—I just chose the books I'd loved as a kid. But by the time we got to the last few titles, I continued on purpose. I could have stopped while Laura and Mary were still young girls. I could have stopped before Mary got sick and lost her sight. I didn't, because I *wanted* them to hear a story where the family banded together to help each other. I thought it'd reinforce the sense of joyful duty we've been trying to instill in them. The books have so many great examples of both the kids and parents sacrificing for the good of their family. Back then, family was all you had—and I don't think that's really much different today. Family is the most important thing, especially for Bas. He's never going to stop needing us. I wanted to help them understand that. Except I thought I was being smart, planting a tiny *seed* of an idea." She forced herself to look at the wreckage she'd caused, displayed across her husband's face.

"I'm sorry," she choked.

"Hey," he said, pulling her close. "Everything is okay. You heard them. They knew...they already knew." His voice was gruff, and although she knew his tears wouldn't fall, she felt responsible that they were trying.

"But if I hadn't read them those books," she mourned, "they might not have realized for years. Wouldn't that have been better?

Think about Vince," she said, her voice cracking. "In a heartbeat, his grow-up plans changed to incorporate a sidekick role for Sebastian. Our six-year-old just changed his life goals." She sniffed as a fresh wave of tears coursed down her cheeks, but Matt was smiling.

"Seriously?" he asked. "Do you even listen when Vince talks? In the past week alone, we've had conversations about his future aspirations to be a treasure hunter, a grocery store owner, a professional dog walker, *and* a swim instructor." Matt shook his head, grinning. "Don't worry about Vince. He's going to be incredible. In fact, he's rather amazing already."

"They all are," Mom agreed. "You heard them. I told them they're inheriting the responsibility of a lifelong dependent, and they just smiled and took it in stride. All of them."

Matt reached for a towel and then narrowed his eyes at her playfully. "You thought you were planting a 'tiny seed'?"

Mom looked down, chagrined. "Honestly? Yes. I was trying to do some long-term planning. My half-cooked idea," she explained, "was that in about ten years, I'd sit down the Big Three and broach the subject by reminding them of the Little House books and Mary's story." She looked sadly at Matt. "We should be attempting some long-term *financial* planning, too, but in doing our budgets, I know that it's hopeless right now. I keep telling myself that the endless tuition for dance, violin, swimming, trumpet, saxophone, science camp, and everything else are investments that'll somehow pay off in time to save the day." She sighed. "Along the same lines, I thought this series was a good first step in planting a 'tiny seed' of future responsibility in the kids' minds."

Matt stroked her arm. "You aren't wrong. The sports and music experiences are so important." He kissed her head. "You just forgot that all those hours at dance, swim, and violin lessons act like fertilizer for tiny idea seeds."

Mom sighed. "Yup—they're too smart. And now they know. They can't go back to not knowing. It'll always be there, in the back of their minds. And I'm terrified it might change the way they feel about their brother."

Matt pulled a bed sheet from Mount Laundrious and offered her two corners.

"I didn't tell you about a call that came in during my afternoon shift yesterday," he said thoughtfully, stretching out the dog-patterned fitted sheet. "I didn't want to. But now I do." He looked at her steadily as they brought their corners together. "I'm going to tell *you* now, and tomorrow at dinner I'll tell the kids. Because their worldview has changed and they know what they'll have to do someday. This call will help them to understand why their job is going to be so important."

"What happened?" Mom asked, quickly finishing the fold and grabbing another sheet.

"Well," said Matt. "you know those nice houses on Ellicott Creek—where they all have deep front yards, setting them back from the road?"

"You mean the road where cars zip by, constantly breaking the thirty-five-mile-per-hour speed limit?" Mom asked.

"That's the one," said Matt. "Meanwhile, on the other side of the street is a ten-foot-wide stretch of wilderness fronting the creek." He paused. "You should have seen it rushing yesterday with all that wind. I've never seen the level so high or the current so strong." He shuddered. "Well, apparently, a lady was watching the creek out her front window when she noticed a man in the slice of woods across the road from her house. He was wandering around like he was confused, out in that crazy wind in just a t-shirt and sweatpants. She assumed he was a drunk and didn't call the police until he lay down on the side of the road." Matt grabbed the corners of a *Star Wars* quilt being handed to him. "The cops arrived and talked to him for fifteen more minutes before they called in our ambulance."

Mom saw the pain in Matt's eyes and braced herself for whatever was to come.

"By the time we got there, they'd cuffed him. But they'd left him sitting on the ground. They called us because he wasn't answering any of their questions. They thought maybe he'd taken a cocktail of drugs, or was having trouble with his insulin levels." Matt took a deep breath and puffed out his cheeks. "At least they realized something wasn't right, I guess."

Mom froze mid-fold. "What *was* wrong with him?"

"The guy was seated on the gravel with his arms behind his back. But I could see his hands twitching and from the way he held his head, I just knew. I knew before I stepped out into the wind."

"What was it?" she asked again, dreading the answer but needing to hear it anyway.

"I brought him a blanket and wrapped him up. He was freezing. I did my initial assessment right there, and when I asked him how he was feeling, he told me, 'The dog got away.' Then the guy started to cry." Matt shook his head angrily. "He wasn't a drunk. He hadn't taken any drugs, and he didn't have diabetes. He wasn't even loitering. Not on purpose, anyway. He'd escaped from the adult daycare about a mile away. No one had noticed him leave, and he hadn't been missed. He'd just been wandering around unsupervised between a raging creek and a winding two-lane road where speeders hit fifty miles an hour with regularity."

"How did you know where he'd come from?"

"Lucky guess. I've responded to that place a few times, and the calls are always terrible. So I had the police contact them to see if they were missing anyone matching the guy's description. The site director showed up five minutes later to collect him."

Mom stared at Matt in horror. "Are you kidding me?"

Matt sighed again. "I wish I were. It happened yesterday. But it can *never* happen to Sebastian. I presume the guy was trying to follow a dog. After checking the security cameras, the site director had a good guess about when he'd gone on walkabout, and the poor guy had been on his own for over two hours! Who knows *when* they would have noticed he was missing if that lady hadn't called in, mistaking him for a staggering drunk. It's a miracle the guy wasn't hit by a car. Or that he didn't drown in Ellicott Creek, or get wet and die of hypothermia." Matt's eyes flashed. "That can never be Sebastian. *Never.* And the Big Three need to know that." His expression was fierce. "I'm *glad* they figured it out today. Because we can't live forever, and someday it's going to be their responsibility to make sure that's not our Bassie. The more we talk about it, the better they'll understand."

Mom realized she was mindlessly holding a black leotard. She set it on the Marian pile and stepped over to hug Matt.

"It won't be Sebastian," she said. "It won't. We'll take care of him, and then they will. I'm working like a maniac so we can pay off the bills and set money aside. Maybe some big bonuses will come in for me. If you don't let me spend on another trip to Disney, we might be able to buy those two houses around the corner. They're going up for sale soon, and you know they want to sell to us. Then we'd be sure the Big Three could afford to keep him. Bas could live in the smaller house, or if that's more responsibility than he can handle, he could stay with whichever kid takes the big house, using the little one as a rental for income." She nodded with conviction. "We'll think of something. That won't be him."

Matt looked at her with a heartbroken expression. "Remember when that young boy died during my shift—the one wearing the same footie pajamas Baby Vincey had?" He blinked. "I had nightmares for months. I still do sometimes."

"Of course, that'd leave a mark," she empathized. "You couldn't save that precious child. You tried so hard, but it was just too late. And the baby was the same age as Vince, wearing Vince's clothes. You'd have to be a monster not to be affected. It was terrible."

Matt looked at her as though she were missing the point. "But the guy yesterday—he was probably older than me. He wasn't terribly clean. He had a beard. Still, when I looked at *him*, hunched and handcuffed on the side of the road in the freezing cold, all I could see was Sebastian."

She hugged him harder, speaking into his shoulder where he couldn't see her face. "It's our job to make sure that's never Sebastian," she said. "We'll fight for the best education. We'll keep paying the insane rates for his adaptive swim program. He can stay in dance class with typical kids, and this summer he'll play soccer. We'll take him everywhere, letting him experience as much of the world as he can because that's how he learns best." She pulled away to face him, her expression composed. "We'll give him as many life skills as we can, and maybe someday he can have a job. Plus, we're figuring out a plan for him stay with his siblings once we're gone. If we can't afford those houses around the corner in time, we'll find another set when we *can* afford to move. And we'll teach Bas how to be safe. If anyone can do it, it's us. That's why Sebastian came to our family. We're his best shot."

She smiled and kissed Matt on the lips.

He gazed back at her. "Okay, then," he said resolutely. "I'm on board with that strategy. Are you?"

"What do you mean?" she asked. "I'm the one who just described it!"

"Ahhh…" he said slowly. "But let me ask you a tough question." He waited until she nodded. "I put Sebastian in fire-truck pajamas after his shower today. But he wasn't wearing them when I came up to say good night." He stared at her. "What happened to them?"

"They got wet in the shower," she replied, holding his gaze.

"One more question then," he said casually. "How did you punish Sebastian for getting into the shower fully clothed again?"

She looked away, knowing he was asking something he already knew the answer to.

"I didn't," she admitted. "Because he doesn't understand." Her confession sounded like a challenge.

"That's where you're wrong," Matt replied quietly. "Was that the fourth or the fifth time this week? He *could* understand. He just needs practice. But *we* have to give him chances to practice." Matt took her hands into his. "He needs limits, and we need to be firm in maintaining those limits. He's four. It's time to start using time-outs."

Mom dug slowly through Mount Laundrious for a matching pair of socks.

"How?" she asked. "How do I use time-outs with Sebastian? He wasn't being mean, or even sneaky. He just wanted play in the warm water with his toys and his brother. He doesn't understand why he shouldn't, and a time-out isn't going to teach him." She stubbornly stared down her husband. "Life is hard enough for Sebastian. If taking an extra shower makes him happy, I don't really mind putting him in dry pajamas. It's not worth breaking his innocent heart with a time-out that he doesn't understand."

Matt inhaled deeply. "I get it. But think about that man, handcuffed in the cold," he countered. "He didn't understand that leaving the adult daycare center was the wrong thing to do, either. And he wasn't being mean or sneaky. He just wanted to pet a dog. That didn't make it any less dangerous for him. Sebastian needs to find a way to understand the limits in his world. You know he can learn. He's got a tremendous memory when the information is important to him. Maybe time-outs will make the rules feel important. If he can't play with his toys for a few minutes, if we won't answer his questions, or sing him songs, or give him hugs and kisses..." At her horrified expression, he paused before starting again. "Sebastian is four. But in most areas, it's generous to say he's on par with a typical two-year-old. So, let's go for two-minute time-outs. Just two minutes." He squeezed her shoulders encouragingly. "You can stand his devastation for two minutes, can't you? If it means he's not going to grow up to be that lost and frozen man handcuffed on the roadside?"

Reluctantly, she nodded. "Of course I can. You're right. He's probably ready for time-outs. It just feels wrong, making him cry when he doesn't understand why he's in trouble." She managed a small, resigned smile. "We can use the microwave timer so he'll get an auditory cue when his punishment is over. He'll like that."

Matt smiled back. "Or the timer on our phones, if we're out and about somewhere."

She blew out a slow breath, thinking about the enormity of the task. "I'll start tomorrow. If something dangerous happens, or if

Sebastian pours all the dog food into the water dish again, I'll put him in time-out."

"You can do it." Matt encouraged. "He's ready. You'll see."

Mom turned back to Mount Laundrious and broke out in a laugh.

"We live with a stealthy ninja, and she's a fat dog named Alice. How'd she manage to sneak past us? I didn't even hear her nails click on the floor!"

Perched like a dragon protecting her hoard, Alice opened her eyes and looked at them disdainfully from atop the remaining heap of towels, jeans, and sweatshirts.

"At least we got the bedding folded before she hopped up there," Matt said. "There's nothing worse than pulling up the sheet in bed, only to have a waft of Alice-stink smack you in the face."

Mom giggled in agreement and tugged on a pant leg dangling off the front of the couch. "I'll try to at least rescue some of this bottom stuff before it gets a layer of orange dog fur."

"Mind if I dig through the paper stack in the kitchen for a minute?" asked Matt. "I lost the referral form for my medic student. He gave it to me a while back, and I never filled it out."

"Go for it," she said. "I'm on a laundry rescue mission here."

"But I don't want to leave you alone if you're still upset," he said, pulling her in for a kiss.

She gave him a squeeze. "I'm good. The kids know now and we can't take it back. And maybe it's even for the best. Because I feel like we finally have a semblance of a plan, and that's exciting."

MONDAY, 10:45 P.M.

From her laundry post in the living room, Mom heard Matt shuffling papers in the kitchen.

"Hey, sweet girl," she cooed, scratching Alice's belly. "I don't suppose you'd like to shift off of our clean clothes?"

Alice grunted like a contented pig, indicating it was a lost cause. Mom grasped a beach towel the kids needed for swim practice tomorrow and yanked. Alice gazed at her lazily and stretched out to get even more comfortable on the shrinking mountain.

As Mom was balancing the rolled towel on the pyramid of bathroom laundry staged to be carried upstairs, Matt reappeared, brandishing a stack of thick, lumpy manila envelopes.

"These are all addressed to us and they're not even opened. What are they?"

Mom froze, her outstretched arms steadying the folded towels.

"Were they under the green stepstool?"

"Yeah, I think so. What are they?" he asked again, sliding his finger under the taped-down flap.

"They're from the researchers—the ones in Seattle *and* the ones in Toronto."

Matt froze. He carefully retracted his finger from the packaging. "Oh."

She nodded. "Right. I sent Bas's medical history packet to both groups last summer after we ran the gamut of tests on him at the National Institutes of Health. Research is tremendously important. But I haven't had a single day in the last five months where I felt brave enough to open those envelopes and spit in those tubes myself."

She reached over and petted Alice again, avoiding Matt's gaze.

"Tell me about the chances again?" he asked sincerely. "What are the chances that one of us somehow gave this to Sebastian?"

She blew out her breath. "AUTS2 is autosomal. I looked it up. That means if someone is a carrier, they have a fifty percent chance of passing it on to their child."

"But we're not impacted," Matt argued. "And neither are the Big Three. So doesn't that mean it was probably a spontaneous mutation?"

"De novo?" she asked, using a term she'd become familiar with over this journey. "It's possible. But we have members in our Facebook group who are braver than us, and some of their tests have shown the same mutation as their kid. They have AUTS2 Syndrome and never even knew it."

Matt frowned. "But how can that be? Even without medical diagnostics, AUTS2 symptoms aren't exactly something you can ignore."

Mom spread her hands. "It depends on where in the AUTS2 zone the mutation takes place, I guess," she said. "Some people are barely impacted. Others aren't as lucky."

"Well, I'm not super-smart, but I get by," he analyzed. "And you're almost a genius! And neither of us has trouble focusing long enough to eat significant quantities of food—I don't even want to think about what *my* body mass index is. Do you really think it's probable one of us carries a genetic mutation causing intellectual disability that we passed on to our baby?"

"I'm terrified of the possibility," she admitted. "That's why I haven't spit in the tube." She closed her eyes and shook her head. "Why don't you put them back under the green stool? We'll do it—we'll send them everything they're requesting. But not tonight. Maybe next week. Or next month. But I can promise I won't forget."

He smiled at her gently. "In that case, shall I just throw them out?"

She grimaced. "You can toss the envelope from the orthopedist if you want. That appointment is over, and they know what they need to. But don't you dare chuck the other ones. That information is critical. The medical community needs data for global research. Since there are so few subjects in the sample, we *have* to participate. Plus, it's important for our family. If one of us is a carrier, that has major implications for Jack, Marian, and Vince. We can't hide from it forever. If Bas inherited it, there's a fifty percent chance the other kids did, too."

"Which means they could pass AUTS2 Syndrome onto their own kids someday?"

"Right. Even if they're unaffected, the same chances would apply."

Matt looked at the stack of envelopes as though realizing he was holding a nest of vipers. "I'll put it back."

"Could you grab Alice's medicine while you're there? She didn't get it yet today."

"Sure thing," he agreed.

When he returned, he smilingly held out a pill wrapped in bologna, along with two beers.

"It's too late for that!" Mom protested. "It's eleven o'clock. I've got the hour-long mystery conference for Sebastian in the morning, and the kids will be home with me all day."

"That's too bad," Matt said sternly, "because we're going to watch an episode of *The Office* and drink a beer together." He plunked the cold can into her hand. "It'll take thirty minutes. And we need it."

She'd passed exhaustion four hours ago and had been riding an emotional roller coaster that refused to slow down long enough for her to get off.

If I'm going to choose how to spend thirty minutes doing whatever I want, the winner should be sleep, she reasoned. *Or work—my projects sat neglected all day except for the forty minutes I put in sitting on the floor during violin lessons, and my clients will be looking for drafts tomorrow. Not to mention I have three deadlines looming on Friday.*

Unthinkingly, she took a long sip from her can of beer. It was frosty and delicious.

"I didn't even know I opened it!" she cried, laughing. "I was standing here, listing the reasons in my head why I should not sit down and watch a show with you, and then I tasted the beer in my mouth that I'd decided to hand back to you untouched."

He grinned and pointed to the couch. "Sit down. I think we're on the one where they hand out Dundie Awards."

She yawned and took another large gulp. "In that case, you'd better go grab us each another can. That's one of my favorite episodes."

DAY THREE

TUESDAY, 2:31 A.M.

The dolphin was calling her. The sky was sunny and the sand was warm under her feet. Sleek and shining, the dolphin splashed near the shore, inviting her into the clear, calm water. His frolicking sent ocean spray all over the beach as he made cheerful sounds that she found comfortingly familiar.

Where have I heard those sounds before? she struggled to recall, still basking in the warm sun with the tropical beauty of the beach around her.

The dolphin called out again, begging her to join him—communicating in what she now realized was a strange mix of unusual dolphin squeaks and English words. *Do dolphins use words?* She didn't think so, and the squeaks weren't normal, either. Something wasn't quite right. *But the sun felt delicious and the sand was so warm...*

This could be a dream, she thought hazily, *but those sounds are real. I know they are.*

To test her suspicions, she cautiously tried opening her eyes. Instantly, the sun went out and the darkness of her bedroom enveloped her. Her attention was drawn to her digital clock, its steady glow competing with the still-audible dolphin-splashing in the background for her perception of reality.

She blinked as she considered the digital display, showing the time as 2:35 a.m. Then she was bolt upright in her pitch-black bedroom, untangling herself from the sheets and blankets, and sprinting for the bathroom. Because the clock read 2:35 a.m., and while most of the world dedicates the prime hours between late night and early morning to deep, restorative sleep, she didn't have that luxury. Because Sebastian's mind didn't rest. Somehow, it just couldn't.

She briefly tried to work out how long he'd been awake unattended, but gave up when her sleep-deprived mind couldn't even determine how to start on what was probably very simple addition. Or subtraction. Or maybe square roots. In the fuzzy place between awake and asleep where she moonlighted as a hostage each night, she heard the dolphin again calling to her. But he wasn't at the beach now; he was standing in the bathroom. And unlike most dolphins, he wore dinosaur pajamas.

Her mind snapped awake as she took in the scene. Sebastian was playing in the toilet bowl, diving his plastic sea lion and dolphin toys in and out of the water while bellowing his best aquatic animal impressions. The floor once again hosted an inch of standing water, and Sebastian was saturated from the tip-top of his head to the bottoms of his feet.

She closed the bathroom door, shutting herself inside, and turned on the light. Moving on autopilot, she tugged towels off the back of the door, pitched them onto the ground, and turned on the shower. Sebastian hadn't reacted to the sudden light, but the sound of water spraying tore his attention from his game. His face lit in a delighted grin.

"Hi, Momma! I'm Sebastian! It night, and you so tired. Momma sleeping. Sebastian play with dolphin and sea lion. They swimming in cave. Momma sleep!"

"Kindness. Courage. Understanding." She'd meant to chant the mantra internally, but it slipped out in a pleading whisper that startled her.

"You sad, Momma?" Sebastian sounded worried. "You sad?" He tottered towards her now, his unsteady bare feet sliding across the soaking floor. "I just love you so, so much, Momma."

She bent down and picked him up, holding her baby tightly while tears streamed noiselessly down her cheeks. She knew the wetness soaking through her pajamas was toilet water and that the stabbing pain in her shoulder was a plastic dolphin tail, but she didn't care. Rocking Bas slowly in the bathroom as it filled with steam, she begged forgiveness from the pure, innocent creature the universe had entrusted to her.

"I love you, Sebastian. I love you so much, and I'm sorry I didn't wake up in time. I'm so, so sorry, Bassie." She took a deep breath and tried to temper the desperation she could hear in her voice. "Momma needs more sleep than you, but I don't mind being tired. I don't mind, my little love. I'll wake up to keep you safe, always."

"You sad, Momma?" Sebastian asked again. "I kiss you." He planted a wet, sloppy smooch on her cheek. "What dolphins eat, Momma? They eat fish?"

"Yes, Sebastian," she replied softly, pulling the shower curtain aside, stepping in the tub, and situating them both—still fully clothed—under the warm water. "Dolphins live with their families in the big blue ocean, and they eat fish."

As she scrubbed the toilet germs from her child and herself, all the while answering questions about the habitats and eating preferences of the world's fauna population, she wondered idly if this was the type of situation Matt had intended to result in a time-out. She decided she didn't particularly care at the moment.

When she and Bas were both clean, dry, and wearing fresh pajamas—Sebastian's third pair of the night featuring aliens in flying saucers—she took his hand and guided him to her bedroom. She gave him a sip of water from the cup on her nightstand and wearily rubbed antibacterial ointment across the wound on his back. The clock now read 3:15 a.m. and she smiled, because that meant she had less than an hour before Bas settled down for his second truncated round of sleep.

Hearing a snore from the first floor, she suddenly realized Matt was not in bed. *I could wake him to come up*, she considered, *but tomorrow is Tuesday and his alarm will start buzzing at 5:30 a.m. That's an hour before I have to get up, and I need all the sleep I can get.*

Decision made, she crawled into bed and positioned Sebastian on Matt's pillow.

"Sea lions eat fish, and dolphins eat fish, Momma?"

"Yes, Bassie-Boo. They both like fish."

"They mammals, Momma? Babies drink milk?" His arms—reflecting his exhilaration at mastering a new vocabulary word and its meaning—stiffened straight outwards and caught her in the stomach.

"That's right, Sebastian. Sea lions and dolphins are both mammals. Just like dogs and cows and people. Their babies are birthed, and they drink milk."

"Red the Dog a mammal?" Bas asked as his toes, flexing up and down excitedly, pulled at her pant leg, reminding her of the now-soggy Band-Aids she'd forgotten about on her knee.

"Yup. All the *Dog Town* puppies are mammals. Another way to tell is because they have fur." She kissed his head gently. "Now, Sebastian, my love. It's time to be quiet and go to sleep. It's night-time and we both need to rest."

"Alice a mammal, Momma? Thomas Jefferson a mammal?"

"You got it. Both our doggies are mammals." Though Mom was desperate for sleep more than anything, she couldn't pass up the critical-thinking opportunity that popped into her head. "What do you think about Bully Fish, Sebastian?" she asked, referring to their dearly loved pet fish who lived in forced isolation due to his unpleasant habit of pecking tank-mates to death. "Do you think he's a mammal?"

Sebastian's arms and legs relaxed as he devoted all of his energies to solving this new riddle. "I no know, Momma."

"Yes, you can figure it out, Bassie. Think about it carefully. Remember: Mammals breathe air and they have fur. Now think about our Bully Fish downstairs in his tank. He's orange, he has a notched fin, and he's as big as your hand. But is he a mammal? Does he have fur? Does he breathe air?"

Sebastian's body lay perfectly still as he considered. "Bully Fish has SCALES!" he cried happily, his arms flapping. "He breathe water with GILLS!" he shouted, his whole body rigid with delight. "He not a mammal. He just a big mean FISH!"

"That's exactly correct, Sebastian," Mom whispered, hugging him close. "Your brain is so smart! But now it's tired." She kissed him one more time. "No more talking now, please. Save your questions, and you can ask them in the morning when the sun is shining."

"Momma? Turkeys gobble?"

She sighed. "Yes, honey. Turkeys gobble. Now it's time for sleeping."

"Momma? Turkeys gobble me up?"

She opened her eyes to smile at him. "No, sweetie. Turkeys make a gobble noise. But they don't eat people. Turkeys eat seeds and berries and bugs."

"Oh. Turkeys not scary? They no have teeth?"

"No, Sebastian. A turkey won't hurt you. It can't bite; it just has a pointy beak."

"I love you, Momma," he tried to whisper in his familiar hoarse shout.

"I love you too, Bassie," she said.

What a funny conversation, she reflected. But before she could giggle, her eyes closed and unconsciousness overtook her.

TUESDAY, 6:30 A.M.

It seemed as though she'd just closed her eyes when her phone alarm gave its piercing 6:30 a.m. shriek. She silenced it and was on her feet in under two seconds. Stretched out and dreaming peacefully, Sebastian looked like he belonged in a magazine advertisement for mattresses. *Or overnight diapers*, she thought wryly.

Absurd images and fuzzy memories clawed their way to the front of her mind. *Was he really playing in the toilet last night?* Seeing his fists gripped tightly around a plastic sea lion and dolphin, she knew he had. She squinted in concentration. *Do I really need to take another shower then?* She padded towards the bathroom and caught a glimpse in the hall mirror of her reflection, which featured a wild disarray of creased blond hair. *Yikes! Another shower it is then*. She grimaced in pain. *If that throbbing is any indication, my knee could use a scrubbing anyway.*

Pulling on dry socks ten minutes later, she tried to push away the cobwebs of exhaustion by running the day's schedule through her mind. *Breakfast, conference, voting, bowling*. She pulled out her phone and flipped to the photograph she'd taken of their calendar. *Marian has her tap solo lesson. The Big Three have swim practice. Right. Busy day.*

She finished tying her maroon trainers and stood to retrieve her glasses from the sink counter. Looking in the foggy bathroom mirror, she grinned. By chance, the gray sweatshirt she'd grabbed read "Be Courageous" across the front in gray stitching.

All right, Conference Day! Bring it on, she resolved. *It'll take more than a meeting bloated to three times its regular twenty-minute size to scare me.* Nodding smartly at herself, she wiped her glasses clean and flipped off the light. *They can all sleep a little longer if I set up breakfast.*

She gently pried open the bathroom door to sneak into the hallway...and had to use her Supermom reflexes to avoid trampling Vince, who was sitting cross-legged in the threshold.

"Good morning, Momma!" he tried to whisper. "No school today and you promised donuts for breakfast!"

"Hey, Vincey," she mouthed, pointing to the stairs.

Shoot! I forgot the donuts. I promised donuts, and of course Vince the Eternally Hungry remembers. I forgot to get donuts.

Down in the dark living room, Vince grabbed her hand. She stepped on the button that turned on the floor lamp.

"Good morning, Thomas Jefferson," she greeted their slobbering largest dependent curled up on the couch. He lifted his head lazily and blinked at them.

Vince hugged the dog around the neck, kissing his enormous muzzle, and then scurried towards the kitchen.

"I'll open the door," he called over his shoulder. "Thomas told me he's got to go out."

Dreading the looming donut-deficit tantrum, she hurried after Vince.

Maybe I can turn on the television and fly really quickly to the store, she considered. *Or maybe I can just leave a few minutes early for the conference, grab the donuts, and swing back to drop them off before I leave for real?*

None of those were good options because time was already running short. Taking a deep breath and preparing herself for a bargain that would involve offering frozen waffles now for an ice cream trip later, she rounded the corner into the kitchen—and stopped short.

Vince was seated at the table bench, gleefully shoving a full-sized sprinkle-covered donut into his mouth.

"These are my favorite kind, Momma! Thanks!" he rhapsodized, his mouth stuffed with sugary goodness.

Incredulously, she stared at a full dozen donuts nestled in a paper box sitting on the table next to a vase of red and yellow flowers.

"Daddy did this for us, Vincey," Mom confessed. "It wasn't me. I forgot all about it!"

"Daddy went to Dickie's Donuts for these," Vince said excitedly. "He knows they make my favorite flavors. When I get bigger, I'm going to work there to learn their secret recipes and then I'll start my own donut shop. Bassie can help clean up the tables!"

Mom was still smiling in wonder. "I can't figure out how Daddy did it!" she said. "Maybe his ambulance is posted nearby today."

"Call him, Momma!" urged Vince.

"I've got to finish a few chores, Vince. Here." She handed him her phone. "It'll be good practice for you to call him. Tell him he's a hero—and see if he'll tell you how he managed it!"

She stepped into the laundry room at the back of the kitchen and unloaded the dryer. Carrying an armload of towels towards Mount Laundrious on the couch, she heard Vince's voice and smiled. Matt must not be with a patient, so was able to answer.

Vince met her in the dining room on her way back to the kitchen.

"He snuck back home in his ambulance, Momma! You were right!"

"That daddy of yours is pretty excellent," she said.

"He said the peanut stick is for you, because they only had one. So you'd better eat it up, Momma. Jack will snatch it if you're not fast."

"I'll get to it in a minute, Vincey." She smiled. "First, I've got to finish the laundry tasks and get you guys some mandarin oranges."

"I'll get the cans out!" he said quickly. "I know right where they are. Lazy Susan's hiding them, but I'll find them! Susan will see. It's no good to be lazy."

Mom giggled. "That spinning Lazy Susan cupboard is rather clever when it comes to making things disappear. Lucky thing you're the very opposite of lazy." She snatched the peanut stick—Dickie's specialty creation—out of the box and kissed the top of Vince's head. "I'm going to run upstairs to get Jack and Marian. I'll be back down in three minutes."

She sprinted to the stairs and took them two at a time. When she rounded the landing, she was shocked to see Sebastian standing above her in the hallway.

"Good morning, Momma!" he said sleepily. "I'm Sebastian."

"Good morning, Sebastian!" she replied, climbing the remaining stairs and pulling him into a hug. "I'm Momma. You're up earlier than you needed to be, my little man.

"No school today?" he confirmed hopefully. "We watch fish movie?"

"That's right," she said, taking his hand. "Let's wake everyone else up and go downstairs for some donuts."

"What? Donuts? Yay!" he chirped. "Thank you, Momma, for getting us donuts!"

She turned on the light in the bunk room and shut off the fan. As she pulled open the drapes, she broke into song.

"Good morning to you, good morning to you! Good morning, sweet kiddos, good morning to you!"

Jack sat up immediately. "Today we go bowling?" he asked groggily.

"Yup! But first we're going to watch the fish movie, remember? I've got to leave for the conference in about twenty minutes."

Marian jumped theatrically out from under her covers, fully dressed for the day.

"I was only pretending!" she crowed. "I woke up when Vince did, but I didn't tell anyone! You thought I was sleeping, but I'm already dressed!"

"You're goofy!" Mom replied, shaking her head. "Come on down and give me a hug. Daddy snuck to Dickie's Donuts this morning and brought us back a dozen fresh donuts for breakfast!"

"Wahoo!" Jack and Marian shouted in unison.

"I'll take Bassie down right away," Marian offered. "I'm starving!" She took her baby brother by the hand and led him out of the room towards the stairs. "Bassie-Boo, after we eat our donuts, do you want to find all our ocean toys? We've got a sea lion and a sea turtle you could hug."

"And a clownfish!" he shouted happily.

Jack was still pulling on his shirt, and so—in deference to the fear all her kids harbored of monsters—Mom busied herself picking up stray bits of laundry and tissues from the carpet to avoid leaving him alone upstairs.

"Hey, Mom?" Jack climbed down his ladder fully clothed. "You started your own business so we didn't have to go to daycare, right?"

"That's right, honey," she said, wondering where he'd boarded this train of thought. "I quit my job when you were six months old and became my own boss instead. You were chubby and adorable, and I missed you too much to sit in an office all day— especially when I thought I could do the same work at home." She ruffled his hair. "I was terrified, but Daddy was sure it would work out fine. And he was right. It was the scariest leap I've ever made, but it was worth it."

"You did that for us," Jack said, giving her a squeeze, "even though it wasn't easy." He smiled into her eyes. "That's how you can know we won't ever let Sebastian be alone. We know what it means to take care of our family."

He rose up onto his toes to give her a kiss on the cheek and then headed downstairs, leaving her standing dumbstruck, gripping a handful of socks and Kleenex.

Us against the world, she thought happily, *and I'm betting my money on us.*

TUESDAY, 7:25 A.M.

"I'm heading out!" she called to the living room at-large.

She knew all four kids were crowded onto the loveseat, but she could barely make out their faces among the sea of stuffed animals. She'd been amazed—and slightly alarmed—to realize the quantity of aquatic-related fuzzy creatures they owned, seeing them amassed in their full glory.

Still, look how happy the kids are, she thought, *hugging the dolphins and narwhals, manta rays, seals, sharks, sea stars, fish, whales, and seagulls.* She shook her head and sighed. It truly was a ridiculous number of fluffy sea-themed companions.

The movie was starting, but all four voices chimed out cheerful good-byes.

"I've got my watch phone on, Momma," Marian said in an important voice that reflected the full weight of her perceived responsibility.

"Me too," Jack said, smirking at his sister's over-the-top earnestness.

"I should be back before the movie's over," Mom assured them. "Then we'll cast our secret ballots at the voting booth and hit the bowling lanes."

She ducked into her new green winter coat and headed for the van.

There's nothing like wearing something new to boost your spirits. She laughed out loud. *Who knew I'd end up being* <u>excited</u> *that the dogs tore my old coat to shreds looking for Sebastian's half-eaten granola bar?*

She started the van and plugged her phone into the dash radio.

I can listen to whatever I want!

At the first red light, she scrolled through her playlists to find the one littered with songs she'd never play around the kids. It was titled "Clean the House." *If I'd named it "Not for Kids," they'd have clicked on it first chance they got*, she thought smugly. Singing along with the scandalous songs of her teenage days, she glanced at herself in the rearview mirror and reveled in her own brilliance. *THIS mom can still outthink her children.*

She cracked open her energy drink and laughed again. *This is my life now: Driving alone in the van, listening to racy nineties music and drinking a caffeinated beverage is as good as it gets. Who'd have guessed THIS is what I was so eager to grow up and experience!*

Traffic was sparse, and she pulled into the hidden parking lot behind Sebastian's school five minutes early. She chugged some water, bit into two pieces of minty gum, and slathered on some lip balm.

I should have brought a snack! she mused, glancing again at the conference invite with the thick black circle designating three full time slots for her.

I have no idea what I'm heading into, she thought as icy adrenaline flooded her stomach and spread to her limbs. *But really, does it matter?* "Be Courageous," right?

With that, she burst out of the van and hiked across the lot to the security entrance, where she buzzed to capture the attention of the staff upstairs. The intercom cackled.

"I'm here for Sebastian's conference," she enunciated clearly.

The door clicked open, and she crossed the still-dark entryway to the stairwell, realizing the Jewish Education Center portion of the building must be closed for Election Day. As nerves threatened to overtake her, she focused on putting one foot solidly ahead of the other while blasting eighties power ballads through her mind.

She was upstairs now, facing the long hallway. Sebastian's classroom was the last one down (of course!), so she kept her feet moving, refusing to allow herself to slow.

The faster we start, the sooner I'll know what's going on and the quicker I can get home to the kiddos.

When she was halfway down the path, the school's director stepped out of her office and headed in the same direction, just six steps behind her.

I could turn and say hi—it's probably rude not to—but I don't have the energy to spare, and I really want to get to the meeting. She smiled to herself. *I'm long past worrying what other people think anyway.*

She kept her course and her speed, and arrived at the classroom ten seconds later.

She was early, but Sebastian's teacher, speech therapist, and occupational therapist were already assembled around the half-moon table adjusted to preschool-student height. She was thrilled to see that the preschool chairs were unoccupied and that larger, adult-sized seats had been dragged in. That's when she realized that not one, but three large chairs sat empty and waiting.

Who else is coming? she fretted.

Smiling and bidding all a good morning, she chose the empty seat in the middle and turned to hang her coat over it just in time to see the director enter the room carrying a thick folder and clipboard.

Mom's heart rate quickened. *This is my third conference here for Bas, and the director has never joined us. Why is she here now?*

"We're just waiting for Sebastian's physical therapist," someone added.

To Mom's shock, she heard her own voice quip, "I realized too late I should have brought us donuts and coffee. We'll need them if we really have a full hour's worth of items to discuss!" Quickly plastering a fresh smile on her face, she was relieved to hear everyone chuckle.

"We just wanted to make sure everyone gets a full opportunity to discuss Sebastian's progress," replied the director. "With so many of us coming, we figured the extra time would be nice."

The physical therapist walked in just then, and the official meeting began.

"I'll go first," offered the occupational therapist. "Sebastian is strengthening his fine motor skills, but as you know, his muscle tremors make it difficult to accomplish small, focused tasks like writing or coloring. He's an absolute joy to work with, and he's always willing to try whatever I ask of him—but he's also super silly, so sometimes it's difficult to tell if he's just pretending not to be able to do something."

"That's true for me, too," interjected the speech therapist. "He likes the buzzing raspberry sound the vocabulary game makes when he chooses incorrect matches, so he gets them wrong on purpose and then laughs and laughs."

Mom smiled slightly, wondering if they were hoping she'd somehow be able to curb his mischievous enthusiasm.

Sebastian's sense of humor shows he's really IN there, she argued back mentally. *Jokes and silliness require intelligence, and I'm just so elated when his personality shines through. Maybe we don't reel him in as often as we should, but I'm not sure I can punish him for having fun. By every measurement tool but the calendar, he's barely even two years old.*

"I've had *some* success explaining to him that he needs to 'do it right' the first few times," the OT interrupted her thoughts, "and then I offer him a few minutes of free play at the end, when he can mix up the answers and pretend to get them wrong. He's a little boy who loves to play...that's how little boys *should* be."

"Plus, he's hands-down adorable," the speech therapist added with an affectionate grin.

Mom felt her static smile brighten. *Sebastian's a handful, but at least they still like him!*

"How are his skills for writing and coloring coming along?" Mom asked. "Especially considering the school district is going to push for him to be in kindergarten next year. Is it looking like he might be able to have success in the integrated classroom with some typical peers, or is he on the self-contained special education classroom trajectory?"

The OT looked uneasy. "Bas is making amazing progress. When I think of how far he's come in a year, it's really mind-blowing."

"I know it," Mom agreed. "He's a superstar for sure. But as far as kindergarten planning goes..."

The OT hesitated. "He's trying so hard. But trying isn't going to make those muscle shakes go away. And they have a ripple effect: With his muscles so weak, his grip is immature. *That* leads to his lines being extremely wobbly. He's not even to the point of drawing something basic, like a square or even a circle." She tried for positivity. "Sometimes he can identify those shapes, though." She bit her lip. "But sometimes he's just too silly for me to tell if he really knows them or not."

Mom donned a brave smile, freezing time around her breaking heart.

These are things you already know, she lectured herself. *If it's not a surprise, you're not allowed to start crying about it. There's no room for sadness in this conference. Move along.*

Aloud, she said, "Bas *loves* going to OT. He comes home and talks about using glue, and squeezing the pig that pops out a ball. And he genuinely looks forward to spending time with *you* every day."

The occupational therapist smiled. "He's such a sweet soul. And I've got to tell you: Last week, as we were making our way down the hallway here, practicing our ducking and crawling through the rainbow pop-up tunnel, he was lagging behind, so I turned to see what was going on.

Sebastian looked up at me and said, 'I just love your cutie little buns!'"

The whole room burst into giggles.

"Oh dear," said Mom, her cheeks heating up.

"It was the best compliment I got that whole week!" the OT sang. "I even posted about it on Facebook—not using anyone's name, of course!" she added quickly.

Mom snapped her gum unconsciously, smiling at the group. "I'm going to focus on being thrilled that he made a seven-word sentence!" she said, chuckling as she felt the blush slowly leave her face.

"He really has come so far," the speech therapist agreed. "Last year at this time, he really didn't say much of anything except 'baap-baap.' Now he can tell us all about what he does when he's not at school. And your family does so much! I think I want you to adopt *me*! Sebastian's been more places than I have, and he's four."

Mom smiled. "He seems to comprehend things best when he participates in them directly," she explained. "So we try to give him as many experiences as possible."

"He retains what he learns, too," the classroom teacher said. "All those trips to the zoo and the aquarium and the farm and the drive-thru safari have paid off. Sebastian knows so much about animals. The other day, he pulled one of the books off our shelf and started telling us all about manatees and flamingoes and harbor seals. He knew *everything* about them! What they eat, where they live, everything!"

Mom grinned, picturing Sebastian at home right now, relaxing amongst the heap of stuffed sea creatures. "Animals are Sebastian's favorite topic of conversation," she agreed. "We do our best to answer his questions. Although it's not always easy to recall what sea lions eat and where armadillos prefer to live," she admitted. "Especially at four o'clock in the morning."

"He's still not sleeping through the night?" the director asked in alarm.

"No." Mom sighed. "Bas doesn't have an easy relationship with sleep."

"He won't nap in the classroom either," his teacher added.

"I wonder if exhaustion is a contributing factor to his recent stutter pattern," the speech therapist interrupted. "Have you noticed it at home?"

Mom nodded. "It takes over when he's either tired or excited. It's frustrating for him, but we're all very patient."

"That's the best thing you can do," the speech therapist confirmed. "Just be patient. Maybe as his stamina grows, it'll sort itself out. Stuttering can be common during a vocabulary explosion, too, and there's no question he's adding words every day."

Mom smiled. *So far so good.* But she felt like a shoe was waiting to drop. She wished they'd hurry up and explain why this meeting was so long and well-attended.

Just brush it off and go with the flow.

"Last weekend Sebastian was trying so hard to tell me something," Mom said, "but he couldn't get it out. We all waited, but finally he just stopped and said, 'M-M-M-Momma, m-m-m-m-my words stuck.'"

Everyone chuckled.

"It *was* funny," Mom said, "and he meant for it to be. He laughed along with the other kids and added a 'W-W-W-W-Wocka-Wocka' for good measure." She paused. "But it was terrible, too. We don't want him to stop being able to communicate. That's been the biggest difference-maker: his words. So many AUTS2 kids *never* find a way to vocalize what they're thinking. His stuttering makes us terrified that he'll regress."

The speech therapist shook her head. "He's not moving backwards; that's for sure. His sentence length is growing, as is his word variety. He still relies on stock phrases, but new sentences are popping out all the time."

"I love his stock phrases!" the physical therapist interjected. "I hope they stick around. Sebastian has some of the sweetest stock phrases I've ever heard. He's always telling me 'You smell so good!' and 'You my best, best friend.' Bas is truly just the sweetest little guy. Just hearing his tiny voice say 'Hey! What's the big idea?' melts my heart." She smiled warmly. "He's making progress in *my* room, too. He can pedal a tricycle now, and as long as I play his favorite music, he's very willing to practice whatever skill I request. His jumps are getting longer, but he still doesn't bend his knees when he lands, so I'm not pushing that too much. I don't want him to get hurt. As I'm sure you've noticed, he's getting better at running, too. He can move his legs faster now, so we're just working on lengthening his stride and moving his arms in a more natural position."

"His daddy will be glad to hear that!" said Mom. "He says Sebastian runs like Steven Segal."

As the room burst out laughing again, the classroom teacher spoke up: "Does Sebastian call his dad 'Big Tuna'?" she asked. "Because he's always talking about someone named 'Big Tuna' and then calling himself 'Little Tuna.' It's so funny!"

Mom smiled broadly. "Yup. Sebastian invented 'Big Tuna' during our beach vacation last summer, and it seems to have stuck."

"That's the funniest thing!" the director said.

"The worst part," Mom said, "is that I posted about it on Facebook, and now all of Matt's work friends call him Big Tuna, too."

"Oh no!" the group chorused.

"Thank goodness my husband's a trooper," Mom said. "He claims everyone should get a new nickname the year they turn forty and that he's lucky to have had his bestowed by his son."

At the teachers' *"Awwwww"*-ing, she rolled her eyes and added, "Matt knows his friends would've figured out a way to incorporate 'fart' into his nickname, so he feels like he dodged a bullet with Big Tuna."

After more ensuing laughter, the director turned serious.

"We've heard some details about Sebastian's progress," she said, "so now we'd like to talk to you about Sebastian's classroom placement."

Ice filled Mom's stomach again. She gazed steadily at the woman, waiting for her to get on with it.

"Sebastian has come so far and gained so many skills," the

director said, "that we no longer feel his current class is a good fit for him."

Mom tilted her head. "I don't understand."

"Sebastian is a superstar in this room," the teacher spoke up. "His classmates don't really speak. Bas has grown so much in the past year, we can't move fast enough with the curriculum to keep him engaged and learning at the rate he could. It's like he's treading water instead of swimming toward the goal."

Mom knew this sounded positive, but she still heard panic leak into her voice: "What's he supposed to do then?"

Someone needs to write a handbook for parents on special needs journeys, she thought. *Regular parenting is hard enough, but what on earth do we do now? Sebastian's not ready for a classroom with typical four-year-olds.*

"This is still the right school for him," the director clarified, placing a comforting hand on Mom's shoulder. "He would simply do better in a classroom that moves a bit faster and provides more challenge for him."

Mom let out a huge mental exhale. *He's not getting kicked out of the school! There's still a place for him here.*

"So," she replied, taking a calming breath. "What classroom do you have in mind?"

"We all think,"—the director indicated the other staff members, who nodded—"that Sebastian is ready to be promoted to the classroom next door. Instead of six kids and three teachers, that room has space for twelve kids and three teachers. It would provide more opportunity for the type of social interaction Sebastian is capable of, and the class delves more deeply into academic content related to the national and state standards."

A classroom with higher expectations sounds great. And everyone here is smiling like it's great. So why are their eyes so worried?

"It's the right move to help him on his journey toward being kindergarten-ready," the occupational therapist encouraged softly. "In *this* room, Sebastian is the role model for all the other kids. In his new classroom, other children can model academic and social behaviors for *him* to aspire to. Sebastian will make huge leaps."

Fast. Fast. This is moving so fast. I wish Matt had taken the day off after all, rued Mom. *This is a big decision and it seems like they're looking for an answer right away.*

"Will he get to keep all of the same therapists?" she asked.

"Absolutely," assured the director. "Maintaining some stability in his schedule will help smooth his transition—although honestly, Sebastian doesn't ever have problems making friends." She smiled. "He loves everyone."

The number of kids in Sebastian's classroom would double. Is that a good idea? Mom started second-guessing. *He doesn't choke or fall as often as he used to, and his language has exploded. But should we really move him out of the room that has supported all that progress?*

"The team in the room next door is incredible." The speech therapist seemed to read her mind. "They've been teaching together for years, and you're going to love them. The kids have so much fun, they don't even realize they're learning. It's a wonderful place for them to grow."

The physical therapist also jumped in. "This is a *good* thing," she reassured. "We rarely get to have a meeting like this. Kids don't often show they're ready to transfer to a *less*-restrictive environment. It's a big deal. We're all very proud of Sebastian."

Mom closed her eyes. She needed to think. *This is our team. These people know Bas, and they love him. They work with him every day, and they want him to succeed. Maybe their eyes are worried because I look like a deer caught in the headlights. Everything they're saying sounds like they have Sebastian's best interests at heart.*

She opened her eyes.

"When would the switch take place?" she asked hesitantly.

"He's ready now, but the paperwork takes time—we usually have to assume sixty days. That means, if you give approval today, you could count on a transfer by the second semester of the school year, right around mid-January," the director said confidently.

What? After half the year is over? What's the point?

"But since you think he's ready now and that room has space, sixty days of his treading water seems like forever," Mom said, solidifying her decision. "How can we make it go faster?"

If this new classroom is where he needs to be, then we need to get him in there NOW.

"We can get all the paperwork ready here in just a few days, but your home school district needs to approve it. They will require you to schedule a formal Individualized Education Plan meeting with your director of special education and all the regular representatives. There's a lot of red tape involved, unfortunately." The director sighed.

Sebastian doesn't have sixty days to waste. If this is what you're committing to, then make it happen. Time to earn your sweatshirt: Be courageous.

"Hmmm. Do you mind if I make a phone call?" Mom asked, pulling out her cell phone and scrolling through her contacts. Not waiting for an answer, she selected her home district's director of special education and hit *Send*. "It'll only take a quick minute."

Though she hadn't really given them a choice, they all nodded as they watched her in silence.

A few seconds later, the magic of caller ID gifted her with a personalized greeting: "Hey there! How are you? How's Sebastian?"

"Hi, Amy!" she replied, grinning. "You're a mind-reader, because that's what I'm calling about. I'm sitting here in Sebastian's school conference, and we have unbelievable news. His entire team is on board with promoting him from his 6-1-2 class to a less-restrictive 12-1-2 class. He's ready now and they've got space for him, but we need the district paperwork that serves as his golden ticket."

"Yahoo!" shouted the voice on the other end of the phone. "I've been watching your family on Facebook, and I was wondering if something like this would happen soon. Kudos to you, Momma! Congratulations to Sebastian! This almost *never* happens—it's wonderful!"

"Thanks," Mom said, laughing. "That's what they've been telling me. Anyway, if we can get the paperwork done on this end by Friday, how soon can we get him started on the exciting next level of his journey?"

"Right away!" Amy enthused. "I'll do the forms right now and drop them off at your house tonight. We don't need a formal meeting if everyone is in agreement. If his school indeed gets their piece done this week, there's no reason he couldn't start in his new room Monday morning. No sense in holding him back if he's ready to move on!"

Mom was smiling so large, she could barely respond. "Awesome. You're awesome. Thank you so much! I'll see you tonight then!"

Hanging up, she confirmed to the astonished group everything they had already surmised.

"That's just incredible," the director said in astonishment. "It never happens this fast! Do you want to meet his new teachers? I think they're next door right now, waiting for their conferences to start for the day."

"Sure!" Mom agreed.

"We were so worried about how you'd react," the classroom teacher confessed. "Parents *never* want their child moved to a less-restrictive environment. The fight to *get* services is so tough to begin with, that no one wants to relinquish a single inch of what they've won. That's why I put you on the schedule first, so I could get the nervous part of the day over with."

Bingo. Worried eyes explained.

"I admit it's a terrifying decision," Mom said. "The stakes are so high! You're Sebastian's team, though." She smiled. "You *are* the expert opinion I'd go in search of. You work with him every day, and you see what he's capable of. Since you all feel like he'll learn more, faster, in a different classroom, we're going to trust you." She nodded, still convincing herself. "This is such a critical time for him. We don't know much about AUTS2, but it does seem like these kids level off their learning trajectory before reaching middle school. So we need to get him as far as possible before then."

"This is *absolutely* the right move for Bas," the physical therapist assured her. "I spend a lot of time working with the kids in his new room. It's going to be a great fit for him."

"And if his academic growth will indeed slow down later, then you're exactly right," the director chimed in. "His learning progress in his preschool years is critical."

"We expect great things from Sebastian," the OT said.

"The world needs more personalities like his," his speech therapist added.

"He's going to be amazing!" the teacher gushed.

Mom blew out her breath and smiled, finally relaxing. "Matt and I are so glad we chose this school. Thank you all for working so hard to help our little guy be the best that he can be."

The director smiled back at her. "We all *love* Sebastian," she said, as everyone else continued nodding. "He's a doll."

TUESDAY, 9:15 A.M.

Mom was still walking across the parking lot when Matt answered his phone.

"Sebastian's being promoted!"

"What?!" he asked. "What do you mean?"

"They recommended moving him to a classroom for kids who need a bit less supervision and can learn a bit faster!"

"What?!? When? Really?"

"Really! They said it almost never happens but it's the right move for Bas. It'll push him to be closer to being ready for kindergarten." She hesitated. "So, I gave permission—I hope that's okay!"

"What? Of course!" he said. "That's amazing! When does he start?"

"Ha!" she said happily. "It normally takes sixty days, but I called our special ed director right from the conference, and she's so ecstatic, she's bringing us the paperwork *tonight*."

"Tonight???" Mom could hear Matt smiling through the phone. "*That's* why we live in small-town Western New York!"

"Right? I'm still reeling. Sebastian can start in his new room this Monday."

"And to think—we were so nervous!" said Matt. "I'd never

have guessed in a million years that they'd book a triple timeslot to talk about *good* stuff!"

"I know!" Mom said. "I loved the inspirational flowers you left me, by the way. I was going to call you, but I needed to psych myself up for the conference. And all for nothing! You'd think folks who work with special needs families would have a better understanding of how little room we have for unnecessary worry."

"Right?" Matt agreed. "I mean, as much as I love roller coasters, we've been riding the Emotion Express for about four years now. It'd be cool to cruise on a straight stretch once in a while."

Mom laughed.

"I wished you'd been there with me, though," she added soberly. "It was a big decision, and they were worried I'd refuse. But his entire team is in support of this, so if he's ready for a challenge, I don't want to hold him back."

"You see?" Matt soothed. "Sebastian is going to surprise us. You wait. He's going to do some amazing things. I wish I'd been there, too, but the result would have been the same. It was the right decision." He sighed heavily. "Dispatch is radioing; I've got to go. Fingers crossed I get out on time tonight! I love you."

After he hung up, she filled the remaining ten minutes of her drive home with excited shrieks and random exclamations.

"He did it!"

"We made the right decision!"

"Everyone loves him!"

"Sebastian is being promoted!"

"He did it!"

She pulled into the driveway and parked the van under the towering maple trees. Then she sprinted towards the gate. Alice and Thomas Jefferson ran out to meet her, and she reveled in a joyous reunion with her faithful dogs before continuing into the house.

The kids' movie had reached its satisfying ending, with colorful fish swimming happily in all directions across their enormous television screen.

"Momma! You came back! I missed you so much!" Sebastian dragged himself out from under a large stuffed manta ray and a three-foot-long yellow pike fish pillow. "We go bowling now?"

Mom lifted Bas into the air and spun him around. "Sebastian! Your teachers said you're doing such a good job at school that you get to move to a different classroom next week! You're graduating!" She spun him in a circle again but got only halfway around before she found herself at the center of a kid huddle.

"Congratulations, Bassie!" Vince shouted.

"That's so wonderful, Bassie-Boo!" Marian cried. "Con-*grad*-ulations!"

"You're so smart, Bassie!" Jack added. "We're so proud of you!"

Sebastian had no idea what all the commotion was about, but he knew he was at the epicenter and his little face shone. "We the best family EVER!" he added to the shouting.

Mom clicked off the movie and channeled "Love Shack" through her phone to the blue TARDIS speaker on the shelf, launching an impromptu dance party celebration. Sebastian ran around in lopsided circles amid the melee before ducking into the cocoon of his blue therapy swing, which hung from the center beam of the room. With expert skill gained from thousands of hours of practice, he quickly became a blue and yellow blur, spinning around so fast that only his hair color and the swing itself could be discerned. Jack and Vince leapt around with raucous fervor while Marian turned cartwheels into the dining room.

As the song blasted into the second verse, Mom froze to soak in the manifold joy of a day off from school, her precious children, and this most incredible news.

This is now, she thought happily. *This is now, and now is a moment worth remembering.*

The Big Three fizzled out before the song was over, but Sebastian continued twirling away at record speeds as the music came to an end. Red-faced and panting, the others lay collapsed in various poses of exhaustion among the heaps of aquatic stuffed animals littering the couch and living room floor.

Mom gave them a moment to bask before getting down to business. "Catch your breaths, and then please start hauling our fluffy friends upstairs," she said. "I think it's just wonderful that you collected them all for Sebastian to watch the movie with, but if we leave them strewn about, Alice and Thomas Jefferson will think they're having Dog Christmas. We'll come home to knee-deep stuffing and plush animal carcasses."

The kids sighed and started gathering armloads of fuzzy buddies.

"I'm going to flip a load of laundry and take out the kitchen garbage, and then we can head out to our voting-slash-bowling adventure!" Mom effused.

"Doesn't Bas have to help us?" Vince asked plaintively.

"Let's let Sebastian keep swinging," Mom decided. "The spinning helps him have a better day, and we want him to have fun at bowling, don't we?"

Vince heaved a sigh. "Fine. But Jack and Marian have to make as many trips upstairs as I do. Because Marian will pretend to have to go to the bathroom, and Jack will hide in his bed with a book as soon as he gets a chance to slip away."

As Marian and Jack began to protest, Mom silenced them with a look.

"Vince speaks truth," she said. "No one is allowed to shirk their duties right now. You can travel in a group of three, please. And remember: The sooner we get our chores *done,* the sooner we'll get to the *fun!*"

The trio began their first grumbling trip upstairs, bickering loudly about who was carrying the most and who'd unfairly taken a lighter load.

"And don't just chuck them on the floor, please," Mom called after them, "or Dog Christmas will simply take place on the second floor! They need to go in the hammock on the loft room wall."

"I swing, Momma?" Sebastian asked, slowing his speed and

then shifting to whirl in the opposite direction.

"Yup! You can stay right here and swing, Sebastian. In a few minutes, I'll help you get on your doggie feet, your trainers, and your coat so we can head out into the cold on an adventure. But for right now, swing away, my little man."

TUESDAY, 9:55 A.M.

Mom hurried towards the kitchen. She opened the garbage cupboard and was blasted by the stench of used diapers. *And THAT is why I'm taking out a bag that's only seventy-five percent full. It smells like a neglected zoo in here!* Gagging slightly, she dragged the bag down the back steps and heaved it into the black garbage bin outside the back door. Complimenting herself on a job well done, she headed back inside to tackle the laundry.

She'd dumped another layer on Mount Laundrious and was back to the task of shifting wet clothes into the dryer, when she realized that the only other living souls in the living room were Thomas Jefferson and Bully Fish. The blue therapy swing hung limply from the ceiling beam, and it wasn't swaying even slightly.

"Sebastian?" she called. "Where are you, Bassie?"

She could hear the Big Three arguing upstairs over whose job it was to pick up the stuffed animals that had fallen, but she hadn't heard a peep from her youngest. She peeked her head into her office, hoping to find him hiding in the corner, but the room was empty. She took the stairs two at a time, trying to outrun whatever mischief Sebastian was certainly chasing.

Please let him be in the middle of their argument! she pleaded—hoping against hope that the "fallen animals" the Big Three were fighting over were being flung from the hammock by their youngest brother. But she saw only three heads.

"Was Sebastian in here with you?" she asked more loudly than intended.

The argument stopped mid-sentence. Marian slid down the reading-loft stairs while Jack simply vaulted over the side, neatly avoiding a collision with Vince as he crawled out from the play space underneath.

"He hasn't come in here at all," Jack said.

"I *think* he was still in his swing on our last trip down," Vince murmured.

"Yeah, but that was a while ago, because you boys won't pick up the toys from off the floor," Marian complained.

Mom turned on her heel and headed down the hallway, sparing a quick glance toward her bedroom before heading to the more likely targets. Jack and Marian ran past and called out from the bunk room, reporting that Sebastian hadn't climbed up their ladders. Vince shouted from the closet, declaring it empty. Ignoring the small room crowded with chapter books and clothes, Mom stepped into the bathroom.

"*Oh, Sebastian…*" She sagged. "What are you doing?"

Bas was standing at the wall, wildly unspooling a nearly full roll of toilet paper. His feet were hidden under a pile of tissue that must have recently been two jumbo-sized rolls, but she was certain he was up on his toes in excitement. She stepped closer and saw that another roll was soaking up the water of the toilet bowl, its long paper trail snaking out over the seat and onto the floor where it joined its fallen comrades.

Sebastian is the only person in this house besides me who replaces the toilet paper roll, and THIS is what he does with his talent!

"Sebastian! Stop!" She reached out and grabbed his hand as it prepared to give the toilet paper on the holder another wild spin. "This is *not* the right thing to be doing! Now what will we use when we go to the bathroom? You wasted all our toilet paper!"

He looked at her with surprise. "We roll it back up, Momma."

He bent down and plunged his hand into the pile, fishing around until he pulled up his arm in triumph. "Here, Momma!" he shouted, proudly handing her a brown cardboard tube. "I find it for you!"

She sighed. *This is the moment I promised I'd do something about.* Her internal voice recited a pledge to the universe: *Sebastian will never be wandering around lost in the cold, chasing after a dog between a raging creek and a dangerous road.*

"We *cannot* roll the paper back onto the tube," she said sternly. "I love you, Sebastian, but this was the wrong thing to do." She bent down and picked him up, holding him like a football under one arm. "You were supposed to be in your swing," she continued, "and if you were going somewhere else, you should have told me."

She headed down the stairs now, past the Big Three, who peeked out of the bunk room, eyes wide and mouths agape.

"You could have helped Jack and Marian and Vince clean up the big mess," she went on, "but instead, you made another big mess. You *know* we're not allowed to unroll toilet paper—it's wasteful. But you still did it. It looks like you unrolled *three* full rolls. And you put one in the toilet, too! That's not how it works, Sebastian."

They were in the kitchen now, and she pulled the tray off his highchair, plunked him into it, and snapped the tray back on. "You made a big mess *and* did something you know you're not supposed to do, so now you have to sit in time-out."

Sebastian's face, so expressive in its pure emotions, was the picture of devastation.

"What time-out, Momma? You hold me, Momma?"

"Time-out means you sit here for two minutes all by yourself, and you don't talk, you don't play, and you don't sing. You just sit here and remember that you're not allowed to play with toilet paper."

She turned to the microwave and busied herself pressing buttons so she wouldn't have to see the pitiful expression on his face.

"You sit there until the timer on the microwave goes 'ding,'" she told him. "Then your time-out will be over." She turned to face him. "And remember: We don't play in the toilet, and we don't play with toilet paper."

With that, she walked through the kitchen and into the laundry room, leaving Sebastian entirely alone in his punishment. She'd intended to transfer the wet clothes from the washer to the dryer, but she found herself frozen—fighting her resolve as she listened for the sobs he'd been choking back. She tried to peer through the crack between the door and the frame, but the angle was wrong because she'd dragged his highchair near the microwave so Bas could have a front-row view of the timer as it counted down.

After an eternity of twenty seconds, the silence was broken.

"DIIIIING!" came Sebastian's small, hopeful voice from the kitchen.

Mom started and choked back a laugh.

"You hear that, Momma?" Sebastian asked in a tone dripping with innocence and wonder. "What that sound is, you think?"

Mom bit her cheek and counted slowly to five, knowing that if she spoke he'd detect laughter in a heartbeat.

A kid has to be pretty smart to think up a plan like that and carry it out so quickly. Listen to Sebastian being brilliant!

She wanted to run out of the laundry room and hug him, but she'd promised to stick to their time-out resolution, and it was becoming abundantly clear that Matt was right: Sebastian *was* ready to understand time-out.

Making an angry face in the mirror for inspiration, she tried for a stern voice. "I think that was the sound of *you*, pretending to be the microwave. Time-out is *not* over. Sit there quietly."

Her proclamation was met with silence, and she shoved her arm across her face to stifle the rupturing laughter. The now-empty dryer awaited the next load of wet clothes, so her only dry sound-absorbing options were the dirty clothes at her feet.

Who'd have guessed I'd be wishing for a dryer full of clean, dry laundry right now?

A strange noise came from beyond the closed door leading

to the dining room. She cautiously cracked it open and peered out. Jack, Marian, and Vince were in the back corner, shaking in silence as the laughter they knew better than to release escaped in the form of tears down their cheeks. Fearing she'd spoil their efforts if they saw her fighting the same battle, Mom quietly shut the door and headed back toward the kitchen end of the long, narrow laundry room.

The timer *had* to be nearing extinction. This had been the longest two minutes of her day. She held her breath and counted backwards from twenty. Before she got to five, she heard a legitimate *Ding!* from the microwave.

Stepping back into the kitchen, she smiled broadly at Sebastian. "Your time-out is over, Bas. I'll get you out of your chair now."

"You get me out?" he confirmed hopefully. Then, staring in concentration at nothing in particular, he said quietly, "I no touch toilet paper?"

"That's right, Sebastian. That's exactly right." She grinned.

"Here, Momma." Marian had partially composed herself and was holding out Sebastian's doggie braces and trainers. "Thought we could put these on first, so he'll be ready to go. White high-tops for bowling, right?"

Mom hugged Marian quickly and then leaned over the highchair tray to kiss Sebastian's forehead.

"What do you think, Bassie? Can we put on your feet so we're ready for bowling?"

"You love me?" Sebastian asked hesitantly.

"I do!" Mom said, her heart breaking all over again. "I love you very much, Sebastian. Always. Even when you're sitting in time-out learning that we don't play with toilet paper."

She'd started on his second brace when Vince bounded into the kitchen, pushing his arms into his jacket. "All the stuffed animals are away," he said happily.

"Where my Fluffy Red?" Sebastian cried suddenly. "I need my Fluffy Red."

Jack was zipping his parka and cramming his swim team pom-pom beanie haphazardly over his spiked hair, the Survival Bag slung over his shoulder. "I was heading out to warm up the van. Do you want me to find Red instead?"

"That's okay, Jack," Vince called over his shoulder, already on a mission. "I'll find him. I'm pretty sure I saw him upstairs earlier."

"Vince find my Red the Dog?" Sebastian asked. "He looking?"

"That's right, Bassie. Your amazing big brother is going to find Fluffy Red." Mom turned to Marian. "Sissy, will you grab Sebastian's coat when you get yours down?"

"Already got it, Momma. Here's yours, too. Let's go vote!"

"We'll meet you at the van in a minute," Mom said, taking the proffered coat. "We've got to wait for Vince."

"Ruff! Ruff! Ruff!" Vince called. "Here comes Fluffy Red—and Fluffy Vincey, too!"

Sebastian stiffened, and Mom hurried to zip his coat while his arms flapped in anticipation.

"Fluffy Red! Oh, my Fluffy Red! Thank you, Vince! Thank you so much! You my best, best friend!"

Mom ruffled Vince's hair and gave him a kiss on the head; then she bustled him out the door.

Finally, clasping Sebastian tightly, she carried him out of the house, shut the back door, and locked the gate behind them. Then she stowed Sebastian in the van and climbed into the driver's seat.

TUESDAY, IO:I5 A.M.

"Everyone ready?" Mom called. But she knew they were. "We don't *have* to drive to the polling place," she explained aloud. "It's actually at the end of our block. But since it's just our first stop on today's adventure and it's rather colder than I'd like, let's take the van anyway."

"Where are we going?" Vince asked.

"Right there," she said, pointing to the three-story building looming through their windshield. "It used to be the junior high. Grandma and Grandpa went to school here, as did Mamita and Gramps." She thought for a moment. "So did Aunt Pat and Uncle Al, *and* Aunt Sue and Uncle Pete. Back then, our town had more people in it, so they needed a huge building to have room for all the students."

"What's it used for now?" Marian asked.

"They turned it into one-bedroom apartments."

"*That's* right!" Jack said. "I remember now. Old people live there, in the same place they used to learn math and social studies!"

"They live in their old school?" Marian asked in horrified fascination.

"Yup!" said Mom. "Isn't that crazy? Can you imagine growing up to find that your new bedroom used to be part of your English classroom? Anyway, the gymnasium was turned into a big common area, and that's where we'll vote. You'll probably recognize it; we came here for a Christmas party a few years ago."

They parked at the very back of the lot.

"You can tell that old folks live here," Marian said. "Almost all the parking spaces are for people with wheelchairs!"

Mom laughed. "That's very observant, Marian. Now." She shut off the van and turned to look at them. "We have some ground rules for our voting adventure. There will indeed be a lot of old people in there. Some will be voting like we are, and some will just be standing around because they live in this building and Election Day is something different for them to be part of. Rule Number One is that we aren't allowed to ask anyone how old they are."

The kids nodded in unison.

"Rule Number Two is that we aren't allowed to talk about how anyone in there looks different than us. There might be people with walkers, or service dogs, or wheelchairs. There may be ladies who don't have any hair, or folks wearing pajamas. As soon as we get back to the van, you can ask as many questions as you'd like. But not until then, okay?"

"That sounds good, Momma," Vince answered for the group. "We don't want to hurt anyone's feelings."

Mom smiled before continuing. "The last rule, Rule Number Three, is about voting," she said. "People like their vote to be kept a secret. So dividers will be set up, with people hiding inside them to fill out their ballot sheets. We are *not,* under any circumstances, allowed to peek. We aren't even allowed to *pretend* to peek. We are so fortunate to live in a country where we have the right to vote, so it's important that we don't make anyone feel uncomfortable in there, okay? *Everyone* belongs on Election Day." Mom smiled again. "I'm so glad you're here with me! You can't look at a stranger's ballot, but you *can* look at mine. I'll show you how we do it, and then you can all help me submit our vote into the robot counter."

"There's a robot in there?!" Jack asked in wonder.

"Yup!" said Mom. "It's a specialized computer, I suppose, but

I like to think of it as a robot."

"Let's call it Freedom Bot," Jack suggested.

"Freedom Bot!" Sebastian echoed.

"Off we go then!" Mom said as they climbed out of the car. She motioned for everyone to grab hands.

"We'd better be really careful," Jack warned. "It's busy in this parking lot today."

"Good advice, Jack!" Mom concurred. "Sebastian, honey, I'm going to pick you up, okay? I don't want you to get too tired before we go bowling." She scooped him onto her hip and reconnected with Vince's hand. "It's fun to think of all the history our family's had in this building," she said. They all looked up at the imposing structure. "Our relatives have lived in this wonderful little city for a long, long time."

They reached the entrance without incident and claimed their spot at the back of the line, just inside the doorway.

"Remember the rules," Mom said quietly, eyeing the impressive line of elderly voters ahead of them awaiting ballots.

The instant they stepped into the warm community room, Sebastian wiggled to get down. He'd spotted a potted plant decorated with pinwheels a few feet away from the noisy line, and as soon as his feet hit the ground, he made a beeline for it. Bas's "excited run" involved a series of rapid-fire tiny steps, slowed by his constant need to stop and flap his hands. He made swift progress anyway.

"Marian, would you mind going with him for a few minutes?" asked Mom. "This line will be slow, and I'll call you back before we get our ballot."

"Sure thing, Momma," Marian replied cheerfully. She skipped off to join her brother.

"Four kids?" came a gravelly voice from the kitchen area extending along the left side of the room. "Poor thing. You've got your hands full, for sure."

Mom looked up to see a small woman leaning against the counter, stirring a Styrofoam cup of coffee and wearing a look of distaste.

Yikes. Mom thought. *Do I look horribly stressed? Her expression is awful! Children are probably a rarity here, but the kids are clean, polite, and well-behaved, so what's the problem?*

Remembering Jack and Vince were watching, Mom plastered on a smile.

"They keep us busy, that's for sure," she said, realizing her attempt at cheerful was probably closer to an unsettling leer. "But my husband and I signed up for this chaos, and these are the times we'll always remember. We wouldn't have it any other way."

Mom turned away, glancing to making sure Marian and Sebastian were making good choices. Marian was patiently standing guard as her brother dealt with the overpowering rapture of spinning the colorful plastic lawn ornaments. Satisfied all was well, Mom quickly counted the people between her and the table; twenty minutes to go, she estimated.

"There's donuts," the same voice croaked again. Mom realized with chagrin that it was closer now. "The city attorney just dropped them off—looking for votes in his next election, I bet." The woman seemed convinced she'd just exposed a dangerous conspiracy. "The kids could have some," she said, bending her head toward the donuts. "*If* they don't have any of those new-fangled allergies."

Mom felt Vince's hopeful squeeze across her fingers and saw he was gaze longingly at the colorful donut box on the counter. She sighed.

This woman's probably lonely—she's certainly batty. I'm sure she means well. She has no way of knowing that they already had donuts for breakfast.

"That's very kind," Mom said aloud to the woman, now just a few feet away. "Thankfully, we are allergy-free. Jack and Vince, if you want to go get Marian and Sebastian, you may each have one donut."

"Could we just take some to them?" Vince asked. "Bassie isn't going to want to walk away, even for a treat. You know how he feels about pinwheels."

"Good idea," said Mom. "Pick ones they'll like, please. It should be our turn in about ten minutes."

The boys headed for the beckoning box of sugar, and she realized with dread that the woman was now directly beside her, eyes squinting and jaw working.

"Your kids all have blond hair," she declared abruptly.

"Yup," Mom said, forcing another smile as she flipped her own bright-yellow hair over her shoulder. "No idea where it came from."

"Ha!" the woman spat. "There aren't enough tow-heads anymore. Keep it up." Then she glanced around furtively—as if worried she was being followed—and leaned in even closer.

Is she really going to whisper a secret to me? This woman needs to go away.

Although Mom's patience for stranger-interaction was wearing thin, she tried to assume a half-interested look.

In response, the old woman raised one hand aloft, apparently shielding her mouth from insidious lip-readers and then, as though she'd never learned to whisper, shouted, "Too bad about your youngest, though. He's cute, but it's a shame. You'd think they'd get better at detecting defects like that before they're born."

This isn't happening. Not again. Please not again.

Mom stiffened and stared the woman down, feeling heads turn and ears perk up throughout the room. She knew they'd be searching for the shortest blond head, currently positioned above two very stiff arms, flapping away at the pinwheel plant.

The horrible woman wasn't finished.

"You don't have to look like that," she said. "I'm serious. He's cute. At least it's better today than it used to be. My sister—her son was one of the retards, too." She shook her head sadly.

Please make it stop. Please. We're here to vote. We're just trying to vote. Please.

"Terrible thing," the dreadful woman went on. "Back then, they'd just hide them away until they could ship 'em to an asylum."

I need this to stop. The kids aren't hearing this, are they?

Please, please stop.

"The world's nicer now. You can take them out with your family when you go places. Bet he gets to go to school too, huh?"

Shock and incredulity rendered Mom almost immobile as her brain desperately scrambled to design a reaction that wouldn't get her arrested. Her mind muddled by rage, she regurgitated her mantra: *Kindness. Courage. Understanding.*

"Sebastian goes to a wonderful school, yes," she heard her voice answer calmly.

"Our tax dollars hard at work," the woman replied, her raspy voice thick with sarcasm. She leaned in again, her hand lifting once more to shield her mouth. "As if you need school to be a cart-pusher in the grocery parking lot." Then she cackled horribly—like a nightmare with advanced emphysema.

No. No more.

Involuntarily, Mom took a step backwards, bumping into an elderly man waiting behind her.

"I'm so sorry," she said to him, feeling her heart pound in her ears.

She turned back to face the woman and cleared her throat. "Life is hard for Sebastian," she said, "but he's already far better at being a human being than you are. I didn't ask for your vile opinions, and I don't care to hear any more of them."

Ignoring the indignation that spread across the woman's face, she turned her back, rose up on her toes, and called urgently to her children.

"Jack! Marian! Vincey-honey! It's almost our turn!" she lied loudly.

I need them to come back.

As Jack arrived with Sebastian in his arms, she saw that Vince had pulled one of the pinwheels from the dirt and was holding it up for his baby brother to continue spinning.

"We didn't think anyone would mind if we borrowed it for a few minutes," Marian said, licking chocolate icing off her fingers.

"That was great thinking," Mom applauded, taking Sebastian

into her own arms to give Jack a rest.

"See, Momma? See?" Sebastian asked, flapping his arms up and down excitedly. "It spinning! It spinning so fast!"

Mom kissed her precious baby boy and smiled.

Let them look, she thought defiantly. *Sebastian is incredible. Let them think whatever they want.*

"Where's Freedom Bot?" Jack asked.

Mom pointed deeper into the room near the far exit. "There she is! Watch. See the man putting his ballot in? That's what Freedom Bot does. She reads each vote that gets filled in on a bubble sheet, and then she tallies them all up."

"Why's Freedom Bot a girl?" Vince asked, dejected.

"Because," Marian said impatiently. "Lady Liberty? Ever hear of her? We climbed right up to her feet in New York City, remember? And she was wearing a dress—because she's a girl."

Vince stuck out his bottom lip. "I wanted Freedom Bot to be a boy."

"Maybe when you grow up," Jack suggested, "you could design a newly updated Freedom Bot and dress it up in a necktie."

The twinkle in Jack's eye told Mom he was teasing his brother. Vince, however, obliviously began plotting out his future career with voting technology.

"It would have to be bowties, Jack," Vince propounded. "A regular tie would get sucked into the slot where Freedom Bot eats the ballots. But bowties are cool, right? And it'll be yellow."

"Yellow isn't patriotic," Marian argued.

"Maybe not," Vince said stubbornly, "but the bowties will be yellow. That's my favorite color, and when you're the robot designer, you get to pick stuff like that."

"Look!" Mom interrupted, ending the conversation. "It's our turn!"

They moved up to the check-in table and sought out the lady manning the sign-in book for people with last names near the end of the alphabet.

"Shepler," Mom told the woman. "On Hill Street."

The lady leafed through the oversized ledger until she found the correct page. After showing her driver's license for identification, Mom signed next to her name.

"Here's your ballot," the lady said. "I'll slide it into this privacy envelope for you." She handed it to Mom and then directed the group to one of the makeshift polling cubicles. "Oh!" she hollered as they started away. "You forgot your pencil!"

Vince ran back to retrieve it and then the fivesome squeezed into their assigned voting booth. Even with the hassle of pointing out the correct columns and passing the pencil back and forth so everyone had a turn, filling in the bubbles took less than two minutes. Then they all trooped towards Freedom Bot.

Watching the machine quickly eat their form, Marian asked in disappointment, "That's it?"

"That's it!" Mom said. "We did it! Our votes have been cast."

Marian tugged on Mom's arm and then cracked open her coat to reveal where she'd stowed Bas's Fluffy Red the Dog.

"I've been hiding him," she explained, "so we can divert Bas when we have to sneak the you-know-what away."

"Capital idea, Sissy!" Mom said. "Now is the time."

"Ruff! Ruff! Ruff!" Marian barked energetically.

"Bassie-Boo, did you hear something?" Vince asked sweetly.

Marian barked again and Jack jumped into the game. "Let's use our hands to dig around," he suggested to Bas, quickly relieving the borrowed pinwheel from his brother's fist. "I'm sure I heard a strange sound."

As Jack led Sebastian on a dig through his own coat and Marian continued to bark sporadically, Vince snuck away to return the pinwheel.

Sebastian finally reunited with his pal, never even noticing the deception.

"It's Fluffy Red! Red the Dog!" Bas cried. "I missed you so, so much!" He hugged the toy tightly. "You my best, best friend!"

TUESDAY, 10:45 A.M.

Lifting up Sebastian, Mom grabbed Vince's hand and led the way into the parking lot.

"I loved voting, Momma," Marian said happily. "Donuts *and* a robot."

"Plus, a bubble-test quiz we didn't have to study for," Jack chimed in.

"What could be better?" Mom asked, smiling thinly as she continued reeling from her confrontation with the beastly woman.

They were just steps from the van now, in the last row of the giant lot. The Big Three clambered in the passenger side as Mom slid open the driver's side rear door to strap Sebastian into his car seat. She suddenly heard the sound of feet pounding on the pavement, sprinting their way towards the van. She turned to see a stranger waving his arm.

"For the kids!" the elderly man called breathlessly. "Wait! These are for the kids!"

He was upon them now, and she could feel all four children watching curiously through the van windows. Dangling from his arm was a plastic grocery bag, heavy with whatever it contained.

"These kids have earned a treat," he said, panting from his exertions to catch up with them. "They're beautiful, inside and out."

He peered into the van over her shoulder. "That was a long line to wait in, without much to do, and they were perfect. The world needs more kids like that." He extended his arm, pushed the bag into her hands, and said softly, "The world needs more moms like you, too." He locked eyes with her and gave her an encouraging smile. Louder, he said, "I bought these for my grandkids who are coming over later, but they fight with each other all the time, so I'm giving them to you instead." He grinned at their astonished faces and turned on his heel. Then he called back over his shoulder: "I can't wait until I get to stuff my ballot into a robot wearing a yellow bowtie!"

The kids watched in stunned silence as he walked away before they started shouting, "Thank you! Thank you!"

When he'd passed out of sight, Marian suggested, "Let's see what's in the bag."

She pulled apart the plastic to reveal two packages of fresh chocolate-chip cookies from the bakery.

"Cookies!" Sebastian squealed. "My favorite! Cookies!"

"Can we have some?" Vince asked, in wide-eyed awe of his good fortune.

Mom smiled. "Yes." She pulled the packages out of the bag and handed them up to Jack in the front seat. "You're in charge of handing them out," she said solemnly. "Everyone gets four, because they're small and because, well, things like this don't happen very often."

"Wahoo!" shouted Marian. "I told you voting was the best!"

As Mom crumpled up the bag in her hand to stuff into her pocket, she realized it was lumpier than it should be. *I probably have the poor guy's receipt*, she thought, unfurling the bag to look inside.

It wasn't a receipt. There, creased in the bottom of the bag, was a twenty-dollar bill. She sucked in her breath as she reached in to pull it out. Scrawled across the front in hastily printed letters was the message: *Keep smiling, Mom.*

Mom felt tears well in her eyes.

"What is it?" Jack asked.

Wordlessly, she held it out for him to see.

"Awesome, Momma," he said genuinely. "It's like you're always telling us: Good people outnumber the bad."

"What do you mean 'the bad'?" Mom asked in alarm.

"That gross lady," Jack replied matter-of-factly. "With the voice."

"Oh, honey." Mom was stricken. "What did you hear?"

"I heard proof of what you're always telling us: Monsters are real." He swallowed hard. "But they don't have tentacles or slime. It's just like you said—monsters look like people. Her disguise was pretty good, but her words gave her away."

Marian leaned between the two front seats and kissed her mom on the cheek.

"*I* heard my Momma stand up to the monster," she said. "That's what I heard."

Vince joined in the conversation from the back of the van. "I don't know about not having slime, though, Jack. Did you hear her voice? I bet she was loaded with toxic ooze! It was just hiding on the inside."

At that, Mom burst into laughter. The Big Three joined in.

"Wocka-wocka!" Sebastian called from his car seat. And his laughter, blending with theirs, was the loudest of all.

TUESDAY, 11:00 A.M.

They pulled into the parking lot of the bowling alley, but Mom left the van running.

"We're going to wait in here for a few moments," she told the kids. "It's not our turn yet, and I don't want to stand around waiting inside the building."

"Can we have another cookie while we wait?" Vince's voice called hopefully from the back row.

"Why not?" She sighed. "We're already on track to capture the world record for eating the most sugary foods in a single morning, and the only thing on our lunch menu is greasy pizza. I don't think another cookie is going to sink the ship."

"We had oranges with breakfast, don't forget," Vince said, eagerly reaching forward for the cookie Jack was handing back.

"I'm sorry you kids had to overhear any of what that woman said today." Mom turned to look each of them in the eyes. "I wish it weren't so, but she's not alone." Mom bit her lip. "I hope it was the first time you've heard something like that, but I can promise you it won't be the last. Sometimes people are angry and afraid about things they don't understand."

"It's not *that* hard to understand, though," Vince said through a mouthful of cookie. "Our Bassie loves everyone. There's nothing scary about that."

"And he's always happy, and he's never mean," Marian argued. "Are you, Bassie-Boo?" she asked, petting her brother's head.

"I not mean. I Sebastian!" he shouted, throwing Fluffy Red into the air.

The toy missed his lap and landed on the floor of the van, where Marian snatched it up and handed it back lovingly.

"Ruff ruff ruff!" she said.

"She can be wrong all she wants," Jack said confidently. "She doesn't matter."

"That's correct," agreed Mom. "And we don't have to listen to her—or anybody else's—opinions. That's why I stopped her. And again, my sweet babies, I'm sorry you had to hear it."

"I'm not sorry," Marian said proudly. "My Momma is smart and scary. *And* she fights monsters."

"Could we listen to some music while we wait?" Vince asked. "Maybe some Christmas songs?"

"Yuck!" spat Mom. "Halloween was just a few days ago, Vince. It's not even Thanksgiving yet. What do you want to listen to Christmas songs for?"

"How else will Bassie learn them in time?" Vince asked, blatantly leveraging his best angle. "What if the Beef Buff Band has a holiday concert?"

"He's got a point," Marian said, giggling.

"Just a *few* Christmas songs?" Jack urged. "Just until we go in?"

"Ugh. You kids had better know how much I love you." Mom pulled up her holiday playlist on her phone. "Hearing Christmas music before Thanksgiving is going to make my ears bleed!"

As "Rudolph the Red-Nosed Reindeer" jingled through speakers, she cried out, "It hurts!" But the Beef Buff Band was already caroling along.

I should post to Facebook about Sebastian's step-up at school. Mom thought. *How often do we get such incredible news? I have some great pictures from the other day; I could use one of those.*

She scrolled through her phone and found the pose she was looking for: a rare photo with Sebastian looking directly into the camera. *People would be amazed if they realized how many shots we have to take to get one like this.* Image selected, she fought an internal battle. *I'm going to write about Sebastian's amazing progress, and his promotion. I will. It's the most wonderful news we've had in such a long time.* She felt her spirits rising. *He's working so hard, and even if his stutter is so bad by the end of the day that he can barely communicate, it's paying off. I want to share our celebration with our family and friends.* She blew out a slow breath. *I wish that woman hadn't spoken to me. I wish the kids hadn't heard her. I won't let her spoil our day, but it'd be so easy to write something entirely different.* She turned around in her seat to gaze at the kids, singing merrily along to "Deck the Halls." *The world doesn't need more anger. So we won't play a part in spreading it. Sebastian's here to bring joy.*

Resolved, she quickly wrote a message under Sebastian's joyous face and shared it with their family and friends. As the holiday playlist finished blowing through "Jingle Bells" and launched into "I Want a Hippopotamus for Christmas," she closed her eyes.

I cannot believe the kids bought my story about waiting here because it isn't our turn. Haven't they noticed ours is the only vehicle in the lot?

At that moment, a dark SUV pulled into the empty parking space beside them, and the kids nearly exploded in delight.

"That's Aunt Jess's car!"

"I can see Ari! And Rori, too!"

"Momma! Cam is getting out!"

Mom grinned broadly. "Surprise!"

The doors flung open and the Big Three flew out of the van to greet their best friends in the parking lot. Mom turned off the van, grabbed the Survival Bag and her second energy drink of the day, and joined them, unstrapping Sebastian and setting him down to join the animated hugfest between the vehicles.

She'd first met Jessica when Jack and Ari were in preschool together. The seven years since had flown by in a blur, but their friendship had been a welcome constant. The two families had grown steadily, with both moms cheerfully juggling the responsibilities of their many children and their successful businesses. In Jessica, she'd found a kindred spirit who had kids that loved to play with her own. And while she and Jessica relied on each other for practical demands like carpooling and summer adventures, she knew their mutual ability to jump into a conversation about whatever was worrying them the most—and finding a way to laugh about it—was something they both needed just as much.

And so, as the years shifted from pregnancies and babies to raising toddlers, kids, and pre-teens, they'd progressed from friends to family.

Jessica came into view from the other side of the SUV, lugging an infant carrier and beaming. "Greetings! We are so excited to have a bowling adventure with Team Shepler today!"

"Life is always better with friends," Mom agreed.

Together, they herded their combined eight kids across the freezing lot and into the warm bowling alley. Euphoric over being together unexpectedly, the children jumped and danced and waved their arms around with glee.

"Sorry we're late," said Jess. "Cole needed a last-minute outfit change."

"What's life without an outfit change or two?" Mom laughed. "We were early anyway. I was supposed to hit the pharmacy for flu shots between voting and now, but I got flustered and forgot."

"Oops. Well, no one really wants to get a shot anyway, do they?"

Mom shook her head. "Of course not! That's why I was stacking it ahead of bowling. It was a complex bribe. But now I've lost my advantage." She rolled her eyes. "That probably means I'll have to take them out for ice cream later."

"Oooh! We'll join you!" Jess said eagerly. "We want to take full advantage of our Tuesday off! It seems like there isn't enough time during the school year, you know? It's so much fun to get the kids all together." She put the baby carrier on the carpeted floor. "I'm missing our warm summer days of fun."

"It's a deal." Mom nodded. "Bowling, pizza, and ice cream. These kids are lucky."

"Living our best life!" agreed Jess as they watched their delighted offspring orchestrate complicated secret handshakes with one another while Sebastian ran around them in circles.

No one else was in the bowling alley, so Mom walked right up to the register. Smiling at the man behind the counter, she signed up for seven bowlers to use two bumper lanes, eat two pizzas, and drink two pitchers of caffeine-free soft drinks.

"Kiddos! Come on over and get your bowling shoes!" she called to the eager group.

She didn't have to ask twice. The kids all came running at once and crowded around the counter, eager to get their red-and-blue rental shoes and find house balls they could lift.

"Momma, my feet are bigger than yours!" Jack said proudly. "If you tried to wear my bowling shoes, you'd look like a clown!"

"Jack, *you're* gonna look like a clown in them, too," Ari teased, tossing her long blond ponytail over her shoulder. "They're blue-and-red boats!"

"I love my shoe boats," Jack proclaimed, striking a theatrical pose.

Marian laughed and gave Ari a squeeze. "I love having another girl around!" She giggled.

"You have me, too!" Rori announced, bouncing in between the two bigger girls. "*Three* girls are bowling today!"

Marian and Ari each took one of the younger girl's hands and swung her into the air.

"Ari, bring her back!" Jess called to her oldest. "I can't remember what size shoe she's in. I need to check."

Vince and Cam pushed towards the counter.

"We both need a size four," Cam said importantly. Vince nodded.

"Vince, you wear a size two," Mom said.

"So do you, Cam!" his mother called.

"Actually," Vince said seriously, "we both feel like, since we're getting older, our feet have probably grown."

"That's right," Cam concurred. "Look at how tall we both are. We probably need the size four by now."

Mom shook her head and turned to the man collecting shoes. "They'll both try size two for a start, please."

The boys started to whine, but Mom shot Vince a threatening look and he quickly grabbed his best friend's hand and led him away, size two bowling shoes in hand.

"Look for numbers five and six!" she reminded them as they headed towards the lanes.

"I'll take Cole and start putting names in the computer," Jess offered. "Who do you want Sebastian to bowl with?"

"I'm not sure." Mom pondered. "Jack and Ari?"

"They'd probably love to help him. And that would put Marian with my Rori. Sounds perfect. That way Cam and Vince can be together too."

"Great!" said Mom. "Sebastian and I will be right over. We need to sort out his shoe situation, and I forgot to tell them we need ball ramps."

"I stay with you, Momma?" Sebastian asked in panic.

"You sure do," Mom soothed, scooping him up. She could tell that the lights, sounds, and commotion were overwhelming him, so she needed to calm him down. "Let's go find out about getting some dinosaur ramps, okay?"

Hugging him tightly, she crossed her fingers and approached the counter.

"Hi! We forgot to ask for two of those ramps that the younger ones can use to roll the ball down the lane."

"Dino ramp!" Sebastian shouted. "I roll that ball down the dino ramp!"

"I'll bring them out," the man said curtly, not bothering to hide his disgust at Sebastian's flapping hands. Then he looked closely at the boy's white trainers. "He needs shoes if he's going to bowl."

Here we go.

Mom summoned her best smile. "Our Bassie here needs to wear these braces on his feet so he can walk safely." She pointed to the thick orthotics poking out the top of his shoes. "Do you have any high-top
bowling shoes? Or maybe some extra-wide ones in a size eleven?"

Please be willing to make an exception. Please. You can see he needs extra support. You can see something is different.

"They only come in one width and one style. Do you want a size eleven then?"

"He's going to have a very difficult time bowling if we can't cram his braces into the shoe. I put him in white trainers with white soles on purpose; is there any chance he could just wear these? I want him to be safe."

Please. What damage could he possibly do? Please.

"House rules. You have to wear bowling shoes if you're going to bowl. What size do you want for him?"

Seriously? My kid's going to push a six-pound ball down a big plastic dinosaur ramp sheltered by bumpers. Is that really considered bowling?

"Size nine, then."

"I thought you said he was an eleven?"

"I not eleven. I Sebastian!"

Really? You're going to deny my son the accommodation he needs and then force me to give you an education on adaptive footwear?

She sighed grimly.

"It's tough to find shoes that fit because the braces add so much bulk. We've found that going up two sizes usually does the trick. But since you don't have extra-wide or a high-top style, and he's not allowed to wear his custom trainers, I'll just have to try to strap his feet into bowling shoes without his medically necessary orthotics. We're aiming for the exact right size, pulled as tightly as they'll go, and we'll hope for the best."

"They're held together with ancient Velcro." The man plunked a tiny pair of multicolored shoes on the countertop. "You're not going to have much luck making them tight."

"You get the dino ramp?" Sebastian asked hopefully.

The man just stared...so Mom grabbed the shoes and answered for him.

"He's going to get *two* dinosaur ramps, Bassie! That way everyone who wants a turn can use one. Doesn't that sound perfect?"

"Yes!" Sebastian shrieked, looking so worked up, she worried he might cry.

"Let's find everyone else, then, and get these nice shoes on you so you can start bowling!"

The lanes were on, the rosters were ready, and the kids had found ten bowling balls whose bright orange, green, and pink colors indicated their child-friendly weight. She sat in a plastic molded bucket seat and began releasing Sebastian's feet from their supports.

"Can't his braces fit inside the bowling shoes?" Jack asked as he and Ari looked on in concern.

"They're too narrow," Mom lamented.

"But that's why I grabbed his white trainers," Marian said, clearly affronted. "Why can't he just wear his regular shoes?"

"Right?" Ari agreed. "This isn't the Olympics or anything."

"I'm not sure," Mom said as she tightened the decrepit Velcro as far as it would go across Sebastian's little foot. "The rules are: You've got to wear the shoes if you want to bowl." She smiled at her youngest son and tapped his nose. "You want to bowl, right?"

"Yes!" he shouted. "Sebastian go bowling with all his best, best friends!"

"There you go, then." She sighed again. "Be careful, Bas. You don't have your doggie feet on—just these goofy bowling shoes."

They heard a rumble, and saw Vince and Cam pushing the plastic dinosaur ramps toward their lanes from the far side of the alley.

"Got tired of waiting!" Jess called from behind the boys. She was holding baby Cole in one arm and waving at them with the other. "We could see them down there, so we decided to help ourselves."

"Great thinking!" Mom called over Sebastian's squeals. "Let's get this crazy train rolling!"

She knew from experience that Sebastian would need her help for the first few frames. He knew how to lift his ball and carry it to the ramp. He knew how to push it down towards the pins. But he struggled to deal appropriately with his emotions during the process. Before Sebastian came into their lives, she hadn't known it was possible to be too happy.

But she did now.

As soothingly as possible, she wrapped him in a tight hug and said, "Let's get your green ball, Bas. It's your turn."

Stiff and flapping, as high onto his toes as the bowling shoes would allow, Sebastian shouted, "G-G-G-G-G-Go, puppy, go!"

Jack and Ari stood patiently at the return, rolling the other balls away so Sebastian could lift his without smashing his fingers. Then, bright-green ball in Bas's arms, Mom helped him up the ledge and onto the bowling surface. The bigger kids hurried to the ramp, finagling their final adjustments.

"Should be perfect, Bas," Ari assured him.

But then, in the lane next door, Vince let his first ball loose. It ricocheted off the bumpers and hit the pins with a spectacular clatter...which was immediately echoed by the hollow thump of Sebastian's six-pound green ball crashing to the ground. His arms, stiff and flapping, hadn't been able to keep hold of it.

Hugging Bas's rigid body tightly, Mom spoke gently into his ear. "The pins make a loud noise, don't they?" She repositioned him to face his brother's lane. "See? Vince knocked down six of them! Now he gets another try—and it's going to make that sound again.

Watch." Huddled together at the end of their lane, they watched Vince capture a lucky spare with his wild, zigzag throw. The second crack was just as loud as the first, but Sebastian was already adjusting.

"It my turn?" he asked hopefully.

"Yes, Bassie-Boo. Here's your green ball," Jack said, holding it out to his youngest brother.

"I roll it!" Bas shouted. "I hit the pins, too!"

Carefully, and with considerable effort, he hefted his ball onto the top of the ramp. Mom hovered protectively, but she didn't intervene. *He needs to be able to do this himself.*

"Give it a push, Bas!" Ari coached.

Like an explosion, Sebastian shoved the ball down the ramp. Immediately, his arms stuck out to the sides and his hands began jerking up and down. His eyes widened and his smile stretched so large it looked almost painful. There he stayed, frozen in position, until his ball reached the pins and knocked three to the ground.

"I get them!" he shouted, somehow managing to jump into the air despite his knees remaining stiffly locked. "I get those pins!" He released a roar. "That my dino ramp yelling. He so happy, too!"

Sebastian's enthusiasm was uniquely contagious, and before the pin-setter finished sweeping away his conquest, he was surrounded by the other kids.

"Great job, Bas!" Cam said. "Here. Give me five!" Sebastian slapped his hand and, impossibly, his smile got bigger.

Marian picked Bas up and spun him in a circle, and then Vince did the same.

"Okay, kiddos," Mom admonished. "He's going to be too dizzy to roll his second ball!"

Jack and Ari rumpled Bas's hair, and then Rori pushed to the center of the crowd.

"Great job, Bassie!" she congratulated in her small voice. "That was such a good roll!"

Thrilled with the praise, Sebastian hugged his friend, their tiny heads reaching almost the same height.

"T-T-T-Thank you so much!" he said.

"Bas, you need to roll your ball again." Mom maneuvered him back towards the return. "Here it comes."

Sebastian grabbed his ball and carried it carefully back to the ramp, where Jack and Ari were again orchestrating minute adjustments.

"It's lined up perfectly," Jack assured them.

"You're going to get them all," Ari predicted.

Once again, Sebastian hefted his bright-green ball onto the dinosaur's back and shoved it with all the power his thin arms could muster.

"Green puppy, go!" he called as his hands flexed at the ends of his stiff arms.

With a satisfying crack, his ball made contact, and all of the remaining pins fell.

"That's a spare! You got a spare, Bas!"

"I bowling!" Sebastian cheered. "I bowling!"

Mom led him off the wooden ledge and back onto the linoleum of the waiting zone. Rori had just finished her turn and jubilantly greeted her friend.

"Hi, Bas! Aren't we lucky? Isn't bowling fun?"

Overstimulated and struggling to cope, Sebastian just jumped stiffly in place, grinning madly.

Losing interest in her silent peer, Rori ran to climb on her mother, who shifted Cole to make room for both kids.

"Bas and I are going to track down a pitcher of water and some cups," Mom told her friend with a weak smile. "He needs a minute to regroup."

"Absolutely. Take your time."

"I'll bowl for Bas if he's not back in time," Rori said helpfully. "I don't mind at all!"

"Thanks, sweetie. Come on, Bassie; I'll hold you."

Mom lifted him from where he stood, frozen with emotions he couldn't process fast enough. Bas went limp in her arms, and she cuddled him gently, singing reassuringly in her softest voice.

"Let's go for a walk," she said.

TUESDAY, 11:30 A.M.

They were heading back with the drinks before Sebastian spoke.

"Where dinosaurs live, Momma?"

"In the past, Sebastian. Dinosaurs live in the past."

"No dinosaurs now?"

"Nope. Dinosaurs are extinct. That means they're all gone. But scientists think they evolved into birds, like chickens."

"Where *that* dinosaur live?" he asked, pointing at the red plastic bowling-ball ramp.

"*That* dinosaur," she said, kissing his cheek gently, "lives here at the bowling alley."

"He loves me?"

"Well, the dinosaur ramp loves to be used for bowling, and you roll your ball down his back. So, sure, I guess...the dino ramp loves you!"

"Yay!" Bas exclaimed, tipping his head to the left as he tried to process the world around him. "I roll my green ball again now?"

"Yep, it's your turn, Bassie-Boo," Jack answered. "Come on! I'll help you."

Sebastian eagerly grabbed his brother's outstretched hand and headed for the ball return. Mom sat down heavily next to her friend.

"Who's winning?" Vince asked, staring intently at the two finished frames on the scoreboard. "How can we tell?"

"We're all winning," said Mom. "Because bowling is fun."

"No!" Marian corrected. "*I'm* winning right now."

"The game isn't over until the tenth frame is done," Jess responded. "Get going, Cam. It's your turn."

"Can I hold the baby?" Mom asked hopefully.

"For sure!" Jess answered. "My arms could use a break."

Cole smelled marvelous, and Mom kissed his fuzzy head contentedly.

"Do you miss it?" Jess asked.

Mom hesitated. "Not really. Sebastian is the end of the line, and we're good with that. I love holding babies, but I'm also loving that I can hand them back when they start to cry or smell."

"I don't ever want to be done," Jess confessed. "I hate that we are. Every time Cole outgrows something or moves into a new phase, it's awful. I want to keep him little forever."

"I guess that's one of the great parts about having Sebastian," Mom said slowly. "He takes so long to move along, that we never mourn the milestones. It's always a full-blown celebration."

Jess's smile faltered. "He's growing, though!" she recovered. "And making progress all the time!"

"Oh, I know," said Mom. "Today we found out he's being promoted at school to a less-restrictive classroom."

"That's wonderful!" cried Jess. "Congratulations!"

"Yup!" said Mom. "But—" She nodded over to the table behind the chairs. "My baby is four, and I'm still dragging a diaper bag with me everywhere."

"Stop!" Jess laughed. "That's just your purse."

"Nope. It doesn't even have my wallet in it. We call it the Survival Bag. Because mentally, I'm done with diaper bags. But see?" She shifted it open. "Diapers, wipes, a change of pants, two granola bars, and three toys. We can call it whatever we want, but if we're honest, it's still a diaper bag."

"You'll get there," Jess encouraged.

"Yes. And when that glorious day arrives, I'm not going to miss diapers and wipes. Just like whenever Sebastian finally loses interest in toys designed for infants that have littered my living room for ten years straight now, I'm going to throw them in the garbage and take myself out for lunch."

They laughed.

"I'll go with you!" said Jess. "So you can help cheer *me* up about it! I don't know if I'll be able to pitch *any* of the things Cole outgrows. I'll probably hold onto them forever."

The kids were nearing the tenth frame when Marian hurried over, dragging Sebastian by the arm.

"Momma, someone's stinky."

"I not stinky! I Sebastian! I bowling!"

"You can come back to bowling in a few minutes, Bas," said Mom. "Let's go get you changed first. You're smelling the place up. It can't be comfortable."

"Should we have someone bowl for him when it's his turn?" asked Marian.

"No. It'll only take us a few minutes because the bathrooms are right there. Jack and Ari won't mind waiting. Good thing we have the

Survival Bag." Mom sighed under her breath. "Come on, Bassie. You've got to walk there, or we're going to need your spare pair of pants, too. I'll hold your hand, so you don't trip in those shoes."

They walked together to the ladies room and pushed open the door.

Please let there be a changing table. Please let there be a changing table. Please let there be a changing table.

She scanned the walls and then checked in the stalls. No changing table.

"You no flush?" Sebastian whispered, squeezing her fingers.

"No one will flush," Mom said patiently. "I promise. But, my little man—they don't have a changing table here, so we're going to have to do this standing up."

"You help me, Momma?"

"Of course I will, honey." And for the second time in two days, she found herself on the floor of a public restroom, sitting this time instead of kneeling because her injured knee couldn't support her weight.

Just don't think about it. You're on the floor of a bowling alley bathroom, but we're not going to think about it. Don't smell anything but Bas. Don't look at anything but Bas. Just focus and get the job done. You never know—maybe they clean the bathrooms on Monday nights. But since there's a very good chance these bathrooms are only cleaned every other *Monday night, you can change your pants as soon as you get home.*

"Practice makes perfect," Mom said with relief just a few minutes later. Sebastian was clean and she'd scrubbed their hands with warm, soapy water. "Let's get you back to the lanes. I bet it's your turn!"

TUESDAY, 12:15 P.M.

The pizza arrived two frames into the second game.

"Where's the Coke?" Cam asked.

"Sorry, buddy, I didn't order any. Jack can't have caffeine, so we all stick with Sprite. I've got water as a choice too, if you'd rather."

"Sprite is good. Could I also have a cup for Vince? He's getting the slices for us."

"You betcha," she said.

Sebastian was standing stiffly in rapt attention, watching his ball roll towards the pins. Jack and Ari flanked him on either side.

I've got time to cut up his pizza into bite-sized chunks before he gets back, she thought. Then she saw the plastic knife, and her heart sank. *No worries,* she consoled herself. *I've ripped pizza before; I can do it again.*

"What are you doing?" Rori asked in fascination.

"I bet you don't usually see a grown-up tearing up food, huh?" Mom laughed with the beautiful little girl. "Sebastian has trouble chewing, so we cut up his food into small pieces. That way he doesn't choke as often." She held up the plastic knife. "But look at this flimsy thing! If it tries to fight the pizza, the pizza is going to win. So, I'm just ripping it apart with my fingers."

Rori began laughing deliriously. "When Cole's old enough to eat solid foods, maybe you could rip up a slice of pizza for him," she suggested.

"Momma, is it a good job to work at a bowling alley?" Vince asked as he and Cam dragged out chairs and squeezed into their seats. "I was thinking maybe I'll work at a bowling alley. Did you see that fancy vacuum cleaner scooting down the other lanes? That thing would be a lot of fun to operate. And if he gets really good at recognizing his numbers, Bas could hand out the shoes. He'd get to spray them, too, so they don't smell. You know how much he loves to spray stuff."

Mom giggled. "You and Cam love to spray stuff, too," she reminded him. "Are you sure you'd let Sebastian have that job?"

"Well, I could help him whenever I wanted, right?"

Marian plunked into the nearest empty seat, blotting her pizza with a napkin.

"I really don't like the grease," she explained. "Where are Jack and Ari and Bassie?"

Mom pointed to the lane and saw the kids heading towards them.

"Here they come!" she said.

When the bigger kids spotted the food, like all children of large families, they instantly worried someone else was going to eat their share if they weren't quick enough. Jack and Ari sprinted up the stairs, momentarily forgetting about Sebastian skipping along behind them. Mom knew what was going to happen, just as surely as she knew she wouldn't reach him in time.

Seeing himself being left behind, Sebastian tried to run to catch up. His awkward gait was exacerbated by the clumsy bowling shoes, and he tripped over his own feet. But instead of reaching his arms forward to break his fall, they shot out sideways. He teetered for the briefest of moments, but without his braces, he simply didn't have the strength to balance himself.

Mom watched the drama unfold in slow motion as she tried desperately to outrace disaster, scrambling around chairs and children, all while still gripping the plastic knife. But it was too late. She heard the sickening thump of Sebastian's forehead colliding with the bottom stair-ledge and arrived in time to catch him before he slid to the floor.

"Ice!" Mom shouted, vaguely aware of Marian running past in a blur.

Bas was crying hysterically, but not, she knew, because of pain. Sebastian was afraid. He'd fallen, and it had terrified him.

"I've got you, Bassie. Momma's here. I've got you." She was on the floor, rocking him on her lap as she hugged him tightly to her chest. "I tried to get here in time. I'm so sorry, my love." She pulled him away to view the damage and felt herself reeling. The lump on his forehead was already sticking out almost two inches. *The skin is going to split again if we don't get ice on it right away.*

"I fall. I fall on the floor," Sebastian choked out through his peculiar, tearless sobs.

"I know, Bassie. I was running to get to you. That was very scary."

"You scared, Momma?"

"I was afraid you were going to fall and get hurt. I ran so fast, but I didn't get here in time. Are you scared, lovey?"

"Yup," Bas cried. "I scared I fall. My head make a noise."

Mom heard footsteps and felt a bag of ice on her shoulder.

"No one came even through Marian was calling," said Jess, "so we helped ourselves to the ice machine behind the counter." Without hesitation, Jess had passed baby Cole to Ari and taken off after Marian. "How bad is it?"

Mom pulled Sebastian away from her and delayed a beat

before placing the ice bag on his still-growing lump.

"Oh my," said Jess, recoiling slightly. "I've seen some bad ones, but that's the worst." She swallowed. "What else do we do?"

Mom sighed. "I don't know. We'll keep the ice on it for a bit and see how it looks."

Sebastian was clinging to her, his sobs escalating. "That too cold. That too cold for me!" He began to thrash, and she held him tightly.

"Sebastian, I need you to listen. You have a big boo-boo on your head. The ice will help you. I know it's very cold, but it needs to be cold to work. If we don't keep the ice on, you are going to have to see Big Tuna in his ambulance."

"No!" Sebastian screamed. "No mam-lance. No!"

"All right, then. If you hold still and keep the ice on your head, your boo-boo will get better all on its own."

Her little boy hugged her, whimpering softly. "I happy, Momma. I not hurt. I happy. I bowling. I no go on mam-lance. I so happy."

This, more than the swelling head wound, made Mom's eyes tear. "You *are* hurt, Sebastian. You can be happy and hurt at the same time. Happy is a choice; hurt isn't." She repositioned him, stood up, and carried him carefully to the table.

"Here we go," she said. "I tore up your pizza for you, and I got you a nice glass of water. You can sit here with Momma and eat while we keep the ice on your head. By the time you're done with lunch, you'll be able to finish your bowling."

"I didn't mean to leave him behind, Mom," Jack said, his face stricken.

"It's not your fault," she reassured him. "Clumsy bowling shoes and no doggie braces. It was bound to happen."

"What dinosaurs eat, Momma?" Sebastian sniffed pitifully. "They eat pizza?"

"Dinosaurs would have *loved* to eat pizza," Marian interjected, her level of zealousness betraying just how worried she was about her brother. "Eat your pieces there, Bassie-Boo, and we can go roll your ball some more!"

"What type of pizza would an herbivore dinosaur have liked?" Vince asked loudly. Without waiting for anyone to answer, he yelled, "Pizza with spinach and pineapple. Wocka-Wocka! Get it, Bassie? Herbivores eat plants!"

"Wocka-Wocka!" Sebastian replied. "Vincey telling a joke!" He burst into high-pitched laughter.

"*ROAR!*" Cam yelled, joining in the fun. "But I'm a T-rex carnivore dinosaur, and I want pizza with pepperoni and sausage!"

"Oh, but think about insectivores though," Jack said with the anticipatory tone that precedes a good fart joke. "*Their* pizza would have been the best. Can you imagine? Insectivore pizza is probably loaded with crunchy grasshoppers and beetles and slippery worms and slugs!" He pantomimed slurping something long and slimy off the top of his third slice of pizza. Just as he'd intended, the girls gagged.

"Marian," Ari said, "I don't know how you live with him." Then she turned to Jack. "That's just gross!"

TUESDAY, 12:45 P.M.

In no time at all, the pizzas were gone, the pitchers were empty, hands had been washed, and bowling had resumed. Sebastian's plate, of course, still held more than half of his original slice.

"How's he doing?" Jess asked, looking worried.

Mom pulled away the ice to reveal a shiny lump extending across Sebastian's forehead.

"Well, at least the skin didn't split."

"I think it looks better than it did," Jess said hopefully. "Like the swelling is down already."

"I so happy, Momma. I not hurt," Sebastian repeated, his mouth lifting in a grimacing smile.

"I need to shine my light into your beautiful eyes," Mom said. "Okay?"

"My eyes have a boo-boo?" Sebastian asked in alarm.

"I don't know, but I'm going to check. If your eyes look okay, then you'll be almost done with the ice."

Mom turned on her cell phone flashlight and aimed the bright beam into his eyes.

"Not exactly a formal medical tool," she murmured to Jess.

"Seems legit to me!" Jessica laughed.

"Motherhood takes some inventiveness, right?"

They both stared into Sebastian's eyes, watching them react to the light.

"They seem to be constricting and dilating the way they should," Mom said, satisfied. "At least they're both the same size and changing at the same pace."

"I go bowling?" Bas pleaded.

"Eat four more bites of pizza and let Momma put your doggie feet and trainers back on, and then, yes. Then you can go bowling."

"Momma, I totally agree—no one's paying any attention to us anyway." Marian called from her chair near the scoring computer. "It was wrong of them to keep Bas from his doggie feet, anyway."

"I'm right there with you, Sissy. I just hope no one notices."

They had only three frames of the game left by the time Sebastian was ready to rejoin the fun. His hair had parted around the massive lump stretching across his forehead, but he didn't seem to notice.

"I bowling!" he called cheerfully from the lane.

"I can't believe that doesn't hurt," Jessica said in wonder. "I'd still be crying if it were me. Or I'd at least be sitting with the ice right now. There's no way I'd be up and bowling. The headache has to be tremendous."

"Ah, but as you know, Sebastian doesn't process pain in the same way we do. I mean, I know he must have felt something," Mom said, "but it just doesn't seem to matter to him."

"I still can't decide if that's horrible or wonderful," Jessica said.

"I know exactly what you mean," said Mom. "It's horrible—always horrible. But still." She stopped to watch Sebastian jump on stiff legs to celebrate his strike. "I'm glad he isn't suffering right now."

Vince was tugging on her arm. "Momma, have you noticed the scores lately?"

Mom and Jess glanced up to the screens and broke into laughter.

"I know!" Vince cried. "Do you think it's broken?"

"I think it's working perfectly," Jessica replied, watching Jack and Ari carefully adjust the dinosaur ramp for Sebastian's final frame.

Sebastian hefted his green ball to the top of his ramp and shoved it as hard as he could. It sailed down the ramp and sped towards the end of the lane, crashing into the pins with a terrific crack.

"That's a strike!" Cam celebrated. "A strike in the tenth frame!"

Sebastian ran towards them on his tiptoes, his stiff arms flapping wildly.

"You get two extra rolls, Bassie-Boo!" Jack called. "Get your ball and come back!"

"How is he *doing* that?" Marian asked in awe. "Sebastian has the highest score of all of us! He's even beating me, and I had a one-fourteen!"

"He's going to *destroy* your score," Mom gloated. "Because a strike in the tenth means two extra balls."

"Go, Bas, go!" Rori cheered. "Go, Bas, go!"

"Sebastian has a hidden talent," Vince enthused. "Bowling!"

"We both lost," Cam marveled. "And I don't even mind."

"Really, though," Marian asked. "How *is* he doing it?"

"Watch," Mom said, pointing at Jack and Ari as they carefully shifted the ramp for Sebastian's final ball.

"Ha!" Marian shouted. "Now I see. But still, it's Bas who pushes it down the dinosaur ramp."

"He's a bowling star!" Vince exclaimed. "Do you see his final score? One-thirty-five!"

"Sebastian is the Ultimate Champion!" Cam cheered.

"I think a celebration is in order," Jessica said, hugging her son.

"Agreed," said Mom. "Anybody want ice cream?"

TUESDAY, 1:10 P.M.

A blue Volkswagen Beetle drove past and Mom cringed.
Please don't notice. Please don't notice.

"Punch Bug, no punch-backs!" Marian shouted.

Darn!

Marian repeated the phrase over and over as she flailed around trying to jab each of her brothers in the arm.

"Punch Bug, no punch-backs!" Jack and Vince echoed in endless refrain, also flailing wildly to hit their siblings.

"No punch me!" Sebastian shouted over the cacophony. "I just kiss Fluffy Red!"

"That's enough!" Mom called. "I keep telling you, that's not how you play the game."

"It's how *we* like to do it," Jack said impishly.

"The drive to the ice cream shop is less than two miles, and we're only halfway there!" Mom complained. "We shouldn't have achieved this level of annoyance already."

"Beep, beep, I see a Jeep!" Marian cried out.

"Finger wag, I see a flag!" Vince rejoined.

"Ugh!" Mom shouted. "Stop the insanity!"

"Stuck in the muck, we passed a truck!" Vince cried.

"No more!" Mom said threateningly. "NO. MORE."

They drove in silence for eight seconds before Marian spoke. "Momma?"

"What is it, honey?" She knew Marian wouldn't move forward without audible confirmation that everyone was listening.

"Momma, I was thinking." Marian considered how to proceed. "I love to hang out with our friends. But sometimes it's not fair."

"Well, a lot of things aren't fair," Mom said warily. "But I'm not sure what you mean."

"It's Sebastian," Marian said with a sigh. "We have pictures of him at home, as a teeny-tiny baby, lying on our dining room table with Rori. And in that picture, she's just a teeny-tiny baby, too."

"I love those pictures," Mom said wistfully. "Our babies were adorable in their footie pajamas. But how does that relate to fairness?"

"Those pictures show that Rori and our Bassie are almost exactly the same age."

"That's right." Mom nodded. "In fact, Marian, you and baby Cole are the odd ones out. Jack and Ari are just a few months apart, Cam and Vince are just a few months apart, and Rori and Sebastian are just a few *weeks* apart."

"I know—and that's what's not fair, Momma," pressed Marian. "Sebastian and Rori are both four. But Rori can eat her pizza just as fast as everyone else. No one has to rip it into tiny shreds, and she doesn't choke. She doesn't need help bowling. She talks as well as we do, and she doesn't ever trip and fall. It's not fair, because that's not how it is for Bas. Our Bassie-Boo got a bad deal."

The van was silent. Mom glanced in the mirror and saw the Big Three staring at the back of her head, awaiting a brilliant response. Sebastian's voice was the only sound, softly repeating his best approximation of 'Punch Bug, no punch-backs' while showering Fluffy Red with happy kisses.

Just tell them the truth, she thought. *They're asking.* But it hurt to have to burden them with cruel reality.

"Life isn't fair," she spoke the words. "Not for anyone. Each person is different, which is what makes the world so interesting. And because of that, I'm honestly not even sure what 'fair' would look like. So here's the thing." She parked in front of the ice cream shop and turned off the van. "We shouldn't worry about 'fair,' because we'll never get there."

"But that's so sad," Marian said, her eyes glassy with tears.

Mom glanced back at her children's crestfallen faces and felt her heart break. She forced a bright smile.

"There's so much more to life, though!" she said. "It's not *about* fairness, sweetie."

"What's it about then, Momma?" Jack asked.

"Hmmm…" Mom considered how to explain. "Everyone has a different answer to that question. But Daddy and I think life is about finding joy."

"What do you mean? Vince asked.

"Joy, happiness. It's not about crying or being angry that things are unfair. Because the world is always going to feel unfair, no matter who you are. So in our house, we choose to make life about finding joy. Lack of fairness doesn't mean you can't find ways to fill your life with love and laughter."

She smiled at her children and then reached out to stroke Sebastian's hair, careful to avoid the lump across his forehead.

"Bassie has challenges to face, and he'll be pushing against them his entire life," she went on. "That isn't fair. But he's not the only one. Our Jack had a terrible run of things for a bit there, with a scary heart surgery in a faraway town. Marian, you've had *two* hospital stays because of hernias. And Vincey, you broke your arm right in half! You were trapped in a cast for so long, you missed out on your first season of wrestling. None of that was fair. None of it! But our lives aren't measured by fairness. They can't be. Life is about joy. And through that filter, Sebastian has the advantage. He has a tremendous capacity for joy."

"He doesn't keep it to himself, either," Jack said thoughtfully. "Bassie spreads happiness all day long. He makes everyone happy, everywhere he goes."

Vince giggled. "Everyone except Momma when he's unrolled the toilet paper!"

"But even then!" Marian protested. "Remember when he did the *'Ding!'*? Momma was laughing, too. I heard her!"

"You're right, Sissy." Mom chuckled. "It was hysterical. But that's our Bassie, right? He's never mean, he's always kind, and he wants to share his joy with everyone. If happiness is what life is all about, then we could all learn a lot from your baby brother."

"I not a baby," Bas said indignantly. "I Sebastian!" Then he peeked over Fluffy Red's head and squealed, "We here? We eat ice cream?"

"Yup! I see Aunt Jess pulling in the lot now. Let's go!"

They piled out of the van and waited on the sidewalk, jumping up and down with exuberance.

"I wish every Tuesday was Election Day," Vince said.

"Best day EVER!" Sebastian echoed.

Mom hugged them close until their friends joined them. Together again, the seven children burst through the glass doors and traipsed into the brightly lit ice cream shop, singing "Jingle Bells."

"Look at that employee's face!" Jess whispered, following five steps behind the kids, carrying Cole in his seat.

"Oh, dear." Mom smirked. "The poor girl was enjoying a quiet and relaxing shift."

"She's looking at our babies like they're a herd of rhinos!" said Jess. "I'm almost offended."

"We do make an entrance!" Mom laughed. "And isn't a herd of rhinos called a crash? I'd say that's rather appropriate."

"The girl must not have much experience," Jess reasoned, "or she wouldn't look so terrified. As soon as they get their orders, it'll be perfectly quiet again."

"As long as they don't start singing 'Silent Night,' they can be as loud or as quiet as they want!" Mom joked. "Anyway, that girl is very young. It's not her fault she's oblivious to our trade secrets. Only the most experienced moms know how to fully appreciate the Ice Cream Silence."

Forty minutes later, Mom's entire crew was back inside the van with full bellies and sticky faces.

"I've got wipes here!" she called. "Everyone take one and clean yourselves up a bit, please. You've got chocolate, sprinkles, and whipped cream everywhere."

"What are we doing now?" Marian asked. "There's still over half an hour before my solo lesson at dance."

"We have one more important errand today," Mom said grimly.

Please don't let this go as poorly as it did last year. I'm certain I'm not strong enough to hold Jack down anymore; he's almost as tall as me. I'm not even sure I could keep Vince still if he really struggled.

"What is it?" Jack asked worriedly.

"Well," Mom said calmly, "remember last year when Sebastian had to stay in the hospital for a week because he got the flu?"

"It was awful," Vince said. "We weren't even allowed to visit him."

"Do you remember the year before, when Sebastian got the flu and then he got meningitis and was in the hospital for even longer?"

"He almost died," Jack stated.

"That's true," Mom said slowly. "The flu can make everyone sick, but it's especially dangerous for Sebastian. His immune system doesn't work the same way yours or mine does. That's why he got his flu shot as soon as it became available to our pediatrician, way back in September."

"But we didn't get *our* flu shots," Marian said. "What if we get sick and expose Sebastian? He'll probably get the flu anyway, even though he's had his shot."

And today's "Connect the Dots" Award goes to Marian!

"That's why we have one more errand today," Mom replied solemnly. "Nobody likes to get a shot, but it's really important that we do it anyway. They have flu shots at the pharmacy—I saw the sign when we drove by this morning. I thought we could all pop in there and get it taken care of. To keep all of us safe."

"You too?" Jack queried.

"Me too," Mom replied. "I'll even go first."

"Nope," Vince said. "I'm going first. The sooner we get our shots, the better."

"Ladies first, Vince," Marian said. "That means me. I want to go first."

"I *don't* want to go first," Jack said. "And I can't promise I won't be afraid." He bit his lip and shifted nervously. "But I'm not going to try to hide under the chair or run away."

"I get a shot?" Sebastian asked.

"You already had yours, Bassie," Mom said. "So, no. You don't need to get a shot today."

"That's irony—right, Mom?" Jack asked, his voice quivering. "Bas is the only one who wouldn't want to cry from the pain, and he doesn't even need one."

"I'm not going to cry," Vince boasted. "It only hurts for a minute."

"I'd rather have my arm hurt for a minute than get sick for a week," Marian enjoined.

"I'd rather be sick for a week," Jack said grimly. "But I don't want Bas to be sick."

"Well, then, let's go in," Mom encouraged.

"Wait," Marian said. "We're here already? Are you sure this is the place?"

"This is it," Mom said, climbing out of the van. "Tricky of me to choose the ice cream shop across the street from the pharmacy, huh? Come on, Sebastian. You aren't getting a shot, but you can't wait in the car by yourself."

Marian grabbed her hand. "Are you going to cry?" she asked her mother, sounding frightened.

"I don't know," Mom said. "I feel nervous too, Sissy. No one likes to get a shot. But it's important that we do anyway, right?"

They all walked together through the automatic doors and

began the long, slow march toward the back of the store. No one was at the pharmacy counter, so she held up Sebastian to hit the bell.

"Hello!" called the pharmacist, dressed smartly in a white lab coat. "What can I do for you today?"

"Hi! We need flu shots. Sebastian here already got his, but the rest of us are due." She pulled out her insurance card. "Is there a chance we could get them right now?"

"Come on back this way," the pharmacist said, beckoning. "We can get you taken care of immediately." He led them into a small room with chairs and a doctor's table. "Wait here while I go grab the syringes." He stopped halfway out of the door. "Should I get some helpers to make sure everyone stays calm?" he asked.

Mom considered. "I'd like to think we're all prepared to hold still, but it might be a good idea anyway."

"Got it," he said. "I'll bring back the syringes *and* a helper."

"Momma, am I going to be able to dance after this?" Marian asked. "Will my arm be okay?"

"You're going to be just fine," Mom said, giving her daughter a quick hug. "It'll take about four seconds, and it'll hurt for maybe two minutes. The hardest part is the worrying."

"I'm scared, Momma," Jack said.

"That's okay," said Mom. "There's nothing wrong with being scared. But remember: When you're getting the shot, you need to hold still."

"I'll be the first kid to get their shot, Momma, but I'll let you be the first *person*," Vince said quietly. "That way you won't have to be afraid for as long."

Mom smiled. "I'm happy to go first, Vince. I hate getting poked, but I know getting a shot is better than being sick—or worse, watching one of you be sick."

"Sea lions get shots, Momma?" asked Sebastian

"Not usually—if they live in the wild, on the rocky coast. But if they live at the zoo or aquarium, then yes. Those sea lions get shots just like you and me."

"I-I-I-I get a shot?"

"No, Sebastian. Not today. Momma is getting a shot. So are Vince, Marian, and Jack. But you already got yours. Today, you just have to give us hugs."

The door opened and the pharmacist was back, followed by another pharmacy worker balancing a silver tray holding four shots.

"Who's first?"

"I am," Mom said, rolling up her sleeve.

"You'll all be done and licking suckers in less than five minutes," the pharmacist reassured them, taking in the terrified expressions of the children staring at him.

Mom kept her face perfectly calm during the procedure, and it was over in a moment.

"I need to bring you all along with me every time I get a shot!" She laughed. "It's so much easier to be brave when you're surrounded by the unblinking faces of the children you love most!"

"Oh, Momma! I love you so much!" Sebastian shouted, running to her for a hug.

"I'm next," Vince said confidently. "And I don't even have to roll up my sleeve, because it's already short enough!"

Jack and Marian watched through spread fingers, flinching in sympathy as Vince valiantly held still for his flu shot.

"You did it, Vincey!" Sebastian cheered. "Y-Y-Y-You so, so brave!"

"My sleeve doesn't want to roll up." Marian's voice was panicky.

"You're right," agreed Mom. "It won't work that way. Let's just pull you shoulder out of the neck hole." She turned to the pharmacist. "Will this be okay?"

At Marian's terrified expression, the assistant stepped over with the basket of candy.

"What kind of sucker would you like?" she asked, pushing the colorful sugary distractions under Marian's nose. "You two boys can choose one, too," she said. "You're already done."

"Suckers!" Sebastian squealed, reaching his hand into the

bucket and pulling out a blue-raspberry candy. "Th-Th-Th-Th-Th-These are my favorite!"

"Hey!" Marian squeaked, but her shot was already over. In amazement and relief, she turned to her big brother, who was hovering near the door, contemplating escape. "I hardly even felt it, Jack! It's not bad at all!"

Suddenly Sebastian—who had an uncanny knack for recognizing sadness or fear—ran to Jack, holding his sucker aloft.

"Y-Y-Y-Y-You sad? Y-Y-Y-You want my sucker?" he asked, his voice full of concern. "I sh-sh-sh-share it with you, Jack." Then, not waiting for a response, he flung himself into a hug that nearly knocked his biggest brother off his feet.

Laughing, Jack found his balance and returned the embrace.

"Thanks, Bassie-Boo. You eat your sucker. I'm going to earn my own right now." And with that, he pushed up his sweatshirt sleeve and sat down in the chair. "I'm ready," he announced, "but I can't look."

"Just watch us, Jack!" Vince said happily. "The Beef Buff Band can put on a distracting show for you. We've been practicing!"

Marian launched into "Deck the Halls" and immediately Vince and Sebastian added their voices and dance moves to the impromptu performance.

"See, Jack?" Marian mouthed silently, wildly flailing her arm in exaggerated pantomime. "Doesn't even hurt!"

Absorbed by the spectacle, Jack didn't notice his own procedure until he felt a cotton swab being pressed to the injection site.

"All done," the pharmacist said with a smile. "And I must say, the Beef Buff Band could do some contract work here at the flu clinic."

"You'd be surprised at the number of grown-ups who would welcome such an adorable distraction," the assistant agreed. "They'd probably give you tips in gratitude!"

"Tips!" the Big Three repeated, their eyes round. "Did you hear her, Momma?"

"I think we'll stick with playing our violins next to the Salvation Army buckets at Christmastime. That way, we know the tips are being put to good use."

"But, Momma," Vince whined. "We could save up our tips and go to Disney!"

"My darling, it'd take a lot more than flu-season tips to get us back to Disney," Mom said.

"But—" Vince argued.

"I've got a tip for *all* the members of the Beef Buff Band," Mom interrupted. "Here it is: Put on your coats before we walk out of this room."

"Hey!" Vince said. "That's not a tip!"

"It most certainly is," said Mom. "It's a wonderful tip. And if you follow it, you won't be freezing when we go outside. It's quite cold out, and you're wearing only a t-shirt."

The Big Three groaned but put their coats back on.

"I can give you tips all day," Mom said spiritedly. "Here's another good one: Never forget your mother's birthday. Oh, and after a shower, use a towel to dry your body before putting on clothes."

"Momma," Vince said sadly, "that's not the kind of tip we wanted."

"Really?" she said in mock astonishment. "That's too bad, because I could give you tips like that for hours."

"Momma!" Marian rolled her eyes.

Mom grinned at them. "Anyway, you'd better say thank you for the suckers."

"Thank you for the sucker!" Sebastian shouted, waving it around like a sticky disaster waiting to happen.

"Thank you!" echoed Jack, Marian, and Vince.

"Anytime," the woman said kindly. "You were all terribly brave. You should be proud of yourselves."

"It's pretty easy to do when you know how important it is," Jack said thoughtfully. He grabbed Sebastian's free hand and headed towards the door.

TUESDAY, 2:50 P.M.

"Where to next?" Marian asked when they were all strapped in.

Mom glanced at the clock on the dashboard. "We've got only ten minutes until your private dance lesson, Sissy, so up next, we're all going to the studio."

"Why do we *all* have to go?" Jack whined. "We're going to drive right past our house on the way! I could stay home with Vince and Bas. Isn't there time to drop us off?"

"Maybe," said Mom, "but I don't want to leave you home alone again today. Besides," she added, "your sister is almost done with her routine. I want us to watch it together."

Jack crossed his arms and sighed.

Mom stared at him sternly. "It's only thirty minutes. You'll survive. We all wait much, much longer for you."

"Football games take *forever,* Jack," Marian jumped in. "And we're either sweating in the blazing sun in a hundred degrees, or we're freezing to death in rain that's so cold it's almost snow. There's never an in-between. At least dance is inside and comfortable."

Jack still wasn't appeased. "I didn't even pack my book, though!"

"You're not supposed to look at a *book,* Jack!" Marian said.

"You're supposed to look at *me*!"

"I don't really want to go either, Jack," Vince whisper-shouted from the back seat. "I love going for my own class, but waiting isn't much fun."

"It's not going to be that bad," said Mom. "You'll see. Dig around in the trunk and under the seats. I'm sure you'll find some toy cars or books, or something else you could bring in."

The kids begrudgingly followed her direction.

"Ha!" Vince exclaimed. "I found the dinosaur bag, Jack—from last week!"

"I'm pretty sure the dinosaur bag is from when we went to the playground," Marian disagreed. "That was way more than a week ago. It was warm, remember?"

"The dinosaur bag is perfect," Mom said. "And the longer it's been since we've seen it, the better." She ended the argument with a smile.

They pulled into the empty parking lot and loaded up their belongings.

"We might only be staying for half an hour..." Marian grunted as Jack dropped her dance bag onto her shoulder. "But anyone watching would think we're moving in!"

"What do you keep in there?" Jack gaped. "It weighs twenty pounds!"

"Just my dance shoes, my team jacket, my stretch bands, and my notebook," Marian said as they made their way in through the double doors. "Oh, and my weights!" She giggled.

"Weights?" Vince asked.

"Wrist and ankle weights. We wear them during warm-ups. That's probably what makes my bag so heavy."

"You think?" Jack teased.

"Wh-Wh-Wh-Wh-Where we going, Momma?" Sebastian asked in concern. "We go to-to-to-toooooooo dance?"

"Sissy has a short class, and we're going to watch." Mom lifted him out of his car seat, and they hurried to catch up with the Big Three. "Your dance class is on Thursday. That's in two days. Right now, we're going to peek at Marian through the window."

"What I do, Momma?"

"You can watch Marian spin around in her noisy tap shoes, or you can play with Fluffy Red. *And* your brothers are bringing in a surprise."

"Surprise?!" Sebastian shrieked. "Wh-Wh-Wh-What surprise you bring, Jack?"

With a flourish, Jack revealed from its hiding place behind Vince's back the tote bag filled with plastic dinosaurs.

"Remember these?" Vince asked. "It's our dino friends!"

Sebastian roared, his arms rigid with excitement. "M-m-m-m-my best, best dino buddies!"

"I'm going to get changed," Marian called. "Have fun watching me dance!"

Mom blew a kiss to her daughter, but the boys were already too absorbed in the wonders of their long-forgotten toy bag to notice their sister was leaving.

TUESDAY, 3:00 P.M.

Marian's tap lesson was first up on the teacher's schedule each Tuesday, so they had the studio to themselves. Mom directed the boys to the empty space outside Marian's room, and sat down on the bench facing the two-way mirror.

"Bassie, I'm going to use *this* T-rex and this Stegosaurus," Jack said, holding up the pair of toys.

"And I'm going to use the two Raptors," Vince said. "But all the rest are for you!"

"These my dinos?" Sebastian asked, his flapping hands channeling his delight.

"Yup! You get fifty dinosaurs to play with!" Jack leaned in to kiss his brother's head.

"Just don't take *these* four," Vince emphasized again.

The music floated softly out of the soundproof studio. While Sebastian meticulously lined up his dinosaurs in orderly rows, Mom focused on Marian who was fiercely pounding the floor with her tan taps. Hearing a faint "ping" from her coat pocket, Mom retrieved her phone to check the alert.

A request to join our Facebook group!

She pressed her thumb to the sensor and opened the social media app. *They didn't indicate why they want to join. Time for some detective work.* Clicking on their profile, she scanned quickly through the family photos. Just three pictures in, she stopped scrolling. *Bingo. Look at that precious little guy!* The hairs on her arms prickled, as they always did when she saw Sebastian's beautiful face looking out at her from another mother's child. *I wonder if today is their "Diagnosis Day," or if today is just the day they thought to look up "AUTS2 Syndrome" on Facebook.* She swiftly navigated back to the administrative page and hit "Accept." *No sense in making them wait.*

Management duties accomplished, she headed back to the new member's profile. *Where are you from?* she wondered. *I'm going to guess Australia or New Zealand. Or maybe the United Kingdom...Nope—it's Russia! How exciting!*

Her phone emitted a different sound and she clicked to retrieve the private message in her Inbox.

Hello, it began. *Today we received test results from our geneticist. Our son, who is three and cannot speak, has AUTS2 Syndrome. They weren't able to tell us much, but we found your news interview on the Internet, and then your Facebook page and the support group. Thank you so much for putting information out there. How is your Sebastian? We are devastated. We have questions, and nowhere else to look for answers.*

Mom looked up from her phone to smile at Sebastian, who was pushing his dinosaurs off the bench onto the floor with jerky, energetic movements, simply so he could line them up on the bench again.

I love to help, she thought, *but every single time, my body reacts as if it were OUR Diagnosis Day all over again. It's been nearly two years and I've done this over forty times; I wonder if it'll ever get easier.*

I'm so glad you found us! Mom typed back. *Welcome to the AUTS2 Family, and congratulations on getting your diagnosis. It's a tough day for sure, but having a name to put to the challenges you're facing opens doors to therapies that will be life-changing. There aren't many of us, but we're very close. Please feel free to ask any questions and I'll do my best to answer them. We can also post to the group message board!*

As cascading dots flashed on her screen, indicating a response-in-progress, she took the brief moment to wave at Marian through the window. Jack and Vince were deep into their pretending, and Sebastian was working hard to make all his dinosaurs stand upright despite his shaking hands. The phone dinged.

Can Sebastian chew and swallow? Does he sleep through the night? Can he walk without help? Does he talk? What therapies does he get, and how often?

Mom took a deep breath. *I should probably make a 'Welcome to AUTS2' document to send out to new families,* she thought. *It'd feel too impersonal, though. I remember when it was me finding other moms of AUTS2 who were there first. Those Facebook Messenger conversations were the only reason I was able to sleep for the first month.*

Mom scrolled through her phone to find a video of Sebastian and settled on one from last week that showed him singing, dancing, and laughing with Vince in the living room. She sent it to the new family and began typing her response:

Eating is a common struggle with AUTS2. Around his second birthday, Sebastian nearly had a G-tube placed, but his amazing occupational therapist was able to train him to use his tongue and teeth to chew food. It took months, but it worked. She used a vibrating toothbrush to help him be more aware of the inside of his mouth. We still have to cut his food into tiny pieces, though, so he doesn't choke. Some of our AUTS2 kiddos have had swallow imaging done, which revealed that their throat muscles don't always coordinate the way they should to guide food down. That test was never offered to us, but we suspect Sebastian deals with the same issue. Today, his BMI hovers around 12 percent. It's not ideal, but it's high enough that the doctors haven't insisted on a G-tube.

The phone dinged back:

This video is making me cry. He dances around! He talks! And I hope you don't mind my saying it, but your Sebastian looks just like my son if we put a blond wig on him. They even have the same mannerisms.

Smiling for her new Russian friends, Mom texted a reply:

Therapies make a difference. We have speech therapy, physical therapy, occupational therapy, and aquatic therapy a few times each week. Sebastian wears orthotics on his feet—I'm sending you a picture. They give him the support he needs to walk, and now he even runs (sort of). Music is transformative, too. For over a year, Sebastian communicated exclusively by humming melodies. He's able to focus better and learn more when music is involved.

The response came immediately: *What about sleep?*

I wish I didn't have to answer this one, Mom mourned. *How do I spin this to be hopeful?* She inhaled. *Truth is as important as hope. At least they'll know they're not alone.*

*It takes a long time for Sebastian to fall
asleep, and once he does, he can't maintain it for
more than four or five hours. We start our bedtime
routine at 7:45 each night, and he's in bed, clean,
and calm by 8:15. Typically, he falls asleep by 9:30,
then he's up again from 2:00 a.m. until 4:00 a.m., and
then he sleeps until 8:00. He doesn't nap and hasn't
napped since well before his second birthday. Some
families have had success with melatonin. We haven't
tried it.*

The resigned reply came a moment later.

*We are living the same life here. We're
exhausted, and it's hard to make people understand.*

Mom sighed as fuzzy images of her late-night adventure with
toilet water flashed across her mind. She could commiserate with
exhaustion. But she tried hard to remain positive and comforting.

*I'm so glad you found our group! The search
for a diagnosis is isolating and terrifying, but now you
have some answers and you're not alone—even if
we're literally on opposite sides of the globe. No
matter what time zone you're in, you'll find other
AUTS2 parents awake and ready to talk online
whenever you need them. Because none of us are
allowed to sleep!*

She added a laughing face and a heart emoji to the message
and sent it into cyberspace.

Only five minutes remained in the dance lesson, and as
Marian performed her solo for the tenth time, she looked utterly
exhausted. Mom's phone dinged again, and she hurried to read the
message, knowing she'd have time for only one more response.

*We are so grateful to have found you. Thank
you for bringing a ray of hope to a terrible day. We're*

going to hug our baby and regroup. If it's okay, I'll
reach out again in a few days.

I'll be here, Mom assured them. *Message any*
time.

Tucking her phone back into her coat pocket, Mom stood up. "Jack and Vince, it's time to start cleaning up!"

"W-w-w-we done?" Sebastian asked.

"Marian will be out in just a minute. Let's work together to toss all your dinosaurs into the big bag, Bassie."

"Wh-wh-what *your* favorite dino, Momma?"

"Hmmm. I think my favorite is the pterodactyl." She held up a plastic model. "They could fly through the air!" She zoomed the toy over Sebastian's head. "Remember I told you scientists think dinosaurs evolved into birds? Pterodactyls may have even been covered in feathers!"

"Th-Th-Th-That a chicken dino!" Sebastian shouted, jumping into the air and landing hard on straight legs.

"Yikes!" Marian exclaimed, lugging her duffle into the waiting area. "We've got to bend our knees when we land, Bassie-Boo." She demonstrated an exaggerated squat as she dumped her bag on the floor and then grabbed his hands. "Let's practice!"

Together with Vince and Jack, Mom hastily cleaned up the remaining dinosaurs and began handing out coats.

"That's it, Bas!" Marian cheered. "That's right!"

Both their faces glowed. Mom leaned down to pull them into a hug.

"Great job, guys," she said. "Now put on your coats; it's time to go. Poor Alice and Thomas Jefferson have been stuck inside for hours."

TUESDAY, 3:40 P.M.

Traffic was light with no school buses on the road as Mom sped toward home.

"Is it time for dinner yet?" Vince called from the back row, sounding hungry.

"You've been munching all day!" Mom said. "Don't tell me you're ready to eat again already."

"I could go for some dinner, too," Marian said.

Mom rolled her eyes. "You're all in luck, then, because I'm going to start cooking as soon as we get home. We've got just enough time to eat and practice instruments before we have to leave for swim class."

Nine hours down, eight to go, she mused.

"What are we having?" Jack asked.

"Spaghetti and meatballs, and a spinach salad."

"Leaves?" Sebastian asked. "W-W-We having leaves?"

"That's right!" said Mom. "It's your favorite dinner: noodles, sauce, cheese, meatballs, and green leaves."

"Yummy, yum, yum! I be a d-d-d-d-dino that eats leaves!"

"You're an herbivore!" sang out Vince. "Sebastian the Sauropod!"

"Rrrraaaarrrrrr!" Sebastian replied. "I a hungry dino!"

Mom pulled into the driveway and turned off the van, relieved to be home.

"Make sure you grab everything you took out with you this morning," she reminded the kids. "And also, please grab two things you can throw in the garbage on your way in. The van looks like a trash heap."

"Y-Y-You get me out?" a small voice asked urgently.

"You betcha," Mom said, gently kissing the swollen lump on Bas's forehead. "It's time to go inside! Are you going to do some swinging while I make dinner?"

"We're waiting for you, Momma!" Marian called out. "We don't want another doggie escapade today."

"Good thinking," said Mom as she hurried Sebastian up the driveway. "Let me lock the gate before you open the house. They've been waiting a long time for us to come home."

As soon as the last latch clicked into place, Jack propped the heavy storm door open against his body and swung the interior back door inward. An eager-to-be-outside Thomas Jefferson came barreling toward him and exited through the storm door's thigh-high flap.

"Whoa!" cried Vince.

He'd been standing in front of the dog door, and Thomas Jefferson emerged from it on a mission. Before anyone could react, the furry four-legged missile pushed his way between Vince's legs and lifted him completely off the ground. Balanced precariously on the dog's back with his face at his tail, Vince grabbed frantically at Thomas's furry stomach.

"Help! Aaahhh!" he cried wildly as Thomas made a beeline for the backyard, oblivious to his flailing passenger.

"Hold on, Vincey!" Mom shouted, taking off after their pet bucking bronco.

Sensing the action, Alice burst through the dog door and sprinted for the backyard. Thomas Jefferson was galloping around the perimeter—seemingly oblivious to the child thrashing around on his back as he reveled in being outside.

"Thomas!" Mom yelled, but Alice was one step ahead.

When they first brought baby Vince home from the hospital, Alice was convinced he was her puppy. Six years later, Alice still believed he was her responsibility.

"Help!" Vince cried again, and Alice charged. She cut a diagonal across the yard and leapt at the much-larger dog, nipping at one of his long, droopy ears. Thomas Jefferson halted abruptly in surprise and sat down on the grass, sending Vince sliding into a face-plant in the dirt behind him.

"Are you okay?" Mom called, running to the crumpled heap at the back fence that was her son.

Vince looked up at her sheepishly.

"At least you weren't carrying a carton of eggs this time!" called Marian from the driveway, where she held Sebastian's hand as they looked on.

"What?!" Mom turned back to Marian. "What do you mean?"

Vince hauled himself off the ground, his face bright red.

"Well...maybe Thomas did this to me the other day when we were unloading the groceries," he offered, looking embarrassed.

"But Vince didn't want us to tell you," Marian tattled.

"Nothing broke!" Vince protested, brushing off his pants. "The eggs were in the bag I was holding, but not a single one was cracked."

"We figured it was a sign that you didn't need to know," Jack defended.

A smile spread across Mom's face, and she burst into laughter.

"Honestly, Vincey? That's the *second* time you've been dog-napped by Thomas Jefferson?"

Vince ran to her and buried his face into her coat. "Can we just say that I was trying to keep you from worrying last time?"

"Was that the actual reason you didn't tell me?" she choked through giggles.

"No," Vince said. "It's because I knew you'd laugh. I mean, I figured someone would squeal eventually." He glared at his sister, who stuck out her tongue. "I just wanted to put off having you laugh at me."

Mom pulled him into a tight hug. "Oh, Vincey. I'm sorry if I made you feel bad when I laughed. I'm very glad you aren't hurt. And the trick," she explained, "is to laugh the hardest. Then no one is laughing *at* you, they're laughing *with* you. I think you'll find that there's a big difference." She ruffled his hair and kissed his head. "Just promise me you learned something."

Vince watched Thomas and Alice chase each other spiritedly around the backyard and then looked up at his mom with big blue eyes. "I probably shouldn't stand so close to the dog door anymore."

"Good plan," Mom agreed. She took his hand and led him towards the house. "Let's go inside. It's cold out here, and if you're done practicing for the rodeo, it's time to take out your violin."

TUESDAY, 5:10 P.M.

"Before you get ready for swimming, could you please put away the shredded cheese?" Mom asked Marian.

"Sure thing. Should I put on my bathing suit now, or change when we get there?"

"I haven't heard from Daddy yet." Mom glanced again at her phone. "So put on your suit underneath some sweats, okay? If we don't have to change at practice, we can arrive five minutes later."

"Think Dad'll get out in time for Bassie to stay home?"

"Probably not." Mom shook her head. "But hope springs eternal, right?"

Marian grinned and then headed toward the living room, bellowing at the top of her lungs: "Boys! Momma says we should put on our suits—NOW!"

Mom sighed quietly and turned back to Sebastian, who sat contentedly in his highchair, eating shredded mozzarella cheese one sliver at a time.

"Let's have a big dinosaur bite!" Mom enthused, shoving a forkful of pasta into his mouth. Then she hastily began grabbing plates off the table and dumping them haphazardly into the dishwasher.

There's nothing worse than coming home at night to the

smell of a dinner you already ate, she motivated herself. *Matt's plate can wait in the oven until he gets out, but the rest of this mess needs to go away before we leave.*

"How much time do we have, Momma?" Jack asked, entering the kitchen wearing a fluffy brown bathrobe. "Can I practice my trumpet before we leave?"

"Sure," Mom said. "You've got time. But what are you wearing, exactly?"

"My bathrobe!" He smiled proudly. "I can just throw it back on after swim practice, and I'll be ready to leave in about ten seconds. You won't have to stand around waiting!"

Mom shook her head. "Nope."

"Why not?" he cried. "It's a perfect idea!"

"You're not heading out in a bathing suit and a bathrobe," Mom insisted. "First off, it's November, and, second, practice is at a school, not a Manhattan hotel."

Jack looked crestfallen. "It could have worked," he mourned.

"Pants and a sweatshirt, please," she replied. "And then I want to hear that solo. We've finished three violins and a saxophone. Your trumpet is the only one left!"

A knock sounded at the back door, and she hurried to investigate.

Who on earth would that be?

She heard footsteps on the stairs and then their favorite neighbor poked his head into the kitchen.

"Anybody home?" he called.

"It's my Gary!" Sebastian squealed. "Oh, Mr. Gary! I-I-I-I-I missed you so much!"

"Hello, Sebastian!" Gary exclaimed, kissing his young friend's head. "I'm glad to see you! That's quite a bruise you've got there." He frowned. "I thought you were done falling all the time."

"He wasn't allowed to wear his doggie braces at bowling today," Mom explained.

"That's terrible!" Gary said, shaking his head in dismay. Then he kissed Sebastian's head again. "Are you eating your dinner so you can grow taller?" he asked.

"I-I-I-I-I a dino!" Bas said, flapping his hands at the end of stiff arms. Then he paused, looking concerned. "What sauropods eat, Momma?" he asked.

"They eat leaves, Bas. Here—you eat some leaves, too." She pushed three baby spinach petals into his mouth.

"Yummy, yum, yum!" he exclaimed. "These my favorite leaves!"

"Sauropods?" Mr. Gary sounded impressed. "That's quite the word! No wonder I'm dropping off these papers!"

He extended a paper-clipped packet to Mom, and she jumped up to retrieve them.

"Ahhh! Sebastian's classroom promotion forms!" Impulsively, she grabbed Gary in a hug. "Thank you so much! Did you hear? He's going to start in his new room on Monday!"

"I did hear!" he said. "That's one of the benefits of being the head nurse of the school district *and* a mutual friend of both the director of special education and the amazing Team Shepler."

"Thank you so much for bringing these over!"

"I had to walk past five whole houses to get here," he teased. "It was such a big deal."

"Well, it's a big deal to us," Mom said sincerely. "In some places, it takes *months* to get this paperwork."

"We can't have our Sebastian waiting months to move to the right classroom," Gary said, lifting the boy from his highchair and spinning him around in a circle.

"My Gary!" Sebastian squealed. "I spinning with my Gary!"

Mom heard pounding feet, and Vince and Marian appeared in the kitchen, both in just bathing suits.

"Mr. Gary!" they shouted in unison.

"Isn't it a bit cold to go swimming in my pool today?" Gary joked as the kids leapt to hug him.

"We have swim team practice!" Vince said.

"It's inside," Marian added, "but your pool is still warmer."

"Theirs isn't as fun, either," Vince said. "It doesn't even have a slide. But maybe by next summer, I can beat you in a race down the lane!"

Mr. Gary placed Sebastian gently back in his highchair. Then he spun quickly, grabbed Vince, and flipped him upside down.

"You can try!" he said.

"Hey!" Vince laughed. "I'm having a crazy day here!"

"I don't know why I always forget that you're much heavier than you look!" Mr. Gary grunted as he flipped Vince back over, setting him upright on his feet.

"He weighs more than me by two pounds," Marian agreed, "and I'm two years older!"

"That might be the fifty-seventh time you've told me that," Gary said, spinning Marian in a circle.

"But you still forget!" she chided.

"You're no feather yourself, madam," he said, his eyes twinkling.

"Hey!" she said, punching him in the arm as she spun. "That's not nice!"

"He's kidding, Marian," Mom said, smiling. "We have to cinch the elastic in your pants so far, it looks like you've got two tails hanging out of your waistband!"

Mr. Gary twirled Marian around one more time and then plopped her on the ground.

"But you're a powerful string bean," he assured her. "Pretty soon you'll be able to lift *me*!"

"I'll be the first one able to do that," Jack interrupted, bursting into the kitchen. He also wore nothing but a bathing suit. "I'm so glad you're here!" he told Gary. "I was going to walk over to show you *this*!" He held out a massive contraption made of building bricks. "See? It opens up! Then you can connect *this* piece, and look!"

"Wow!" exclaimed Gary. "Are those hinge pieces?"

"Yes!" confirmed Jack. "Aren't they cool? This thing has sixteen different hinges. Some gears, too—over in this part!"

"Wow, building bricks are a heck of a lot more complex than

when my kids were little," Gary said, marveling at Jack's construction. "Good thing you didn't try to bring it over. What if you lost one of the pieces?"

"I have lots of practice doing modifications," Jack said. "I live with Sebastian, remember?"

Gary feigned shock. "What? Sebastian! You don't break apart Jack's masterpieces, do you?"

"Yup!" said Bas through a mouthful of spinach leaves. "Yup, I do!"

"So we try to hide them up high," Vince explained. "Momma set up these cupboards for us. See?"

"But anything left on the dining room table...Well, Bassie-Boo can reach those without any trouble since he started growing," Marian mourned.

Gary paused. "What you kids need is your own separate house, just for building blocks."

Although he was talking to the Big Three, his eyes were locked directly on Mom.

"Go finish getting dressed, you monkeys," Mom ordered. "It's way too cold to head out in nothing but bathing suits."

"Give me hugs first," Gary said. "I've got to get home."

The Big Three piled in to say good-bye, begging him to stop by again as soon as tomorrow, and promising to visit his house when they rode past on their bikes.

"Any time the gate is open, come on back!" he urged.

TUESDAY, 5:35 P.M.

As the Big Three scampered upstairs, Gary grabbed Sebastian from his highchair for one more hug.

"Y-Y-Y-You my best, best friend, my Gary!" Sebastian said. "I just love you so much!"

"I love you, too, Sebastian," Gary said fondly. "And I'm so proud of your hard work at school. I can't believe the progress you've made in two years."

After putting Bas back into his seat, he turned to go.

"Next October," he said, reminding Mom. "We'll be selling both houses next October. Have you and Matt been thinking about it?"

"We have," she said slowly. "There are a ton of variables, but, yes. If we can swing it, that's what we want to do."

"The green house is huge," Gary said. "Sebastian will be too big to use his therapy swing in your living room soon. You'll need a bigger space. And you could use the little yellow one next door as your office. Or rent it out for extra income."

"Or use it for building blocks," she mocked.

"That's always an option!" He chuckled.

"Honestly, though, it'd be perfect for us," she said. "With two houses right next door to each other, our worries about the long-term would subside. Whichever kid wound up taking the green house could also inherit Sebastian in the yellow one. Or if that's more than Sebastian's capable of, there'd be plenty of room for Uncle Bas in the green house, and the yellow one could be a rental income to offset expenses."

"October," Gary repeated. "If you want them, they're yours."

Mom smiled sadly. "It's not a question of wanting them. We're doing all right financially, but banks don't just let you sign two mortgages on the same day unless you've got a serious down payment and almost no debt. I already called to check: They can't combine the two properties into one loan."

"You're a business owner and you've got almost a whole year," he encouraged, raising a fist in the air. "Take on some extra contracts, and make it happen!"

"We're working on it," she assured him.

"I don't know..." he said, his voice rising in a teasing tone. "Your office light used to be on at all hours. We'd pass by on a midnight walk, and there you'd be, working away. But I haven't seen that light on in months!"

"Ha!" Mom crowed. "That's because I can get my work done during the day now. All four kids go to school full-time—remember? Lately, Matt and I even watch a show at night. It's amazing, really."

"I think it's a wasted opportunity to increase your workload," Gary quipped. "Who needs to hang out with their spouse anyway? And don't tell me you're wasting time on getting extra sleep! We both know sleep is overrated."

"Hardy-har-har," she said. "Now, get out of here!"

"I hand-deliver your paperwork, and you're kicking me out?"

"Stay if you want," she acceded. "But if you do, start being useful. You can finish feeding Sebastian and then get him in a new diaper. That'd buy me extra time to load my laptop with work files, so I could be extra-productive at swim practice tonight!" She winked.

"Y-Y-Y-You change my poop, Mr. Gary?" Sebastian asked hopefully.

"And that's my cue to exit!" Gary said, rumpling Sebastian's hair one last time and sprinting for the back stairs. "Have fun at swim! And don't forget: October!"

"Thank you for bringing the papers!" Mom called after him. "We'll stop over this weekend and the kids can help rake leaves."

"Bye, my Gary!" Sebastian called as he fed himself another microscopic sliver of mozzarella cheese.

There's not enough time for Bas to finish before we have to leave. Mom looked at her phone for the tenth time in the last twenty minutes. *Come on, Matt. Where are you?*

The blast of a musical scale exploding from the living room made Sebastian bounce up in surprise.

"Jack is practicing his trumpet," Mom soothed. "Hear the pretty sounds?"

"Th-Th-Th-Th-That a loud sound," Bas replied shakily.

"Hi, Bassie-Boo!" Vince called as he skipped into the kitchen, his t-shirt inside-out and his sweatpants backwards.

Mom smiled. "Still wearing your suit under there?" she asked.

"Under where?" Vince asked innocently, and then burst into hysterics. "Get it? I said 'underwear'! Get it?"

"W-W-Wocka-Wocka!" Sebastian cheered.

"I'm glad you're here," Mom told Vince. "Want to help Bas eat some meatball bites? I've got to pack him a thermos. Otherwise he'll be hungry during your whole practice."

Snatching the fork from his brother's tray, Vince stabbed a hunk of meatball and zoomed it around the room, dancing it around in time to Jack's music. "Here it comes, Bassie-Boo. Open up!"

Obediently, Sebastian opened his mouth and let his big brother feed him. Mom pushed half the food from his plate into the *Dog Town* thermos and screwed on the cap. Then she tossed the metal container, a plastic fork, and a package of dog-bone-shaped graham crackers into the Survival Bag.

Have thermos, will travel, she exalted. *Now to tackle the rest of these smelly dishes and pack my laptop.*

Marian joined them a few moments later, peering over three

giant rolled-up beach towels stacked in her arms. "Figured the boys would forget to pack towels again, so I grabbed enough for everyone."

"Perfect! Thanks, Sis. I'll take over feeding Sebastian, Vince. Go help your sister get those towels into your swim bags."

The trumpet music stopped, and Mom heard the *zip* and *thump* that meant Jack was putting his horn away.

At least we'll be on time, she thought.

"You don't really want to know, I'm sure," Marian said, faltering, "but I think we forgot about the toilet paper situation upstairs."

"What?" asked Mom.

"The toilet paper—from this morning? That tail sticking out of the bowl must have wicked all the water out, because everything is just a soggy gross mess up there right now."

Sebastian shoved his plate to the far end of his tray. "I-I-I-I done, Momma!" he said.

"Yes, you are," she agreed, wiping his face with a wet paper towel. "Let's put this on the floor for Alice and Thomas and get you into your coat."

"Wh-Wh-Where we going?" Sebastian asked.

"We get to watch swim practice!" she said, trying to infuse excitement into her voice. "First Vince and Marian, and then Jack."

Jack appeared in the doorway. "I put on clothes," he said morosely.

"Just in time," Mom said. "Now put on your coats so we can get out of here. We can't wait for Daddy even one minute more, or you're going to be late."

"What about the toilet paper?" Vince asked.

"It's not going anywhere," she reasoned, yawning. "It'll have to wait until we get back tonight."

Mom grabbed the third energy drink of her day and herded the children outside.

TUESDAY, 5:55 P.M.

They were backing out of the driveway when inspiration struck. Hastily Mom threw the van into drive and pulled forward again, to the house.

"I'll be right back!" she called to no one in particular, before leaping out and running toward the garage.

She returned two minutes later, hefting a small red tricycle with red tassels that dangled from white rubber handlebar covers.

"Is Bassie going to ride that?" Vince asked in awe.

"I think he might!" Mom replied. "The physical therapist said Sebastian's getting good at pedaling, and I realized we have this Sebastian-sized trike just sitting around. What do you think, Bas?"

"I-I-I-I push with feet," he said slowly.

"Sounds promising," Marian said.

"The school is the perfect place to practice," Jack added.

"I know!" said Mom. "It has huge hallways that are empty at night, and if he's on a trike, he won't be running around, falling, and risk smashing his head again." She smiled in satisfaction. "I think it might just be the best idea I've had all month."

To the soothing strains of the violin music the kids needed to listen to as part of their practice schedule, Mom whizzed down the Thruway. She was pleased that by the time she pulled into the back lot of the middle school, the whole clan was a subdued bunch.

"Vince and Marian, you two can head in and get ready with your team. Jack, can you grab the trike in addition to your swim gear? My arms are going to be full carrying the Survival Bag and Sebastian."

"Yup—it's actually pretty light," Jack said with relief as he pulled it from the trunk. "It's just awkward, that's all."

"Make sure you're paying attention to your coach and not doing underwater tricks!" Mom shouted after Marian and Vince.

"I-I-I-I hungry, Momma," Sebastian said pitifully as she pulled him out of his car seat. "I so hungry."

"Here." She offered him a graham cracker package from inside the Survival Bag. "I brought you a special *Dog Town* snack! You'll be needing some energy if you're going to ride your red bike tonight."

"I still can't believe it's this dark outside already," Jack marveled. "It's barely dinnertime, and the stars are already shining."

"Lucky thing we have bright, warm hallways to play in then," she panted as she lugged Sebastian up the long sidewalk, sidestepping the glinting icy patches. "Right?"

"I-I-I-I get d-d-down. I walk," Sebastian offered, but she kept going.

"You can get down as soon as we're inside," she told him. "It's cold and slippery out here tonight."

As promised, she set Sebastian on his feet the instant she stepped into the hallway. He immediately took off, dashing past his tricycle to the right-height wheelchair-accessible water fountain.

"Th-Th-Th-This good water!" he cried jubilantly, soaking the front of his black winter parka. "I-I-I-I love nice cold drinks!"

"Bassie," Jack called hopefully, "I carried your bike in for you. Do you want to race me to the pool door?"

Sebastian looked up from the stream of water and stared at the tricycle suspiciously. "That bike no-no-no-no-no-no work."

"It sure does!" Mom assured him. "You tried it last summer, and it didn't work then—you're right. But that was before you'd learned how to push the pedals. You're good at that now. You've been practicing at school every day. Try it out and see!"

"I'll hold your coat, Bassie-Boo," Jack said, removing his brother's parka and slinging it over his arm. "Then you won't slide off the seat."

"Th-Th-Th-Th-That my bike?" Sebastian asked apprehensively.

"Climb on and try it out, Bas," Mom said, leading him to the shiny red transport. "It's been waiting in the garage for you all this time."

Sebastian stood rooted to the spot, staring warily. "Th-Th-Th-That bike no w-w-w-work."

"Ruff, ruff!" Jack yelped. "Fluffy Red! Get in the basket! Sebastian will drive you to Dog Town!" He pulled the stuffed dog from the Survival Bag and shoved it into the bike basket.

"Red the Dog! My-My-My-My Fluffy Red!" Sebastian shouted, arms stiffly flapping while his thin legs ran quick steps in place. "L-L-L-Let's save the day!"

"*Dog Town* to the rescue!" Jack cried, laughing at the layered meaning.

Now that Bas was willing, Mom helped him throw his leg over the seat, position his feet on the pedals, and grab the handlebars. But as she leaned in to give him an encouraging kiss, he took off like a streak—leaving her standing there, a shocked smile spreading slowly across her face.

"Go, puppy, go!" he called out exuberantly as he flashed down the long hallway.

"I'll stay with him, Momma!" Jack called over his shoulder as he sprinted after his youngest brother. "You can watch Marian and Vince practice!"

Mom walked down the hall behind them until she reached the heavy silver door that led to the pool deck.

I'm propping it open today, she decided. *They can call me a renegade, but I need to watch kids on both sides of this doorway.*

Marian and Vince were already in the pool, halfway through

their eight-lap freestyle warm-up. Swimming had never been Mom's sport—she couldn't even dive—so she stared in amusement and wonder at both of her kids squeezing out cheerful smiles before grabbing each breath. Satisfied they were behaving, Mom let the door close and started off down the hallway towards Sebastian's delighted squeals.

She'd taken only two steps before the boys rounded the corner, headed straight for her.

"I-I-I doing it, Momma! I ride-ride-ride-riding my bike!"

"Mayor Sneak is going to catch you and Red!" Jack cried with an evil-villain cackle. "You'll never get away!"

Sebastian shrieked with joy and pedaled faster, calling "Go, puppy, go!" for the twentieth time that day.

"I'm going to make a video on your way back," Mom called after them. "I'm so proud of you!"

She fumbled with her phone, pulling up the camera app and set it to capture the action.

"I-I-I riding my bike!" Sebastian shouted at the phone as he passed by in a frenzied blur.

"And I'm running out of air," Jack rasped as he lumbered behind him.

"That was a great idea," a vaguely familiar swim mom said, coming out through the silver door. "It's too hot in there today. You've got the right idea, standing out here."

"I wouldn't mind sitting," Mom acknowledged, "but my husband got held over at work, so I had to drag poor Sebastian to practice with us."

"Still, the bike is an ideal solution," the swim mom said appreciatively. "You have two kids on a team?"

"Three," Mom corrected.

The swim mom looked incredulously at Sebastian as he zipped past again. "How old is he?"

"Not him!" Mom corrected, giggling at the thought. "Vince and Marian are both swimming now, and Jack swims on the team that practices next."

"Oh!" The swim mom laughed. "Whew! I couldn't imagine a team for two-year-olds. That would be scary to watch!"

"Actually," Jack said, stopping to catch his breath, "our Bassie is four."

Mom watched the shock pass across the swim mom's face as she glanced reflexively again at Sebastian, who was joyfully repeating "Go, Red, go! Go, Red, go!" as he pedaled past on the mini-trike.

Please not again, Mom beseeched frantically.

But the swim mom recovered almost immediately. "Pretty soon, he's going to need a new tricycle," she said with a smile. She turned to Jack. "But you won't be able to keep up with him once he does," she said. "Those big low-rider trikes are a lot of fun, and they're crazy-fast."

"I wonder if they sell them online," Mom said, typing quickly into her phone. "I was so astounded that he'd mastered pedaling, I didn't notice—but you're right: Sebastian is too big for this tiny trike!"

The swim mom smiled. "Someone in our neighborhood has a metal one with silver-spoked wheels and metallic handlebar tassels—it's possibly the coolest tricycle I've ever seen!"

"Here!" Mom exclaimed. "Look at this."

"That's the one!" the swim mom agreed. "It seems sturdy, and the seat is adjustable. Good thing Christmas is coming!"

"Bassie-Boo needs that right away, Momma," Jack murmured. "Could we order it today? I could help put it together when it comes."

"That sounds like a plan, Jack," Mom said, clicking the *Buy Now* button.

"He's such a good big brother," the swim mom marveled as Jack took off again, reassuming the identity of Mayor Sneak. "I've got three, and none of them can stand each other."

Mom propped open the door to peek in on Vince and Marian. She was just in time to watch them dive into a relay.

"We're really lucky," she agreed. "They genuinely like playing together most of the time."

"I can't even get mine to sit next to each other in the car without fighting," the swim mom lamented.

"Having Sebastian makes a difference," Mom reflected. "He needs a lot of extra help, so it gives them plenty of practice working together."

"He's a speed demon on his bike!" the swim mom said with a grin as the boys flew past again.

"Full credit goes to his physical therapist," Mom admitted. "We tried to teach him to pedal for an entire year, but it was frustrating for all of us, so we gave up. This is the first time I've ever seen him in action, actually making a bike move forward. It seems his schoolteachers have more perseverance than I do."

"Does Sebastian have full days or half days at school?" the mom asked.

"He goes full days. This is his second year, and it's a great fit for him. Most of his classmates are dealing with vision challenges, but they all need extra help. The environment is exactly right for our unsteady little man."

"I noticed his forehead." The swim mom grimaced. "That's gotta hurt."

"He fell at bowling this morning," Mom explained. "But I doubt it's actually causing him any bother. Sebastian doesn't experience pain like most people."

"That's one of Sebastian's superpowers!" Jack added as he jogged past for the seventh time. "If he had an X-Men trading card, it would say he's the hero who's always super-nice and happy, who doesn't need sleep, and who isn't bothered by boring things like pain!"

Mom smiled tightly at the swim mom's quizzical expression.

"Sebastian's DNA is different from everyone else's," Mom explained, "which is, of course, the actual definition of a 'mutant.' His siblings have decided that automatically earns him a spot in the X-Men."

"He doesn't sleep?" the mom asked, her eyes wide in horror.

"Oh, Sebastian sleeps. Just not for more than four or five hours at a stretch. It's common for AUTS2 Syndrome."

"How wonderful that you have a formal diagnosis! So many families never find out what's actually going on with their child."

"For two years, we just called it 'Sebastian Syndrome.'" Mom chuckled. "But having solid medical identification has been a game-changer, that's for sure."

Her phone rang from inside her pocket, and she quickly pardoned herself from the conversation when she saw it was Matt.

"I'm on my way home," he said. "Of course I got stuck with a late call. Today seemed to last forever. I'll be in the driveway in three minutes."

"Great. Your dinner is in the oven, staying safe from Alice and Thomas Jefferson. You've got exactly enough time to get changed and eat it."

"Before what?" Matt asked, genuinely oblivious. "What do I need to do afterwards?"

"It's Tuesday!" Mom said, exasperated.

"We've been through this," Matt joked. "It's your job to remind me every few hours what I'm supposed to be doing next. I can't keep the calendar straight in my head. There are too many activities to remember."

"You need to come up to the middle school." Mom sighed. "Marian and Vince are done with swimming at seven-thirty, and that's when Jack's practice starts. So after you eat dinner, drive over here and pick up Marian, Vince, and Sebastian. I brought my computer loaded with work files, so I'll wait here through Jack's practice and then bring him home."

"Gotcha. I remember that now," Matt lied. "I'll get there before seven-thirty. It doesn't take me that long to eat and change. Then I can hang out with you and Bas for a few minutes, right?"

"He's riding his tricycle!" Mom gushed.

"What? He finally learned?"

"You'll have to see it to believe it," she said.

"I'm just pulling into the driveway. Give me ten minutes, and

I'll be on my way."

She hung up and grinned.

"Guess who that was!" she called to the boys.

"Did Daddy finally get out of work?" Jack asked.

"B-B-B-B-B-B-Big Tuna!" Sebastian yelled.

"He'll be here soon," Mom exulted. "Daddy can watch a few minutes of your practice before he takes everyone else home, Jack."

"I hope we work on dives while he's here," said Jack. "Or flip turns. I'm getting so much faster at both."

"B-B-B-Big T-T-Tuna see me ri-ri-ri-ride my bike!"

"That's right!" Mom said.

"Do you get to stay behind by yourself for the second practice?" the swim mom asked, turning her attention from the open doorway.

"Yes!" Mom enthused. "It's going to be ninety minutes of 'Me Time'!"

"That's wonderful," the swim mom agreed. "Did you bring a book? Or are you just going to close your eyes and listen to the beautiful silence?"

"Ha!" Mom chuckled. "Worse than that: I brought my work computer."

"Oh no! That's not fair."

"The kids were off school and with me all day, so nothing got done." Mom shrugged. "So this will be great. More than an hour with nothing to do but work towards my deadlines."

"I suppose that will at least reduce some stress," the swim mom said.

Mom nodded. "Indeed. And when I finally get to go home, I'll be able to relax for a bit."

"Momma! Momma! Get him!"

Mom turned just in time to see Sebastian careening toward her and the open doorway, which led straight to the deep end of the pool. Instinctively, she jumped in front of the trike, stopping Bas's progress abruptly as he slammed headlong into her legs.

"Y-Y-Y-Y-Y-Y-You save me!" Sebastian squeaked. "L-L-L-Like in *Dog Town*!"

Ignoring her throbbing foot and the handlebar-shaped bruise no doubt blossoming just below her already-damaged knee, she scooped him up and held him tight. "Sebastian. That was very dangerous. Your bike was heading straight for the pool!"

"I-I-I no swim in this b-b-b-big pool, Momma."

"You have to use your handlebars to navigate, Bassie," Jack reprimanded, his voice shaky. "I was getting ready to jump in to save you!"

"I would have caught him!" Marian called, her face just above the gutter in the corner of the deep end. "That was scary, Bas! You're good at pedaling, but you also have to steer!"

"I was panicked, too," Vince said, pulling himself up alongside his sister. "I don't know if I could have gotten to him before he went under."

"Get back to your practice!" Mom told them. "Sebastian isn't going into the pool today. I promise!"

"Maybe we'd better close the door after all," the swim mom said.

"Nah," said Mom. "It's too hot to watch from in there. Sebastian can bike further down the hallway—right, Bassie?"

"I'll take him," Jack offered.

"That's great," said Mom, "but you've got only about ten minutes before you need to get ready for your practice, okay?"

"Sounds good," Jack said. "I don't think I can run for longer than ten more minutes anyway." He snorted. "I'm already tired, and my practice hasn't even started yet!"

TUESDAY, 9:15 P.M.

As soon as they got home, Mom sent Jack upstairs to shower and go to bed. The house was quiet, but she knew Sebastian was still awake upstairs. Otherwise, Matt would have come down already.

Having skidded on a thin layer of mini-chunk dog food when they entered, Mom swept the kitchen floor; then she wiped down the table and counters, and tossed the stove grates into the dishwasher. Next, she double-checked homework folders to be certain she'd signed everything that required her John Hancock and then she stacked a bevy of stray shoes on the four-foot-high rack at the bottom of the stairs.

Tomorrow is Wednesday: Marian has to bring her saxophone to school again. Jack needs clothes for gym class. We have to pack Sebastian a warmer outfit to keep at school in case he has a diaper malfunction. Vince is out of lunch money, so I need to send in a check.

She raced around, hunting for the items that would smooth the snags in their morning routine—putting away toys, clothes, books, and building bricks as she passed them.

The morning will still be nuts. She cringed. *But at least we won't forget anything they really need.*

TUESDAY, 10:05 P.M.

She was pulling laundry out of the dryer when she heard Matt enter the kitchen.

"I know work has been stressful lately," he said, gathering up half the clean pile from atop the washing machine, where she'd heaped it, "but I didn't realize you were switching careers."

Mom stepped back in confusion. "What?"

"Abstract art," he replied simply. "It's a bold choice, I must say. Because you're a terribly talented grant writer, and not many will appreciate your sculptures." He put a hand on her shoulder, his eyes dancing. "Know that I will always support your decisions—no matter how bizarre."

"What on Earth are you talking about?" she demanded, more loudly than intended. "I'm not quitting my job!"

"Taking up a hobby then?" He grinned. "Just when I thought you couldn't squeeze any more into a day."

Mom shook her head. "I honestly have no idea what you're talking about." She pulled the final socks out of the dryer and added them to her half of the pile. "And I'm getting annoyed."

Matt pulled out his phone and scrolled through his photographs. "I wasn't sure if this was a permanent exhibition, or one of those temporary performance pieces, so I left it intact." He held up his phone and showed her a picture of their bathroom floor, covered by a thick white blob that extended from inside the toilet bowl, where it had completely consumed all the water, to the base of the vanity, where it was piled at least a foot high.

Mom finally cracked a smile.

"That wasn't me!" she protested. "Sebastian is the mystery artist in question—and I'll have you know that the renegade sat in his first time-out ever for his creative efforts."

Matt's eyebrows lifted. "Really? You put him in time-out?"

"Don't sound so surprised," Mom said indignantly. She hefted her half of the pile that she'd balanced on a beach towel towards the living room. "I promised you I'd start instituting it, didn't I?"

Matt shot her a sidelong glance. "How did it go?" he asked.

Mom snorted. "Well, you were right: He's ready. The little stinker waited about twenty seconds and then pretended to be the dinging microwave."

"He what?!" Matt followed her out to Mount Laundrious.

"Honestly," Mom said. "He sat quietly for a bit and then he called out a high-pitched *'Ding!'* and tried to convince me it was the microwave timer."

Matt let out a bark and then started laughing so hard no sound came out. He slapped his knee and doubled over, gasping for breath.

"I couldn't let him see me laugh," said Mom. "But can you imagine? That was some fast-thinking to work out a clever trick like that and put it into action!"

"That's the best thing I've heard all day!" Matt reveled. "What else did I miss while I was at work? You didn't tell me anything at swim; you were too busy saying good-bye to your friend."

"I don't even know that lady's name," Mom confessed. "I know what the other swim parents look like, but I never talk to them. I'm always working with my headphones turned up as high as they'll go."

"You should talk to people more," Matt encouraged. "It's fun to make friends."

Mom rolled her eyes at him. "Practice is two or three solid hours of interruption-free work time. I can't waste it chatting with people I don't even know. I already have friends; I don't need new ones."

"What was different today then? I assumed you two were old pals."

"I had Sebastian with me today," Mom explained. "That's what. He's a friendly guy, and—as you saw for yourself—his tricycle skills were too awesome to ignore."

Matt grinned knowingly. "She's going to try to talk to you again," he said. "I can tell."

Mom shrugged. "I actually like her," she admitted. "I should try to figure out her name, I suppose. She was very kind." She pulled a sweater from the pile. "And that's good, because we encountered some real doozies today."

Matt put a hand on her shoulder. "Do you want to talk about it?"

"Not really. It was a very long day. I don't think I'll be heading back to the bowling alley again for a while, though. The kids had a blast, but the guy behind the counter was a jerk. He was rude, and he wouldn't let Sebastian wear his orthotics."

"I was wondering what happened to his forehead."

"*That* guy happened," Mom stewed. "I should have just let Bas keep his trainers and braces on anyway. What were they going to do—disqualify his scores?"

"Maybe we can order him some custom bowling shoes," Matt suggested.

Mom burst out laughing. "There are many things we need to be spending money on." She caressed his cheek. "I'm not convinced custom bowling shoes for a four-year-old rates being on that list."

"Really?" Matt teased. "Marian and Vince said Sebastian outscored everyone today. Maybe he's a bowling prodigy."

Mom smirked. "The big kids set up the ramp for him with

expert precision for every frame. His score doesn't count."

Matt held out his hands. "Still, I can't believe you can think of higher spending priorities."

"Gary stopped by today," Mom gazed meaningfully at Matt. "He brought Sebastian's paperwork."

"Well, that was awesome of him," Matt said. "I'm sorry I wasn't here. I haven't seen Gary in at least two weeks. The weather gets cold, and we all hide inside."

"The kids have been missing him, too," Mom said. "They were thrilled he was here. We should have him over for a movie night or
something," she mused. "Anyway, he was talking about selling us the houses again. He said October."

"That's coming quickly," Matt said softly.

"It certainly is. And I highly doubt we're going to be able to swing it."

"We've been paying everything down, though," said Matt. "Don't you think we'll even come close?"

"What I think," Mom said slowly, "is that our spending forecasts might be wrong." When Matt looked confused, she added, "It was something they said at the conference this morning."

He stopped folding the jeans he was holding. "What do you mean?"

"Well, first of all, Sebastian's team does *not* think he'll be ready for an integrated kindergarten classroom next year. I asked them straight out."

Matt turned back to the laundry. "What would he do then? He's supposed to start kindergarten in the fall, right?"

"We already know the district wants to stick him in the self-contained special education classroom next year. I hate that idea, because his social skills are one of his greatest strengths, and that room won't nurture his spirit. I was figuring we'd just send him anyway, and he'd catch up enough to be able to be in the integrated kindergarten the following year."

"That sounds good..." Matt said tentatively.

"It does. But today I learned that schools don't like to hold kids back anymore, no matter the circumstance. Which means that if Sebastian isn't ready for an integrated classroom in kindergarten in his first year of school, his only options in his second year will be to remain in the self-contained special education environment, or to transition to an inclusive first-grade classroom."

Matt's eyes widened in alarm. "Where does that leave us then?" he asked. "If he's not ready for an inclusion environment in kindergarten, he's not going to magically be ready for an inclusion environment in a first-grade classroom the following year. So that means if he's in the self-contained classroom for kindergarten, he'll be stuck in the self-contained special education classroom for the rest of his school career."

"I know." Mom sighed. "I wish he could be ready in a year, but that's not how this works. We already know: The gap continues to widen. Sebastian's best chance for being in school alongside typical peers is in early elementary. But if we try to send him this September, he's going to blow his shot. There's no way he'll be able to function in an inclusion environment."

"What do we do then—keep him home? Can we do that?"

"Apparently his September birthday gives us an option," Mom said slowly. "We could refuse to send him to kindergarten next year. We could insist on keeping him out to give him one more year to mature."

"Would we just keep him home? That doesn't sound like a good idea at all. You'd be great at the homeschool thing, but you barely find time to squeeze in your work now. It'd be impossible if Bassie were home every day. Besides, we want him to be with other kids."

Mom nodded her agreement.

"What I'd love is to keep him right where he is now. But our district already told us they won't pay for him to stay in the special education preschool another year. The tuition is far too expensive. It's not designed for families to afford; it's priced for school districts." She smiled thinly. "So, I did some research tonight during swim practice. There's a new inclusive preschool opening up in a few months, and it's only about a mile from our house. If we enrolled Sebastian, he'd be with certified special education teachers in a blended preschool classroom. Most of the students would be typical learners, and just a few of the kids would have learning challenges like Sebastian. They'll have specialists on staff, so he'd have full access to speech, physical, and occupational therapy at the same frequency he does now. Plus—" She smiled. "They have a strong focus on music, and all the kids will participate in music therapy a few times a week."

"That sounds perfect!" Matt exclaimed.

"It does." Mom sighed again. "But even though we have an amazing director of special education who's given Sebastian every therapy we've requested, she's been very clear that next year, the district expects him to be a kindergarten student, whether we feel he's ready or not. That means there's almost no chance they'll agree to pay for the integrated preschool. They even brought it up at his IEP meeting last summer, remember? The district wants him to come to kindergarten next year, even if that means he's got to stay separated from typical kids for the rest of his education."

Matt frowned. "Do we need their permission?" he asked. "It's not right! Sebastian is *our* kid. Kindergarten next year isn't what's right for him. He won't even be out of diapers yet."

"Technically," Mom explained, "because of when his birthday falls, we don't *exactly* need their permission. But if they refuse to fund his tuition, we'll have to cover it ourselves." She paused. "And it's not cheap."

"How much are we talking?" Matt asked, his voice heavy with dread.

"Nearly fifteen grand for the year."

"Oh," he said quietly.

"Kills your dreams of custom bowling shoes, I know," Mom said, trying to lighten the mood.

"Where would that leave us?"

"Tight. We'd be all right, but we wouldn't be moving into the big house around the corner."

Matt exhaled through his nose. "But, really, how can we do anything else? If one expensive year of private preschool is really all Sebastian needs to launch him out of the self-contained special education classroom into a learning environment alongside his typical peers, how can we even *consider* not doing it?"

"That's what I was thinking, too," Mom agreed sadly. "I just wanted to be able to move so badly. I don't get to sleep very often, but when I do finally lie down, I waste hours and hours worrying about what will happen to Sebastian after we're gone. I worry about the Big Three having to take care of him. I worry about the financial challenges of having an extra dependent. Buying the two houses now and paying them off was going to go a long way towards calming my worries."

Matt grabbed her hands. "So, let's do both," he resolved.

"Did you plant a money tree that's ready to harvest?" Mom asked sarcastically. "Or come into some inheritance I didn't know about?"

"Nah." He smiled. "Let's think of a plan. There's got to be another way to earn the money we need." He pulled a towel from the pile and began folding it.

"I cannot take on any more projects than I already do," Mom said sternly. "It's almost too much now. I'm beyond exhausted and at maximum capacity. And you can't work extra shifts on any sort of a regular schedule. Things are too hectic here. I need you home sometimes."

"Okay," he said. "No extra projects. No extra shifts. How about your book?"

Mom's eyes narrowed. "What book?" she asked.

"The book you're going to write someday, remember? Maybe it's time!"

"Ha!" She guffawed. "First, in case you weren't listening, I barely have time to sleep—how would I find time to write a book?

And second, I'm not even sure what I'd write about."

Matt shrugged. "You're supposed to write what you know, correct?"

"That's the problem," Mom said. "Right now, I know how to feel stressed out about work—and that doesn't hold a candle to the worries we have at home. I also know where we're each supposed to be every afternoon"—she mock-punched his arm—"because at least *one* of us has to have our schedule memorized. And I *thought* I knew how to protect our kids from the hateful people in this world, but I didn't do a terrific job of that today." She blew out a breath. "I'm basically an activities director on a dryland cruise ship, who is also responsible for piloting the ship and disciplining the passengers. Nothing about that is terribly absorbing."

"That's perfect, though!" Matt encouraged.

Mom scowled at him. "No one wants to read about me sitting at my desk writing grants."

"No," he said somberly. "You're absolutely correct. Please do *not* write about that." He broke into a smile. "But people *would* probably like to read about our family. Our kids are pretty awesome, you know. And even though it doesn't always feel like it, a lot of families out there are facing the same challenges we are. They especially might like to read about us."

Mom paused, considering. "Would you really want to give up our privacy? Because if I were to do it, I'd have to do it right and tell a completely honest story. I don't know if that's fair to the kids."

"It doesn't have to reveal *everything*," Matt reasoned. "You can just pull back the curtain for a glimpse. Remember in college, when you had to write that twenty-page essay about a ten-line section of poetry?"

"Ugh—the Grecian urn poem!" she spat. "I *hated* that assignment."

"Well, the same principle applies here," Matt explained. "Except you don't hate our family the way you hated that urn, so it might even be fun!"

Mom smiled. "I love my family. But I also write all day at my desk for my clients," she said. "So the question remains: When am I going to find the time, or more importantly, the motivation, to spend extra hours writing pages we won't even get paid for?"

Matt smiled. "Just think about it," he urged. "You could start describing a few days of our lives and see how it goes. If it's no good, you don't have to finish."

Mom considered, her hand poised with a sweater suspended midair.

"If I do this," she said, "the time will have to come from somewhere. It's got to be a fair trade." She squinted in concentration. "So I propose a deal: I'm willing to try if *you* promise to do a load of laundry from start to finish, every single day..." She paused for dramatic effect. "*And* clean the upstairs bathroom once a week until I'm done."

"You're bartering laundry chores? Really?" he asked. "That was easier than I thought!"

"Not just laundry," she warned. "I said the bathroom, too." She held out her hand. "And you have to shake on it."

Matt grabbed her hand and pulled her in for a kiss. "We're married," he argued. "You've got to give me more than just a hearty handshake."

Mom laughed and pulled away. "I can't promise this idea's going to work," she warned. "Writing a book is not like writing a grant. But I'll give it a shot. Nothing to lose, right?"

"It'll be incredible—I promise," he whispered. "Now let's have a beer or two and watch something adventurous and distracting on television."

Mom smiled up at him, her eyes sparkling.

"Soon, but not yet," she said. "I'm going spend twenty minutes drafting an outline for this book you think I can write. And that's exactly how long you'll need anyway, because the bathroom is under a soggy toilet paper siege." She rose onto her toes and kissed his cheek. "And you've just promised to be in charge of stuff like that!" She giggled gleefully.

"Hey!" he protested, but she was already gone.

Trailing behind, he peeked into her office and saw her staring at a blank screen, holding her breath. Abruptly her fingers sprang to life, pounding the keys loudly as the sentences spread across the page.

"I can feel you back there!" she called without turning. "Get going! We've got a date in nineteen minutes!"